MOZART

W. A. MOZART at the age of 26 (?)

(From the unfinished portrait by Lange in the Mozarteum, Salzburg)

WOLFGANG AMADE
MOZART

BY

DYNELEY HUSSEY

*O Mozart, divin Mozart ! Qu'il faut peu te comprendre
pour te ne pas t'adorer ! Toi, la verité constante ! Toi, la
beauté parfaite ! Toi, le charme inépuisable ! Toi, toujours
profonde et limpide ! Toi, l'humanité complète et la simpli-
cité de l'enfant ! Toi, qui as tout ressenti, et tout exprimé
dans une langue musicale qu'on n'a jamais surpassée qu'on
ne surpassera jamais.—*Charles Gounod.

Select Bibliographies Reprint Series

BOOKS FOR LIBRARIES PRESS
FREEPORT, NEW YORK

First Published 1928
Reprinted 1969

STANDARD BOOK NUMBER:
8369-5046-1

LIBRARY OF CONGRESS CATALOG CARD NUMBER:
73-94272

PRINTED IN THE UNITED STATES OF AMERICA

TO

IRENE AND DERRICK

WITHOUT WHOSE ASSISTANCE THIS BOOK WOULD HAVE BEEN

A FAR POORER THING

PREFACE

Of no great composer can it be said with more truth that his life and his music are inseparable than of Wolfgang Amade Mozart. In him the two were so closely interrelated that there is no speaking of the one without the other. In the pages that follow I have dealt with both aspects of my subject side by side, keeping to a chronological order, except where it was convenient to treat certain groups of works together. At the same time I have attempted to exclude the mere anecdote, which may be amusing or interesting but is, in Mozart's case, usually worn thin with much telling. For few lives have produced so large a crop of tales, often of a legendary nature, as his. I have tried, rather, to select those facts which shed a light upon his character and that of his works, and thereby to present him and those who came into contact with him as living characters. The resulting portrait differs considerably from that which has been created by sentimental biographers and accepted by fond believers in the angelic young musician whom the gods loved too well. But I hope that the real man I have tried to present will, in the end, prove more attractive, because more human, than the plaster bust. The reader must take the facts on trust, since in a short book of this kind it was obviously undesirable to load the text with references to the authorities.

This revaluation of Mozart's character, which has been in progress for some years in Germany and France, where the works of Abert, Schiedermair, Schurig, Prod'homme and de Wyzewa and de Saint-Foix have contributed in their several degrees to a deeper understanding of his life, carries with it the necessity of revaluing his music also. The formal perfection of Mozart's art, especially when it is viewed across the intervening years that brought about so great a change in artistic ideals, has led many people to regard it as no more than the polished, dainty, highly ornamented and entirely happy product of an age of elegance. His contemporaries thought otherwise. To them the chief characteristic of his music was its passionate melancholy. They found in it difficulties and complexities similar in kind, if not perhaps in degree, to those which a modern audience encounters at a first hearing of a work by, say, Béla Bartòk. To us, who know the late quartets of Beethoven, the symphonies of Brahms, the music-drama of Wagner, the tone-poems of Strauss and all that has followed, the music of Mozart appears to be, at first sight, of a transparent simplicity. But we are beginning gradually to realize that this appearance of simplicity is due to the formal perfection of the

music and that its content is as profound as that
of any of the music which we have been inclined
to regard as " greater," because it was more
obviously portentous.

The identification of Mozart's instrumental
works is always something of a puzzle to the in-
experienced. But I hope that with the help of
the index and the chronological table, which contains in a condensed form the whole of his output, the reader will be able to find what he wants.
Although there are instances in which their
arguments seem a trifle far-fetched and their
conclusions may not be sound, I have accepted
the chronology of Mozart's works given in MM.
de Wyzewa and de Saint-Foix's exhaustive study
of his compositions up to his twenty-first year.
At the same time it seemed more useful to retain
the numbering of Köchel's thematic catalogue,
which is still invariably used for purposes of
reference in this country, rather than to go the
whole hog and give the numbers of the new
French classification.

In dealing with the operas, I found myself in
a difficulty, since they have already been so fully
and ably discussed by Professor Dent in his book,
Mozart's Operas, which is the classic on the
subject. I have, therefore, discussed the operas
in a more limited way than their importance in
proportion to other of Mozart's works would
seem to require. Moreover, I have assumed
in the reader a sufficient knowledge of the

complicated plots of the more familiar operas to enable him to follow the argument. The narration of the stories would have taken up too much space. Those readers, who require information of this kind, must be referred to the excellent accounts of the plots in R. A. Streatfeild's *The Opera* (Routledge), or to the more detailed discussion of them in Professor Dent's book. To this book and to its author's personal kindness in advising me on many points I must here make acknowledgment.

Besides the works already mentioned and such obviously indispensable books as Jahn's *Life* and Ludwig Schiedermair's edition of Mozart's letters, I have made use of the early biography by Edward Holmes, which still makes excellent reading, and of Arthur Schurig's somewhat bitter, but nevertheless corrective, life of Mozart.

Lange's portrait of Mozart is reproduced by kind permission of the Director of the Mozarteum at Salzburg. It represents the composer seated at a harpsichord or pianoforte. Owing to its unfinished state and the drooping pose of the head, it has been suggested that the portrait was painted in 1791, just before Mozart died. The argument is not a strong one. For the unfinished state of the picture proves nothing, and the pose is a natural one for a man seated at the keyboard. On the other hand, there is no record of Mozart having come into contact with Lange, who was a travelling actor, so late in his life. There seems

to be good reason for assigning the portrait to
1782 or 1783, that is to his twenty-seventh year.
But, while the date of the picture is still a matter
for dispute, it is generally accepted as the best
and most characteristic portrait of Mozart.

The photograph, from which the plate was
made, was obtained for me by Mr C. B. Oldman,
who has also with great generosity placed at my
service his extraordinary knowledge of all that
appertains to Mozart and, besides giving me
information on particular points, which is acknowledged in its proper place, has started in conversation several trains of thought which have been
followed up in these pages. Mr A. H. Fox
Strangways has kindly permitted me to reprint
as an appendix the note on Casanova's possible
contribution to the libretto of *Don Giovanni*,
which appeared originally in *Music and Letters*.
Finally, I must acknowledge a debt to Mr H. C.
Colles, the editor of the third edition of *Grove's
Dictionary*, for placing at my disposal a proof of
the revised article on Mozart, which has been
invaluable in checking the facts during proof-
correction.

DYNELEY HUSSEY.

CONTENTS

WOLFGANG AMADE
MOZART

CHAPTER I

ORIGINS AND CHILDHOOD

LIKE most of his peers in the ranks of the great composers, Wolfgang Amadeus Mozart was born of a family which had lately raised itself from a very humble position to one of a slight eminence in the musical world. His ancestors on his father's side were of the artisan class, the grandfather, Johann Georg, having reached the respectable position of Master Book-Binder at Augsburg. This status obtained for the binder's eldest son, Leopold, the patronage of a canon of the Church who destined his godson for Holy Orders. Leopold was consequently educated in ecclesiastical schools and incidentally occupied the position of *discant* in the choir. In 1737 at the age of eighteen he proceeded to the University of Salzburg and became secretary (*Kammerdiener*) to the Count Thurn and Taxis, one of the canons of the Cathedral. He studied Philosophy and Law, but he had by this time decided to become a

B

musician, and in 1743 he entered the service of the Prince-Archbishop of Salzburg as fourth violin in the Court Orchestra.

Salzburg, to-day a sleepy provincial city on the borders of Austria and Bavaria, had in the past its period of greatness and of splendour. Its Prince-Archbishop was, though never immensely wealthy, a person of importance with a seat in the Reichstag and a voice in the counsels of the Empire. In 1750 the primacy of Germany added importance to the position of the Archbishop. To-day the princely splendour has long departed from the city, but its traces remain in the many churches and religious institutions and in the palaces and mansions, which weave about one the last enchantment of the Baroque Age. Situated between Styria and the Tyrol on the main route from Italy into Germany, Salzburg, not surprisingly, presents many features of Italian culture. Indeed, although in the eighteenth century Austrian fashions were apeing the glories of Versailles, it was from Italy that the educated classes had obtained those lighter and more elegant characteristics which differentiate them from the true Germans. By the time that Leopold Mozart came to the city, its greatness was already on the wane, and the archiepiscopal finances, although able to keep up a respectable appearance of pomp, were by no means sufficient to pay for it adequately.

In 1744, one year after his first appointment,

2

Leopold was promoted to the position of Violin-Master. Three years later he married Anna Maria Pertl, daughter of an official of the Archbishop's Court at Hüttenstein. Nothing further is known of her origins except that her mother's name was Altmann, and very little of her personal characteristics. So far as we can gather, she was affectionate both as wife and mother, and she appears to have had, at the same time, a biting tongue. It was certainly not from his dour father, that Wolfgang inherited his gaiety and his equanimity, still less the imagination which lighted up everything on which it played ; and we shall not be far wrong in supposing that he owed some of his best qualities, as also some of his weaknesses, to this unassuming woman.

Of the seven children born to Leopold and Anna Maria Mozart, only two survived ; Maria Anna (nicknamed Nannerl), born on the 30th July, 1752, and Wolfgang Amade born on the 27th January, 1756. The boy was christened Joannes Chrysostomus Wolfgang Theophilus (in German, Gottlieb)[1]. In his Italian days he transformed his last name into Amade. These children were born at a small house, which belonged to Johann Lorenz Hagenauer, in the Getreide Gasse, a street in the centre of the city. In 1917 the house was converted into a museum, where may be seen numerous relics of the composer.

In the year after Wolfgang's birth, Leopold

[1] Leopold wrote Theophilus in the Latin form: Amadeus.

3

was appointed composer to the court (*Hofcomponist*). He rose to the position of *Vice-Kapellmeister* in 1763, but he never obtained the Kapellmeistership, although the post fell vacant on several occasions during his lifetime. According to his own account, printed by Marpurg in 1757, Leopold practised all kinds of composition, but had so far published nothing. His works included a number of Symphonies, Concertos for various instruments, Church Services and a host of incidental music for operas, ballets, and the various festivities of the Court. As a composer he was a capable technician, but utterly devoid of imagination or originality. He could turn out correct music for any occasion according to the rules and regulations laid down by the theorists ; but none of it was living music. He attempted to make up for this lack of genius by composing a number of picturesque pieces of programme-music, descriptive of a " Village Wedding " or a " Sledge Drive ", which are further examples of the ridiculous lengths to which the uninspired will go in their belief that music can compete with the pictorial art. Indeed these pieces are only worthy of mention on account of the purely negative influence they had on Leopold's son, who absolutely ignored this kind of music, and probably despised it utterly in his heart.

However, one cannot say that it would have been better for Wolfgang had his father been a more inspired musician, for the influence of a strong personality, especially in one so closely allied to himself, might have been detrimental rather than helpful to the development of his own individuality. It might even have been disastrous to one who was, as we shall see, so easily impressionable. It was sufficient that Leopold had a sound and thorough knowledge of the technique of music, both as composer and as executant. In the latter capacity he gained considerable fame by the publication of a treatise on violin-technique, which came out in the year of Wolfgang's birth. This work was a decided advance on anything that had been done in this direction before. It dealt not only with particulars of violin-playing, but also with general musical principles, in which Leopold shows himself to be an excellent teacher. He demands of the musician first and foremost, that he shall be patient, studious, and unselfish. He condemns outright any virtuosity which may be to the detriment of expression, and warns the reader against the vain and·fatal desire to make a brilliant show. In fact, his horror of artifice leads him into a preference for the honest orchestral player as against the soloist. Moreover, he expects the musician to be a good Christian and an educated man with a knowledge of Poetry and Rhetoric, so that he may be able to interpret the music with intelligence.

Such ideas, narrow as they may be in some

respects, were no bad beginnings for the training
of a young composer, and, if other proof were
lacking, the practical success of his teaching
would be the vindication of Leopold's methods.
In character, Leopold was obstinate, pedantic,
and humourless. He had the narrow outlook
of an honest bourgeois in a provincial town,
away from the main current of artistic and
intellectual development. He was, moreover,
jealous and vindictive, harsh to his inferiors
but ingratiating to those in authority, while his
pessimistic mind summoned up a host of imaginary
enemies in the event of any casual disappointment
to his hopes. At the same time, he was ambitious
not merely for himself, but for his children ;
for he had a strong family sense, and his love
and care of Maria Anna and Wolfgang, however
misguided it may at times appear, redeem for
us, to a large extent, his otherwise unlovable
character.

May we not, indeed, see in Leopold Mozart
the type of parent who has himself risen a little
above his own origins, and, on behalf of his offspring, hopes for yet further advancement ?
He cannot himself step beyond the place he has
reached, and, in desperation at his failure to
achieve his full ambition, he transfers his hopes
to his son. He will be an eager father, anxious
to help in every way. He will be jealous of any
influence other than his own, and intolerant of
any criticism of the policy he may adopt towards

6

his charge, not least if it comes from the object of his affection. But, with all these faults, he will be self-sacrificing and tender, so long as his will is obeyed and his hopes are not thwarted. It follows that he will be a better guide in infancy and in boyhood than in youth. For he is hardly likely to gain the friendship, as apart from the love and respect, of his son, which alone will foster mutual sympathies between age and youth, and breed tolerance on the one side for the prejudices of a set character, and on the other for the keen adventurousness of a growing mind.

There is a tradition that Leopold and his wife were the handsomest young couple in Salzburg. Unless we are to suppose that the standard was not high, the portraits which remain do not bear this out ; but they represent the father at a later date, when hardships and anxieties, together with his natural dryness of temper, had left their mark upon him. One of the earliest pictures, however, an engraving from a water-colour by de Carmontelle, which was done during a visit to Paris in 1764, shows him and his two children as a good-looking trio ; but one fancies that they are somewhat idealised.

In sum, we may regard Leopold as a capable musician, a loving father, and a narrow-minded man. There was, indeed, little chance of his mind being broadened in the atmosphere of Salzburg. If one can transfer him in imagination to some English cathedral-town, even at the present day,

from which access to the capital is difficult, it
will be appreciated that his opportunities for
the cultivation of the intellect would be few,
and his contacts with new ideas, artistic or other,
would be negligible. The isolation of Salzburg
was far greater in the middle of the eighteenth
century and its inhabitants were living, as it
were, on a rocky bed of dead culture, where once
there had been a splendid living stream. There
was no industry of importance in the city, and
everyone from the impoverished nobility down-
wards lived on pickings from the Court. It may
be imagined what an atmosphere of intrigue
and jealousy, which did not spare the musicians
of the establishment, grew up in such conditions.
In short the moral atmosphere was thoroughly
base and corrupt. Leopold was no different from
the rest in his pusillanimous readiness to impute
evil motives to others, but, on the whole, he
showed sufficient strength of character to rise
out of the general rut. In his letters he castigates
the manners of his fellow-citizens and it is small
wonder that Wolfgang, having once breathed
the free air of the world outside, should have been
reluctant to return to the stuffy atmosphere of
his native town. A writer on Germany at the
end of the century mentions a character in the
marionette theatres, called Hanswurst, whose
part was always spoken in the dialect of Salzburg.
" The *rôle*," he says, " would be ineffective,
would in fact lose all its salt, if any other dialect

were used. This character waxes satirical, but most frequently his jokes are gross and often extremely indecent." The writer is deploring the state of the city in his time, but the passage also serves to explain some of the salacities in the letters of Wolfgang Mozart, who was brought up in a town where they were common currency.

At the time of Wolfgang's birth the reigning Archbishop was Sigismund, a severe disciplinarian and pietist of what was then the Old School. He maintained in his Cathedral the older traditions of Church music against the profane influences which were affecting it throughout Europe at that time, so that Salzburg remained, under his rule, almost the last stronghold of the serious style which had been formed during the preceding century. Leopold Mozart speaks about his patron at times with bitterness, but the Archbishop could hardly be expected to accept his violin-master at his own valuation. Leopold's mediocrity as a composer and, still more, his difficult temperament, which included in its make-up an inordinate vanity, hardly marked him out for preferment, especially as he chose to absent himself so frequently from Salzburg. Biographers of Mozart have sometimes appeared to forget, as Leopold himself did, that Archbishops have other affairs to occupy their time than the exclusive cultivation of music and the foreseeing patronage of budding composers.

9

Sigismund seems to have done as much as was reasonable, considering the revenues of the State, to keep up the music of Salzburg without going out of his way to encourage development in the art, for which he did not greatly care.

During Sigismund's reign, the orchestra at Salzburg numbered thirty-three players, some of whom were Italians. For Germany and Austria depended largely on Italy for the supply of musicians and despised home-products. Burney, writing in 1772 just after the death of Sigismund, states that the Archbishop had altogether " near one hundred musicians " attached to his Court. Unfortunately the standards and the ideals of the orchestra were not high. Burney remarks that they are " accused of being more remarkable for coarseness and noise than for delicacy and high-finishing ", and the Mozarts displayed an extraordinary enthusiasm for the contrasting excellence of the Mannheim orchestra, when they heard it at Schwetzingen. On that occasion Leopold makes the characteristic comment that the Mannheim musicians are " all young men of good character, neither gamesters nor topers, so that their conduct is no less estimable than their performances." Although Burney, who based his remarks on hearsay, tells us that " Hieronymus is very magnificent in his support of music . . . he is himself a dilettante, and a good performer on the violin, he has lately been at pains to reform his band ", the orchestra deteriorated during his reign, for six years later Wolfgang writes from Paris :

> " One of the reasons why I hate Salzburg so much is that the orchestral players are such gross and dissolute ragamuffins ! A decent man with a knowledge of life cannot endure to live with them. Instead of finding pleasure in their company, he must blush for their conduct. That is why, with us, music is neither loved nor esteemed."

It was not long before Leopold perceived that his two children were remarkably gifted. Nannerl, as Maria Anna was nicknamed, soon displayed astonishing facility, and at the age of three, Wolfgang began to show an interest in his sister's music-lessons. Like most other children who have reached the age when their fingers get busy, he enjoyed playing about with the keys of the clavier. But what differentiated this child from others was his pronounced liking for concords and his aversion from discords. It is easy to imagine the joyous gurgles which we are told he gave, when he put down a satisfying third. He soon advanced to the stage when he could finger out from memory bits of the tunes he had heard. The boy was moreover gifted with an ear so keen that he could detect the slightest variations of pitch. There is the well-known story recorded by Andreas Schachtner, a Salzburg musician, that at the age of seven he was presented with a violin by Schachtner, whom Wolfgang asked a few days later : " What's the matter with your butter-fiddle ? When I was playing on it it was an eighth of a tone lower than my own ", and he proved to the visitor that the new violin was in fact lower in pitch than his own. This gift of " absolute pitch " is not in itself remarkable, for it is possessed by quite a large number of people. The strange thing is that its possessors rarely show any great musical gifts in other directions and seldom rise to any position more exalted than that of piano-tuner. The combination of this gift with his extraordinary powers of memory and assimilation enabled Mozart in his later years to write with such facility that there was no check whatever on the free range of his imagination, and from this facility also arises the fact that in his enormous output there is a good deal which has not the life kindled by that divine fire.

In his fourth year Wolfgang may be said to have begun his serious musical studies, and at five he opened his career as a composer. The earliest piece of which we know is a little minuet which was transcribed by Leopold into an exercise book belonging to Nannerl. Leopold has marked it as having been written in January 1762. It is, of course, an exceedingly simple piece, consisting of one phrase repeated at different levels in the scale. It is interesting, however, to note that

the infant composer had already the invention
to vary his monotonous little rhythm by breaking
up the first two quavers of his phrase into a
triplet in the second bar before the repeat.
There are several other pieces of the same date
in the sister's notebook. In the summer of this
year Leopold took the two children to Munich
on the first of those journeys, which were to
broaden the boy's mind and wreak such havoc on
his growing physique. There is no record of
this visit to Munich, a journey of about thirty
miles, except in a biographical notice written
by Maria Anna after her brother's death. According to her account they remained there for three
weeks and then returned to Salzburg.

About this time Wolfgang's growing powers
began to astonish even his fond parents. There
are innumerable stories, more or less authentic,
of his precocity and there is no need to disbelieve
the facts that lie behind them. After all, infant-
prodigies who have accomplished astonishing
things are not unknown, though they are fortunately out of fashion as public performers
to-day. What distinguishes Mozart from the
rest, is that he possessed sufficient character to
go through a period of early adulation without
being spoilt; sufficient pluck to face without
despair the subsequent years of hardship and
neglect; and, above all, a wonderful musical
sensibility which has, in no other case, been
allied in so great a degree with these more

mechanical gifts. It must be remembered, too, that, both from the point of view of performance and composition, eighteenth-century music was extremely simple. No child of six could possibly go through the complicated cerebration necessary for an understanding of modern music comparable with Mozart's early facility in the narrow conventions of his day.

It is not necessary to suppose that Wolfgang was in other respects an abnormal child. It is true that so soon as he discovered the joys of playing with a clavier he abandoned the more usual playthings, but there is no reason to regard this as, in the first instance, anything more than the substitution of one toy for another, the new one being the more acceptable owing to the extraordinary delight taken by his ear in musical sounds. There is plenty of evidence to show that the boy's mind was quite healthy and normal. He was exceedingly sensitive and affectionate, especially towards his father, whom he regarded as second only to God. He was no exception to the rule in his childish aptitude for quaint turns of phrase. How many fond parents have recounted such remarks made by their extraordinary children as Wolfgang's name for the violin, which I have quoted from Schachtner's story! The pages of *Punch* would be halved by the abstraction of the bright sayings of children under the age of five, which it contains, and it would take several Herods to destroy all the infants who kiss their father's noses every night and sing strange rigmaroles to tunes of their own composing like Wolfgang's "Oragna fiagata fà, marina gamina fà."

Nissen, who married Wolfgang's widow and edited his remains with more care for her reputation than scrupulous regard for the facts, relates that the boy never showed the slightest discontent at any order given by his father. "After having played all day, he would readily play again at his father's request. He never needed corporal punishment. He obeyed any sign from his parents so far, that he would not take or eat the least thing without their invitation to do so. However, he worked too hard for his constitution. He had to be dragged from his clavier. This lack of care for himself continued until his death." His docility and obedience to his father are more remarkable than his capacity for taking infinite pains. For it is usual with men of genius to have a most troublesome streak of intolerance towards attempts to curb their will, which inclines them in turn to a reaction against the immediate past, if not to more serious eccentricity. In this respect Wolfgang was indeed exceptional, for he did not break free from his father's severe tutelage until he was twenty-four, and that in spite of his precocious development, which might have been expected to make him revolt at a much earlier age.

Wolfgang's interests were almost entirely musical and Mr H. C. Colles has summed up the difference between him and a typical composer of the Romantic School in the dictum: "To Mozart music was life: to Weber, it was a part of life". He showed little enthusiasm for other arts and sciences, with one exception. At one period of his life he abandoned everything else in favour of a wild passion for mathematics. During this phase he scribbled his figures on every available surface, on tables, stools, walls, and even on the floor. His passion for sums did not subside in after years, for we find him signing a letter to Nannerl "Wolfgang de Mozart, Friend of the League of Numbers", and on another occasion he thanks her for sending him arithmetical stories (*Rechenhistorie*) and asks for more. In literature his tastes were inclined towards the fantastic; he loved a good story and was delighted when an Italian admirer presented him with *The Arabian Nights*. His literary interests, however, were not great, and his letters from Milan, Florence, Rome, and Venice ignore almost completely those masterpieces of architecture and painting, which are the chief subjects in the correspondence of the average traveller. Nor does he seem to have been impressed by the natural beauties of scenery. People and their ways absorbed his whole attention and constantly stirred his sense of Comedy and Drama. . . .

We may imagine, then, a very lively child, full of interest in everybody he came across; a very lovable child, too, with his affectionate nature that responded so readily to any sign of friendship. His craving for the display of such signs, which made him ask a dozen times a day whether he was loved, may have been tiresome; and there are several witnesses to the "naughtiness" of his tongue, a fault which he shared with the rest of his family and with most of the people of Salzburg. His sarcasms and unkind jokes at the expense of others are not, however, a true indication of his character. For, in spite of a readiness to fall in with the prejudices of his friends, he was throughout his life genuinely charitable and tolerant in contrast to his father, and these utterances may well have been a mere screen to hide his sensitive feelings, the true nature of which he did not wish to show. The man who conceals his sensibilities in this way is no rarity, and he is often wrongly judged by his unimaginative fellows as malicious, whereas his boorishness is really superficial and not a true indication of his thoughts.

As I have already stated, Wolfgang was endowed with a keen dramatic sense with a bias towards comedy, so that he was quick to see the humorous side of things. I am indebted to Professor Edward Dent for pointing out to me how, in his letters, Wolfgang quickly sums up the people whom he meets, sketching their characters in short sentences which bring them vividly before the reader. In this respect

c

he is exceptional among composers, who are generally introspective and in their letters show little concern for, or interest in, the characters of other people. Richard Wagner, his only rival among dramatic composers, is also the only one who displays a similar aptitude for characterisation in his writings. The presence of this trait shows how the minds of these two men worked, how they looked at things ; and accounts for their inevitable attraction towards opera as the supreme means of self-expression. But, whereas Wagner took life hardly and brought everything to the touchstone of a pessimistic philosophy, Mozart was of a gayer and more careless disposition ; and, though it must not be supposed that his emotions were shallow, he was naturally disposed to a lighter view of life. We shall see that he was led at one stage of his development even into a certain superficiality and meretriciousness of style, which if not actually insincere, lowers the works of that period in our estimation.

Chapter II

THE FIRST JOURNEYS

THE extraordinary precocity shown by his two children gave Leopold the unhappy idea of taking them on a series of tours, which he hoped would not only complete their education but also bring into the family exchequer some much-needed money. The preliminary journey to Munich in the summer of 1762 has already been mentioned. Later in the same year the family went to Vienna. During the journey Leopold wrote to his friend and landlord, Hagenauer, from whom he had borrowed money to pay the expenses of the journey, a series of letters, in which he gives a glowing description of the children's success. At Passau, the Bishop insists on their staying five days and at the end rewards them with—one ducat! At Ips "Woferl" astonishes the monks by his playing on the organ. At the Vienna customs-house the boy plays a minuet on the violin, which results in the family-baggage being passed through without further ado. In this respect they fared more fortunately than Dr. Burney who came to Vienna just ten years later and complained that the customs-house was "remarkably troublesome, particularly in the article of books". Hagenauer is, moreover,

assured that influential persons are at work to
ensure a great success in Vienna. While we may
be sure that, from pride and from policy, Leopold
did nothing to minimize these triumphs, there
is no reason to suppose that the sensation created
was not great. The Austrian Court was quickly
captivated by the charming boy who was so
clever with his little fingers and could even play
a piece when the keyboard was hidden by a piece
of cloth. Wolfgang could hardly fail to become
the pet of the aristocracy. He was so pretty
in his lilac coat, with his apple cheeks, with his
naïveté and his lively intelligence, as may be
seen from the portrait which is now in the Mozarteum at Salzburg. He had none of the pertness
or arrogance of the average " prodigy ", but took
an evident delight equally in his new suit, in the
attentions of brilliantly dressed women and in
the display of his musical gifts.

The Viennese Court had for many years given
exceptional patronage to music. The Emperor
Leopold I, who died in 1705, was himself a keen
musician and allowed his enthusiasm for the art
to preoccupy him to the detriment of State
business so that on more than one occasion the
palace gates were placarded with the admonition :
" Leopolde, sis Caesar, non musicus ". Charles
VI in his turn included music amongst the many
extravagances which left the Empire financially
crippled at his death. During his reign the
chief musicians in Vienna were Johann Fux,

the author of the celebrated " Gradus ad Parnassum " and the Venetian, Antonio Caldara, who was Fux's assistant and a prolific composer of opera and oratorio. Seventeen years before Mozart's visit Maria Theresa had succeeded to the throne and, after surmounting endless difficulties, had settled down to the enjoyment of it with her consort, Francis of Lorraine, who was somewhat overshadowed by the strong personality of his wife. Maria Theresa had in her youth shown a taste for music and a talent for performance. She sang in an opera by Fux and her daughters frequently appeared in the performances given at the Court. Burney records that he was told " by a person of great distinction " that they sang " very well for princesses ". Francis was also fond of music, so that the ground was favourable for the appearance of the remarkable infant-prodigies from Salzburg.

The seriousness of Wolfgang's musicianship even at this age is attested by his dislike of playing to merely fashionable assemblies. On one occasion he refused to play before the Emperor until Wagenseil, the distinguished composer and clavier-player, who was then in his seventy-fifth year, had been summoned to turn the pages of the music—one of Wagenseil's own concertos—which the boy was to play. On the other hand, when music was not toward, Wolfgang was just a happy child. He played with the young Archduchesses and, when Marie Antoinette picked

him up after a tumble on the polished floor, the
young gallant said : " You are kind, I will marry
you ".

The most interesting souvenir of this visit to
Vienna, apart from the above-mentioned portrait,
is a notebook given to Wolfgang by his father,
containing a number of pieces which Leopold
thought suitable for the boy's education. The
pieces include compositions by Telemann, Philipp
Emmanuel Bach, Hasse, and a solitary *sonatina*
by an entirely undistinguished composer, named
Gottfried Kirchoff. The writing has sometimes
been simplified for young fingers, and the pieces
have been strung together to form suites, no
doubt in order to give them an added interest
in the eyes of the pupil. The choice of pieces
is interesting, because it shows how out of touch
with the recent developments of musical form
the Mozarts were. At a time when the sonata
was supplanting all other forms of composition,
we find in an exercise book compiled for budding
genius, one little *sonatina* of the most mediocre
kind. All the rest are dances—minuets, gigues,
polonaises, and so on. However, if one could
put this choice down to the deliberate intention
of the father, he might be complimented on his
perspicacity. For the presentation to his son of
the more complicated sonatas, which were being
composed at the time, might well have been too
much for the child at this early age ; and, even
if most of these pieces have little intrinsic merit,

they are, at least, examples of musicianly skill and, therefore, suitable for the education of a child.

The Mozarts returned to Salzburg in January 1763, having been absent for a longer period than the Archbishop had originally sanctioned. Throughout his subsequent career the elder Mozart was none too punctilious in the performance of his duty to his patron, when the interests of his son's career, as he viewed them, conflicted with it. The success of the children at Vienna fired Leopold's ambition for wider conquests and six months later the family set out again on a tour of the German Courts with Paris as the ultimate objective. Their carriage broke down at Wasserbrunn, where, to fill in time, Leopold took his son to inspect the organ. " The latest thing is ", he writes, " that . . . I explained the pedal mechanism to Woferl. He set to work to try it on the spot ; pushing aside the stool, he preluded standing up, and there he was using the pedals as skilfully as if he had practised for months."

From Munich, the first big city to be visited, they went out to the Nymphenburg, the summer residence of the Elector of Bavaria—one of the many baroque pleasaunces which had sprung up all over Germany and Austria in somewhat bourgeois emulation of the glories of Versailles— where the boy played a violin-concerto with cadenzas improvised by himself. The visit seems to have been profitable. He had less " honour in his own country " at Augsburg, and an attempt to gain an audience with the Duke of Würtemberg at his summer palace was unsuccessful. This failure was ascribed by Leopold to the machinations of Jommelli, the Kapellmeister, " who takes good care to prevent Germans having access to the Court ". There is not the slightest reason to suppose that there was any real foundation for this suggestion. Jommelli was an amiable man and occupied a position which makes the idea of his jealousy of a child of seven quite ridiculous. Leopold's remarks are merely an example of his own ill-natured readiness to ascribe the worst possible motives to anyone who appeared to thwart his son's career.

At Schwetzingen, which was visited next, they had a better reception, and it was here that, as I have already mentioned, Wolfgang had the opportunity of hearing the celebrated Mannheim orchestra. The experience to the boy must have been much the same as that of a musical lad, who after hearing nothing better than the municipal band at one of our seaside towns, should be taken to a concert by the London Symphony Orchestra. Passing through Heidelberg and Mainz, where concerts were given with good results, the Mozarts reached Frankfurt in the middle of August. Here one concert was announced, but, owing to popular demand, as we are told in an advertisement in the Frankfurt newspaper (a " puff " undoubtedly inspired by Leopold), it had to be repeated three times. Leopold was an excellent advertisement-writer. He knew all the tricks of the business and his announcements only differ from the curt and heavily typed " special engagement " and " positively last appearance " of to-day by reason of the flowery language in which they are couched.

Among the audience at one of these concerts was Goethe, who recorded to Eckermann in his dotage : " I saw Mozart as a child of seven, when he was on one of his concert tours. I was fourteen myself and still remember quite well the little boy with his powdered wig and his sword ". At Aix Wolfgang captivated the heart of Princess Amalie, sister to Frederick the Great, who urged them to go to Berlin, and bestowed on the boy a multitude of kisses—which was all that the poor lady could afford. Leopold comments sourly, " if her kisses were *Louis d'or* we should be well off ; as it is, neither hotel bills nor post-horses can be paid for with kisses ".

The voyage to Brussels was uneventful and their stay in the city deserves mention only on account of the fact that here Wolfgang came across the sonatas of Johann Gottfried Eckard, a composer from Augsburg. Eckard, though himself a mediocre composer, was under the influence of Philip Emmanuel Bach, so that here, for the first time, Wolfgang came into contact with the great traditions of German music in its larger

forms. There can be no question of the effect
of this enlargement of the boy's musical horizon,
for he sat down at once to write pieces in the
newly developed form, worthy examples of which,
as we have seen, his father had not included in
the exercise book. M. de Wyzewa, moreover,
points to an obvious echo of a passage from one
of Eckard's sonatas in the first of Wolfgang's
compositions in this form.

The Mozarts arrived in Paris in the middle of
November. Here they found a powerful patron
in Melchior Grimm, to whom they had obtained
an introduction. Grimm, who was a German
settled in Paris, occupied an influential position
in the literary and artistic life of the city and was
one of the editors of the famous Encyclopedia.
He was, in a superficial way, a brilliant writer
and a man of unusual intelligence and refinement.
His position as the centre of a circle of men, whose
intellectual attainments were in reality far greater
than his own—men like Diderot, Rousseau,
Galliani, and Marmontel—corresponds to that
of the clever publicist of our own day. He was
a good talker and, without possessing a profound knowledge, an acute critic. At the same
time he was, for all his charm of manner, self-
centred and cold of heart. He never forgave
the composer, Schobert, for refusing to acquiesce
when he wished to constitute himself Schobert's
patron and protector in Paris.

Grimm met with no such opposition from

Leopold Mozart, and in December of this year he notes down in the *Correspondence*, which was the most powerful weapon of his influence, his astonishment at and his admiration for the two clever children of the Salzburg musician. In the war which was raging at that time, between the French and Italian composers in Paris, Grimm was one of the most vehement supporters of the latter—a fact which accounts, at least in part, for Leopold Mozart's violent prejudice against everything French. It accounts also for the anger of French critics, who, even after the lapse of more than a century, can forgive neither Leopold nor Grimm for their attitude towards French music ; for the most *savant* and scholarly Frenchman immediately loses all sense of proportion immediately the artistic productions of his country are criticized, and indulges in a display of ill-tempered chauvinism which at once amuses and distresses the impartial observer.

After all, is Leopold Mozart so very far out, when he writes in January, 1764, that the French music of the period is not worth twopence ? " The French," he continues, " are beginning to succumb very quickly, and I am certain that in ten or fifteen years no trace of the French style will remain. It is the Germans who are masters, so far as published music is concerned. Among them, Schobert, Eckard, and Honnauer are particularly appreciated. . . ." In the same letter he speaks of the music for solo voices in the

Court Chapel at Versailles as " empty, cold, and wretched, that is to say thoroughly French ", though the choral works are " good and even excellent ".

It should be remembered that Leopold Mozart is criticizing the music being produced at the date of which he is speaking. The only big figure in French music was the aged Rameau, who was to die in this very year, and whose *Castor et Pollux* was revived during the Mozarts' visit, to the universal boredom of the audience. There was no one to take Rameau's place, and if Leopold was literally incorrect in his prophecy that the French style would disappear altogether, the remark is justified by the almost complete absence of important landmarks in French music during the remainder of the century. Grétry, and Méhul, who did his best work after 1800, are the only names which rise—and that to no great altitude—above the level of insignificance.

Nevertheless young Wolfgang was to benefit from his contact with Parisian music, for it taught him the value of precision and polish, the two qualities which appear in nearly all the artistic products of the French capital. A deeper impression was probably made by the foreign composers, who were settled in the city, and notably by Schobert. For, although Leopold was prejudiced by Grimm against the Silesian composer, he mentions him favourably as we have seen, and his son held him in considerable admiration. Fifteen years later, when he revisited Paris, Wolfgang wrote to his father that he was going to buy Schobert's sonatas for his pupils to play. The most important effect of this contact, according to MM. de Wyzewa and de Saint-Foix, was young Mozart's discovery that " the art of music was in a con- dition to fulfil a poetical function, and that he himself in particular was born to play this *rôle* as much as or even more than any other. For the individual and distinct characteristic of Schobert consisted in the fact . . . of his essentially poetic nature. Instead of expressing fully and conscientiously the reality of what he experienced in his heart, as did Eckard and Honnauer—not to mention Leopold Mozart—Schobert instinc- tively transferred his real sentiments, rendered them more ' beautiful ' and lent them a grace and ' poetic ' sweetness ". These acute critics point out that in the four pianoforte concertos by Mozart, which are deliberate studies from Schobert, those characteristics, which might be regarded as typically Mozartian, are actually present in the originals. These characteristics were in fact completely absorbed into the young composer's being and appear in the works of his maturity. So we may regard Schobert, to whom Wolfgang owes so much of the " romantic " element which appears in his work alongside of its " classic " grace and vigour, as being the first of his real masters.

At the same time he encountered the music of a far greater man, who was to be the prime influence upon his musical development, and upon whom he was in turn to react when his own genius had matured, namely Joseph Haydn. The contact was, however, slight and does not assume importance until a later date. The visit to Paris was undoubtedly a success. Wolfgang and Maria Anna were introduced at Versailles, and the boy captivated the King's daughters. Mme de Pompadour, however, refused to kiss him, whereupon he rather tactlessly protested : "Who is this that does not want to kiss me ? The Empress did ". During their stay Wolfgang made his first appearance in print with a set of four sonatas for pianoforte with violin accompaniment (a reversal of the normal procedure of later days) which were composed in Brussels and Paris largely under the influence of Eckard and Schobert. Among the other relics of this visit is the charming portrait-group of Leopold Mozart with his two children by de Carmontelle, which is well-known through the engraving made by Delafosse. This picture shows Leopold playing the violin in a very nonchalant posture, Wolfgang, on the contrary, sitting very upright at a clavier, very lively and intent on the music, and Nannerl, who wears a powdered wig and an elaborate dress, about to sing.

On April 10th, 1764, the family left Paris and went by the familiar Calais-Dover route—not without the equally familiar discomforts which that route still entails—to London, where they found lodgings with a Mr Williamson in Frith Street, Soho. On April 17th, four days after their arrival, the children appeared before the King and Queen and received a present of 24 guineas—" only ", adds Leopold in his account. However, if the remuneration seemed scanty to the father, the impression made was considerable, and their Majesties condescended to bow from their carriage to the Mozarts, whom they met when driving in St James' Park. At a second appearance before the Court, Wolfgang played at the King's request some pieces by J. C. Bach and Handel at sight, and accompanied Queen Charlotte in an air. He then astonished the assembly by picking up the bass part of one of Handel's airs, and improvising upon it a beautiful melody. " What he knew when he left Salzburg ", comments the father, " is but a shadow in comparison with what he now knows ".

The next step to be taken by Leopold was the public *début* of the children, which would extend the successes gained to a wider circle. The chief places of musical entertainment in London were the " Pleasure Gardens ", among which those of Vauxhall and Ranelagh were the most important. Here music was to be heard both indoors, and outside in bandstands like those in our parks to-day. There is no better description of these places than Boswell's of Vauxhall " that excellent

31

place of public amusement . . . peculiarly
adapted to the taste of the British nation ;
there being a mixture of curious show—gay
exhibition, musick, vocal and instrumental, not
too refined for the general ear—for all of which
only a shilling is paid ; and, though last, not
least, good eating and drinking for those who
choose to purchase that regale ".

The well-known picture by Rowlandson of
Vauxhall Gardens at a later date shows the
assembled company listening, or rather not listening, to Mrs Weichsel singing an air to the
accompaniment of an orchestra. The musicians
are in an outdoor pavilion with a sounding board
over the singer, and below them at a table in
an alcove sits a group of persons, who have been
somewhat dubiously identified as Dr Johnson
and his cronies, Mrs Thrale, Goldsmith, and
Boswell, in evident enjoyment of that regale.

In the centre Georgiana, Duchess of Devonshire,
is holding court, while further over the Prince
of Wales is whispering in the ear of Mrs Robinson
(Perdita) to the annoyance of her husband.
Some commoner people are behaving in a commoner way at tables on the right. At the back
may be seen the enthusiasts gazing up at Mrs
Weichsel's face, as on an August evening in the
Queen's Hall they gaze up at Sir Henry Wood's
back. The orchestra consists of strings, some
oboes, a harassed-looking bassoonist, who has
perhaps lost his place, a jolly player on the

tympani, and two proud trumpeters, who blow for all they are worth on their "loud uplifted" instruments. These last have no music before them and are doubtless playing tonic and dominant in perfect alternation and security.

At Ranelagh, which opened early in the eighteenth century, the great feature was the Rotunda, a vast circular hall whose roof was supported at its centre by a group of ornate arches with a large fireplace in their midst. You may see it, as it was in 1754, depicted by Canaletto in Room VII at the National Gallery. The company circulates, in the huge space between the fireplace and the supper-boxes, like phantoms. For Time, the sure discoverer of impatient work, has made the underpainting visible through the hooped dresses and the brocaded coats. Poor ghosts! Your contemporary, Mr Matthew Bramble, contemptuously likened you to asses in an olive mill "following one another's tails in a circle, while the other half (of the company) are drinking hot water under the denomination of tea". On the right of Canaletto's picture is the orchestra sawing away at its fiddles, while two singers are doing their best to attract the attention of the indifferent audience. But there is another side to that matter, for Mr Bramble remarks, "as for the orchestra, the vocal music especially, it is well for the performers that they cannot be heard distinctly". I cannot make out that there are any wind-players in the picture,

but there is an organist at the back. At this time
the concerts usually began at 6.30 or 7, and consisted of several " acts ", between which " the
company walked in the garden to the music of
clarinets and horns ". The programmes included
Odes upon various special occasions, the birthday
of the King, the advent of a Royal heir, or the
signature of some treaty of peace. But besides
these adulations of Royalty or of politic diplomats,
there were performances of masterpieces like
Handel's *Acis and Galatea*. Moreover, the
promoters were evidèntly not unconscious of the
comic side of certain odes, for among the works
given in 1763 was Bonnel Thornton's burlesque
Ode on St Cecilia's Day, adapted to the Antient
British Musick : viz. the Salt Box, the Jew's
Harp, the Marrow-Bones and Cleavers, the
Hum-strum or Hurdy-Gurdy, " and all kinds of
musick ". The music was composed by Dr
Burney, and Beard was one of the singers.
Dr Johnson found this jest amusing, and to
judge from the lines recorded by Boswell, the
" music " must have sounded something like
that of a jazz-band.

But we must not take this as being typical of
Ranelagh's entertainments nor accept the evidence
of Mr Bramble, who was something of a cross-
patch, without scrutiny. We need turn only a
page or two of *Humphrey Clinker* to find his niece,
Miss Lydia Melford, writing about the music
at Ranelagh with the abundant enthusiasm of a

schoolgirl. To her eyes the Rotunda was the " enchanted palace of a genii ", in which not asses, but " exulting sons and daughters of felicity tread this round of pleasure or regale in different parties, and separate lodges, with fine imperial tea, and other delicious refreshments, while their ears are entertained with the most ravishing delights of music, both instrumental and vocal ". The famous Tenducci was singing on the occasion of her visit, " a thing from Italy—it looks for all the world like a man, though they say it is not. The voice to be sure is neither man's nor woman's, but it is more melodious than either ; and it warbled so divinely, that while I listened, I really thought myself in Paradise ". Miss Lydia was no less gushing about the music at Vauxhall where she heard an anonymous lady, " whose voice was so loud and shrill, that it made my head ache through excess of pleasure ". How little in some ways has the world of music changed since then !

These were, briefly, the conditions of musical life in London at the time of the Mozarts' visit. The father chose for the concert to be given by his children the Great Room in Spring Garden, near St James' Park, and with his usual astuteness arranged that it should take place on the 5th June, the King's birthday. This " Grand concert of vocal and instrumental music " was announced in the *Public Advertiser* for some days in the following terms :

" For the benefit of Miss Mozart of Eleven and Master Mozart of Seven years of age, Prodigies of Nature.[1] This method is therefore taken to show to the Public the greatest Prodigy that Europe or that even Human Nature can boast of. Everybody will be struck with Admiration to hear them, and particularly to hear a young boy of Seven Years of Age play on the Harpsichord with such Dexterity and Perfection. It surpasses all Understanding and all Imagination ; and it is hard to say whether his Execution upon the Harpsichord and his playing at Sight or his own Compositions are the most astonishing. His Father brought him to England not doubting but that he must meet with success in a Kingdom, where his countryman Handel received during his life-time such particular Protection. Tickets at Half a Guinea each, to be had of Mr Mozart at Mr Cousin's, Haircutter, in Cecil Court, St Martin's Lane."

Mr Mozart was, indeed, a clever Press Agent. Our modern publicity man should admire that reference to Handel, even if it does not altogether fulfil the requirements of " Truth in Advertising," for there was little real kinship between an Austrian of that day and a Hanoverian, and Viennese culture was far more Italian than Teutonic. It will also be noted that Leopold takes a year off Wolfgang's age. He had evidently done the same in Paris, for Grimm speaks of the boy in his *Correspondence* as being seven in January, 1764.

The concert was the success which it deserved

---

[1] There is evidently a hiatus here in the advertisement.

to be, and the *Public Advertiser* of June 29th announced that at a concert for " the benefit of a Public, useful Charity " to be given that day at Ranelagh " the celebrated and astonishing Master Mozart, lately arrived, a Child of Seven Years of Age, will perform several select Pieces of his own Composition on the Harpsichord and on the Organ, which has already given the highest Pleasure, Delight, and Surprise to the highest Judges of Music in England or Italy, and is justly esteemed the most extraordinary Prodigy, and the most amazing Genius that has appeared in any Age ".

A long homily on the virtue of charity follows, which shows that the advertisement of concerts cannot then have been the costly matter it is to-day. This must have been a great occasion, for the programme included, besides the appearance of Mozart, some choruses from *Acis* and *Alexander's Feast*. But musical criticism was not so regular as nowadays. For, although there is, about this date, a long account of a forgotten comedy by Mr Foote, I can find no mention in the newspapers of these performances by the greatest executant and composer of his time. One would have expected some description of the event, if for no other reason than that the child was the subject of great public curiosity, like the " Human Frog " and the " Dog-faced Boy ", who were, later on, the chief attractions in the Pleasure Gardens of London.

Leopold intended to remain in England for three months, but his departure was delayed owing to his catching a chill, which developed into a quinsy, after a musical evening at Lord Thanet's. The family moved to the neighbouring village of Chelsea, where the father slowly recovered from his serious illness. During the stay at Chelsea the boy wrote a number of sonatas and his first essay in symphonic form, which was, however, left unfinished. In November a volume of sonatas, which were provided, like the ones engraved in Paris, with an accompaniment for violin or flute, was published and dedicated to Queen Charlotte, who took a lively interest in music and rewarded the composer with a gift of fifty guineas. Among other public recognitions which the boy received, was a request from the British Museum for a contribution to the library. He presented his published sonatas, the engraving of de Carmontelle's picture, and the MS of a specially composed madrigal with English words, " God is our Refuge and Strength ". Moreover, he was subjected to a scientific examination by the Hon Daines Barrington, who published in the *Philosophical Transactions* of 1770 the results of his investigation, which proves conclusively that the extraordinary powers of the boy are neither exaggerated nor legendary.

The visit was eventually terminated in July, 1765, after further concerts had been given,

and, though the financial results were not great—
Leopold Mozart's grumbles at the expense of
English orchestras will find echoes in many hearts
to-day—there is no question that the children's
success was enormous. From the point of view
of its influence on Wolfgang's musical development, the most important event was his meeting
with Johann Christian Bach, the youngest of
Johann Sebastian's sons. This charming musician
and good-natured man was held in great esteem.
His training had been largely Italian and his
style bears little resemblance to that of his father.
J. S. Bach's fame was momentarily eclipsed by
his sons, who were in the van of the development
of the graceful and brilliant baroque style in
music, of which more will have to be said later
on. It is sufficient to call attention, at this stage,
to the fact that at all periods of artistic development the dominant tendencies of the age will
appear in all the arts, and this was the baroque
period in painting and architecture. So it is not
surprising to find in the music of the time a
florid exuberance of decoration. " Bach seems
to have been the first composer who observed
the law of *contrast* as a *principle*. Before his time,
contrast there frequently was, in the works of
others ; but it seems to have been accidental.
Bach in his symphonies and other instrumental
pieces . . . seldom failed after a rapid and noisy
passage, to introduce one that was slow and
soothing. His symphonies seem infinitely more

original than either his songs or harpsichord
pieces, of which the harmony, mixture of wind-
instruments, and general richness and variety of
accompaniment, are certainly the most prominent
feature ". That is how the music of J. C. Bach
appeared to the contemporary ear of Dr Burney.
We may be sure that the impression on the ear
of the young visitor from Salzburg must have
been great, especially as Bach himself was charmed
by the boy's gifts and personality. Just as from
Schobert Wolfgang gained the first inklings of
the poetical and romantic possibilities of music,
so from J. C. Bach he learned his first lesson in
the ornate Italian style of music, which he was
himself to develop to such perfection.

In September the Mozarts were at the Hague,
and Leopold writes to Salzburg a rather over-
anxious explanation of the cause of his delay
in returning to his proper duties. They had been
persuaded by the Dutch Ambassador in London
to visit the Prince of Orange—who, however,
refused an audience. It was now Maria Anna's
turn to fall ill—Wolfgang had had a bad attack
of scarlet fever in Vienna. The girl's case was
more serious and her life was despaired of, so
that the unhappy patient was subjected to lectures
from her father on the vanity of the world and the
blessedness of the death of children. However,
Maria Anna preferred vanity to blessedness,
and lived, whereat her superstitious parent
inconsistently rejoiced. No sooner was Maria

Anna up, than Wolfgang was down—with a severe attack of fever. On his recovery, a new set of sonatas by the young composer was engraved, and the father's book on the violin was published in a Dutch translation. On the whole, apart from his enforced retirement to bed, the months spent in Holland were a period of rest for Wolfgang. He came under no important new influences and all that can be said is that he had moved from the Italian environment of London to a more cosmopolitan atmosphere, where the dominating fashion, so far as there was one, came from Paris.

Paris itself was revisited in July of 1766, whence the family returned, by way of Switzerland, to Salzburg, which they reached at the end of November. The last stages of the journey were in the nature of a holiday and the father had some misgivings about the time that was being lost. " If I knew formerly how valuable time is to youth ", he writes, " I know it more now. You know that my children are used to work. Should they . . . become accustomed to idle hours, my whole building would fall to the ground ". Such words about a child of ten shows a grotesque misunderstanding of the principles of education, which was to have a disastrous effect on the unfortunate victim. The long journeys and the exacting tasks, which the boy had to perform, were enough to undermine the strongest constitution, and it is small wonder that Wolfgang was continually falling ill. The intellectual benefits which were obtained from travel, and the contact with the leading musicians in foreign capitals, were fully counter-balanced by the nervous strain, and it will hardly be denied that, had the ordeal been delayed a few years, the results would not have been less, but probably greater. It must be admitted, however, that, had the tour been delayed, the *réclame* might have been less, since what appeared marvellous in a child of eight would have passed for ordinary in a boy of fifteen. Wolfgang's fame was due to his being a "prodigy," not to the genuinely musical quality of his unusual gifts. From the financial point of view the tour was a success, and, apart from money, the children brought back enough jewellery and other presents to set up a shop, but Leopold must have been conscious that he had done himself no good at Salzburg by his long absence. For in the same letter, he says, "Who knows what sort of reception we shall get on our arrival? Perhaps such a one, that we shall be glad to pack up our knapsacks and set off again". He certainly had not learnt his lesson from experience and the fascination of travel was upon him.

In judging the published compositions of young Wolfgang up to this date, it must not be forgotten that they were, in all probability, touched up and corrected by his father. There is evidence of this in Leopold's remark that some consecutive fifths had been overlooked in one work, which would, he consoles himself, prove to the public that it was the boy's unaided composition. Still further proof exists in the notebook of the London period, which is the only authentic document from which we can judge with certainty the quality of Wolfgang's work at this age. Heuss makes upon it the following comment:

" We see that Mozart, at the age of eight, was by no means the musician firmly seated in his saddle, that we might be led to suppose from his known compositions of this date . . . There is a mass of mistakes. There are, also, too many impossibilities which betray a pure dilettantism. He still lacks control over his inner ear. In sum, this sketch book destroys the idea of a *creative* infant prodigy—and one may be glad of it."

Chapter III

VIENNA AND ITALY

After his return to Salzburg, Wolfgang was kept busy with commissions from the Archbishop and other important persons, who wished to make the best use of the now celebrated young genius. His father fully realized that the boy had much to learn and, in addition to writing a cantata, a symphony, one act of an oratorio, an air for the anniversary of the Archbishop's installation and various pieces of occasional music, Wolfgang was set to study composition in real earnest. The models chosen for him were, according to the account given by his sister to Nissen after Mozart's death, P. E. Bach, Hasse, Handel, and Eberlin. It is strange to find Handel among these names, for Leopold Mozart showed no enthusiasm for his music, which accounts for the small influence it had on the boy during the visit to England, where it was, of course, immensely popular. Hasse was a favourite composer of the Archbishop's and, on account both of his amiable personality and the merits of his music, occupied an eminent position at this time. He was of North German origin, but settled as a young man in Italy where he studied under Alessandro Scarlatti, who treated him, according

44

to his own account quoted by Burney, " with the kindness of a father ". " His later work ", says Professor Dent, " bears little resemblance to the master's. . . . But he doubtless derived from Scarlatti his careful workmanship. . . . He is, moreover, the principal connecting link between the school of Naples and the school of Vienna." His contribution to Mozart's development is, therefore, considerable.

There is an anecdote that the Archbishop, sceptical of the genuineness of the boy's powers, had him shut up for a week while he composed a work to words given by his patron. This story has been referred to the first part of the oratorio, of which the two other parts were composed by Michael Haydn and Adlgasser, but it is more probable that the short cantata, called *Grab-Musik*, is the true subject of the anecdote. The oratorio was successfully produced in Lent, 1767, but neither it nor the comic cantata with Latin words, *Apollo et Hyacinthus*, need detain us. They are *juvenilia*, in which it would be deceptive to pretend to see the first signs of Mozart's greatness as an operatic composer. To this period also belong the first of the series of *Serenades*, *Cassations*, and *Divertimenti* (all more or less interchangeable terms for a suite of pieces), which Wolfgang composed for the Archbishop. Various etymologies have been propounded for the word " *Cassation* ", but they are all more ingenious than convincing. It is more to the

45

point to state that these suites were intended
for performance at banquets or similar festive
occasions. The music was therefore purely
incidental and occasional, and the suite would
not be played right through, but piecemeal at
intervals during the evening. This fact should
be borne in mind when these works are heard
in the utterly incongruous conditions of a modern
concert hall. Before a hushed and serious
audience they often sound trivial and dull.
The equivalent modern conditions are the State
banquets at Buckingham Palace where music
is a mere adjunct to the other ceremonies—or,
for the ordinary citizen, the dinners in restaurants
where an " orchestra " stimulates chatter and
drowns the words.

Leopold Mozart was not content to remain
long at Salzburg and in September of the same
year took his family to Vienna, where the forthcoming marriage of the King of Naples to the
Archduchess Maria Josepha held out prospects
of a profitable season. Misfortune, however,
awaited them, for small-pox was raging in the
city and carried off the bride among its many
victims. The Mozarts sought refuge at Olmütz,
where Wolfgang and Maria Anna developed
the loathsome disease. They were, with most
generous kindness, taken into the house of the
Dean of Olmütz, who was also a Canon of
Salzburg. The boy was very seriously ill and for
nine days lay completely blinded by the swelling

of his face. However, both the children recovered and the doctor received from Wolfgang an air composed by his patient by way of a fee.

In the first days of January, 1768, we find the family back in Vienna. Since their previous visit in 1762 Maria Theresa's consort, Francis of Lorraine, had died, and her son Joseph was crowned Emperor in 1764. At first the Empress-Mother was so disconsolate in her widowhood that she withdrew almost entirely from public business, but her love of rule eventually returned and she shared with her son the burdens of State. Her devout mourning and her position make her in many ways a parallel to Queen Victoria. Like her, Maria Theresa inspired in her immediate entourage the greatest devotion, but was at times the subject of considerable unpopularity among her subjects. Joseph II opened his reign by a vigorous economy-campaign and cut down the expenses of the Court, which naturally did not increase his popularity with the sycophants who had established themselves in comfort about the Throne. Music was, however, encouraged by the Emperor and was, indeed, the only popular form of artistic activity in Vienna during his reign.

Leopold Mozart conceived the idea, no doubt inspired partly by flattering suggestions, that his son should produce an opera. " To convince the Viennese public ", he writes, " of the truth of Wolfgang's talent for composition, I am

determined upon a really extraordinary course :
I have decided that he shall write an opera
for the theatre. And do you know what all the
composers have said at once ? Thuswise ; ' What ?
To-day it is a Gluck who sits at the clavier to
conduct his opera, and to-morrow, in his place,
there is to be a child of twelve ! ' Well, that is
how it will be, in spite of the envious. I have even
succeeded in getting Gluck on our side, so far,
at least, that even if his heart is not with us, he
knows very well that his patrons are also ours,
and so does not dare to show his hostility openly.
. . . It was the Emperor who suggested the idea
of making Wolfgang write an opera and conduct
it himself in the first instance . . . but the
Emperor could say no more, as Affligio (properly
Afflisio) owns the opera-houses. . . . Naturally
there is no question of an *opera seria*, for they are
no longer given here and nobody cares for them.
It will, therefore, be an *opera buffa*, but not a
short one—a work that will last from 3½ to
4 hours. There are no singers here for serious
opera. Even Gluck's sombre tragedy, *Alceste*,
had to be sung by comic-opera singers. And
Gluck himself is engaged upon an *opera buffa* ".
We may note here, once more, the suspicious
mind of Leopold at work. Gluck was an un-
sociable person, and because he did not put himself out in every conceivable way to help the
ambitions of the proud father, he is under sus-
picion of being actively hostile.

There certainly were intrigues against the performance of the boy's work, and Afflisio comes in for a deal of abuse in the letters of Leopold. The impresario placed difficulties in the way of the performance and after a certain amount of rehearsal, the opera was dropped. It must be remembered, however, that the Viennese of the period could hardly be expected to recognize in a boy of twelve the master whom we know, and not unreasonably thought his father's claims exaggerated. Moreover *La Finta Semplice*, which is the title of this work, was in fact not worthy of performance on its own merits. The music contains little indication even of budding genius, and there are no traces of the gift for musical characterization, which Wolfgang was to develop to such a high degree in his later works. Afflisio, who was after all a business man, cannot altogether be blamed for refusing to produce a work which had little prospect of being a success from any point of view.

Leopold set out his grievances in a long petition to the Emperor, and Afflisio was ordered to pay 100 ducats as compensation. The young composer was consoled in turn by the performance at the house of Dr Anton Mesmer of a short comic opera, *Bastien und Bastienne*. This work has for *libretto* a parody, translated from the French, of Rousseau's opera, *Le Devin de Village*. It is a simple little farce and the music composed by Mozart is light and charming, but again

really insignificant. The work has been revived
in recent years, but only as a curiosity. Its
intrinsic value may be judged from the fact that
it is usually mentioned only to point out that
the first four notes of the overture happen to be
the same in rhythm and interval as those of the
first theme in the *Eroica* Symphony.

During their stay in Vienna, the family were
received at Court, where the Empress, who had
herself suffered from the small-pox a few years
before, showed great sympathy for their recent
illness, while the young Emperor brought a blush
to Maria Anna's cheek by the freedom of his
conversation. Owing, however, to the fashion
of parsimony set by the Court, there were few
opportunities for the children to appear. Moreover, Leopold received intelligence from Salzburg
that he might stay away as long as he liked, but
that his pay would be stopped during his absence.
There had been rumours at Salzburg that the
Mozarts were making their fortune, and Leopold
sent the Archbishop a long justification of his
own conduct, together with the usual condemna-
tion of everyone else. One can sympathize to
a great extent with the fond man, absolutely
convinced of his son's genius, in the disappointment he had suffered. He could not get
others to see eye to eye with him, and he was
temperamentally incapable of understanding that
anyone else, who happened to show no particular
interest in his ambitions, was not actively hostile

and in all probability actuated by jealousy. Frivolous Vienna was no place for a man with his serious aim, but he persisted in his attempts to make a success of Wolfgang in this unfavourable environment.

Successes of a minor order there were, the most notable being the performance of a Mass by Wolfgang at the opening of the new chapel of an orphan asylum, at which the Imperial family were present. According to a contemporary paper, the music " was conducted by the composer with the utmost precision and accuracy ". This was probably not the Mass in G major (K. 49) which belongs to this period and is the earliest surviving of Mozart's essays in setting the liturgy. At the time religious music was coming more and more under the influence of the operatic style, and the baroque ornamentations, which are conspicuous in instrumental music, make their appearance also in the music of the Church. This gives to most Masses of the late eighteenth century a superficiality and even a frivolity, which is quite out of keeping with the solemnity of the text. The style did not, however, reach its lowest point of degradation until the following century, when the religious music of men like Rossini became what seems to us little short of blasphemous.

Mozart's early Masses are, to some extent, an exception to the rule. This short Mass in G shows no signs of the new tendencies, but follows the simpler traditions of the previous generation. In the *Missa Solennis* in C major (K. 66), which was composed in Salzburg at the end of 1769, there is a definite tendency to adopt the florid style, though the more austere methods are not wholly abandoned.

The Mozart family had returned to Salzburg in January of this year, and the boy was appointed concert-master to the Archbishop. This position, lofty though it sounds, brought little pay with it and less honour, since it occupied in the table of precedence a place somewhere below the lackeys. The year was spent in further study of the higher branches of composition, the only event being the performance of *La Finta Semplice* by the Archbishop's musicians. Among the compositions of the year may be mentioned the Cassation in G (K. 63), the *Andante* from which is the earliest piece of orchestral music by Mozart which is in the repertory. The movement consists of a charming melody played by the violins over a *pizzicato* accompaniment on the lower strings. There appears in this simple piece for the first time, so far as I can ascertain, that charm and melancholy which are conspicuous in the slow movements of later years.

In December Leopold and his son started out on a tour of Italy which was intended to set the crown on the boy's education. Leopold had wanted to go straight from Vienna to Italy, as is shown in a letter dated 1767, which puts his attitude towards his son in an unpleasant light. He complains that he does not wish to wait until he is too old to undertake the journey and " until Wolfgangerl has reached the age and stature which will deprive his accomplishments of all that is marvellous ". It is clear that the father himself, like the rest of the world, saw in the boy nothing more than a precocious talent, which was to be exploited to the full, before its possessor grew up and settled down as a respectable professional musician. That this was the general opinion of the boy is shown in a passage quoted by Burney from the letter of a correspondent at Salzburg, who says, " If I may judge of the music which I heard of his composition, in the orchestra, he is one further instance of early fruit being more extraordinary than excellent ".

Before this journey Wolfgang had, of course, come into direct contact with Italian music, most notably in London, where the singer, Manzuoli, had befriended him and given him lessons in singing. Moreover, all the German musicians of his day, men like Hasse and J. C. Bach, were profoundly influenced by Italian music. Professor Dent has pointed out that the symphonic point of view developed by the Germans was only obtained by climbing the ladder of Italian opera. Just as we of to-day, unfortunately, get our first notions of music from the pianoforte—though the gramophone and

broadcasting have lately modified the situation
—so the eighteenth-century man regarded music,
in the first place, as singing. And singing meant
Italian opera. The development of symphonic
music from a form adapted to entirely different
ends was not to be perfected at once. Many
operatic conventions remain in the early symphonies, just as for a long time the sculptors
of Athens continued to carve marble as if it
were wood, and the first Italian painters to paint
pictures as if they were making a mosaic of gilt
and coloured *tesserae*.

It was, therefore, as important for a young
musician to visit Italy and study the art of music
there at first hand, as it still is for the student
of painting to visit Rome and Florence and
Venice. You may see foreign pictures in the
National Gallery or hear foreign music in a London
concert hall, but neither can be quite so fully
appreciated as in their native environment.
Mozart's Italian tours are consequently of greater
importance in his musical development than his
journeys to France and England.

The first important city to be visited was
Verona, where Leopold and Wolfgang remained
for a fortnight. They were well received by the
notables of the place and a portrait of the boy,
which is now in the Mozarteum at Salzburg, was
painted by Cignaroli. This portrait shows
already the beginnings of maturity in the boy's
face, though the wistful expression of the eyes

is contradicted by the self-conscious smile, half-repressed, of the mouth.

At Mantua it was very cold and Leopold informs his wife that the boy's complexion has suffered from the winds and the scorching fires. A concert was given under the auspices of the Philharmonic Society at which a number of works by Wolfgang were performed with great success. Passing through Cremona, they arrived in Milan on 23rd January. Here they found a warm friend in Count Firmian, whose elder brother had preceded Sigismund as Archbishop of Salzburg. Through his influence they obtained an entry into Milanese society, and once more Leopold is able to give a joyful account of his son's triumphs. The boy himself sent home, mostly to his sister, lively letters full of boyish fun, and usually written in a mixture of German and Italian. Often these messages are mere postscripts added to his father's letters, for he was kept too busy with his music to write at length. He signs himself in all kinds of fanciful ways, such as " I remain the same—but what?—the same joker, Wolfgang in Germany, Amadeo in Italy, de Mozartini ". But when he has heard some piece of music that has pleased him, he becomes serious and describes the experience at length with critical acumen. Firmian gave the boy a finely printed and bound set of Metastasio's works, and Wolfgang set to music three of the poet's songs for performance at a *soirée* given by the Count. The most important result of the visit was a commission to write an *opera seria* for production in the following year. He was to receive a hundred ducats as fee and free lodgings in the city for the period necessary for the production of the opera. This meant that he had to return to Milan in November. In the meantime he was free to continue his Italian travels.

They left Milan in March and the next important stopping-place was Bologna, where a concert was given at the house of Count Pallavicini. This was attended by all the nobility, but, from Wolfgang's point of view, the most important personage in the audience was Padre Martini, who, says Leopold, "never goes to concerts". The distinguished old musician was evidently impressed by the boy, for the Mozarts were invited to visit him, and Wolfgang was given a subject on which to improvise a fugue. Martini was the most learned musician of his time, but he was no dry pedant. His amiability and sense of humour are apparent in his portraits, and his scholarship was joined with a very considerable genius for composition. His works carry on the old traditions of the Italian contrapuntal style. Burney, who was in Bologna during the Mozarts' second visit later in this year and remained there, at Martini's suggestion, in order to hear Wolfgang play, says that "the excellence of his (Martini's) character . . . inspires not only respect but kindness. He joins to innocence of life, and simplicity of manners, a native cheerfulness, softness, and philanthropy. Upon so short an acquaintance I never liked any man more ; and I felt as little reserve with him in a few hours, as with an old friend or beloved brother ". Of the Mozarts Burney has unfortunately nothing interesting to relate.

It was natural that this genial and kindly old man should win the affection of a sensitive boy. If young Wolfgang had found little to interest him in the exercises of Fux and the teaching of his father—who wrote of his own violin-exercises, " the more distasteful they are found, the better I shall be pleased "—he must have been delighted tc find a master, to whom counterpoint was not an end in itself, but a means to the attainment of a sense of style. The result of this contact was a definite increase in Mozart's store of learning and laid the foundations of his mastery of counterpoint, which in his works never appears, to paraphrase Professor Dent's judgment, as a display of erudition, but as a means of poetic expression, with the consequence that his polyphony, instead of sounding deliberately archaistic, is always essentially Mozartian and imaginative. Like Burney, the Mozarts were greatly impressed not only by the padre's learning and good nature, but by his unique collection of books and music, most of which he bequeathed to the library of the Liceo Filarmonico at Bologna.

A musical figure of another kind, whom the

Mozarts met in Bologna, was Carlo Broschi, called Farinelli, the most famous *castrato* of his time. He had long retired from the stage, and, after having practically governed Spain as the favourite of King Philip V, had settled down in Bologna when Charles III succeeded to the throne in 1761. Farinelli was a genuine musician and a man, if one may call him such, of refined taste and amiable character. Unlike so many great singers, he took a real interest in the art and in the younger generation of musicians. In an age in which song was paramount in music, and whose musical history is the history of song and singers, his prestige was enormous.

From Bologna the travellers went to Florence, where they fell in with their London acquaintance, Manzuoli, who consented to sing in the opera to be produced at Milan. Here, too, Wolfgang met Thomas Linley, an English violinist of his own age, for whom he formed a passionate attachment. Linley was the son of the composer, Thomas Linley, who wrote a number of operas, the most notable being *The Duenna*, of which the *libretto* is by Sheridan. In this work, which has recently been revived with success, the son collaborated with his father. The boy was unhappily drowned shortly after his return to England, and a musician of unusual promise was thereby lost to us ; for, according to Burney, Italian opinion held the English boy in as great esteem as the Austrian. Wolfgang parted from his friend with tears, and set out for Rome, where they arrived in Holy Week after an unpleasant journey.

Here young Wolfgang proceeded to perform another of his astonishing feats. It was the custom for a *Miserere* by Allegri to be sung on the Wednesday and Friday in Holy Week by the Papal choir. The music was reserved for these occasions and no one was allowed to copy it, the choristers being subject to the penalty of excommunication if they divulged its secrets. So Master Wolfgang proceeded to write down this complicated polyphonic composition from memory after the performance on the Wednesday and then corrected it on the Friday, concealing the music-paper in his hat. Leopold was at first nervous about the consequences, if the fact became known. However, he was too much pleased to keep his secret and, instead of punishment, it brought Wolfgang honour. It may be mentioned that in Leopold's opinion the manner of performance was more important than the composition itself.

Neither of the Mozarts display much of the enthusiasm for Rome which is usual among travellers. The following postscript to a letter of his father's is quoted as typical of Wolfgang's epistolary style at this time :

ROME,
April 14*th*, 1770.

I am, thank God, in good health, so is my wretched pen, and I kiss mama and Nannerl a thousand or 1000 times.[1] N.B. I only wish my sister were in Rome, for this city would surely please her because of the harmonious symmetry of St Peter's and of many other things in Rome.—You can see the loveliest flowers in the streets, papa has just told me—I'm an idiot, every one knows that!—Oh! I'm in such distress! There is only one bed in our lodging, and mama will understand that I get no rest alongside papa! So I shall be glad to get into fresh lodgings—Ha! That's a picture of St Peter with his keys, St Paul with his sword, and St Luke with my sister, etc., etc.—I have had the honour of kissing St Peter's toe in *S. Piétro*, and as I have the misfortune to be too small, they lifted me to his height, me myself, your old

Wolfgang Mozart.

A few days later he drops this bantering air and writes to his " *cara sorella* " seriously about his arithmetic and the prospects of Manzuoli singing in his opera. The singer wants a thousand ducats. The composer, it will be remembered, was to get a hundred.

The absence of any descriptions in Wolfgang's letters is worth remarking. He had not an observant eye and it is probable that his attacks of scarlet fever and small-pox had damaged his vision, which must have been further weakened by the severe strain put upon them by constant work both in composing and performing music. So Mozart did not possess the usual attribute of genius, a penetrating glance. His eyes were dull and lifeless. For him beauty was simply a matter

---

[1] This is moderation, often it is nearer 1,000,000,000,000 times!

of sounds, and it was through sound that he perceived it, whereas colour and form escaped the notice of his dreamy eyes.

The visit to Rome was of little musical importance, and after the Easter festivities were over, the Mozarts went on to Naples, which was at first very cold and then excessively hot, so that Wolfgang was able to realize his ambition of getting sunburnt. In one of his letters he describes Rome and Naples as " two sleepy cities ". The climate and hard work were not unnaturally beginning to tell upon him.

The centre of artistic activity in Naples was the house of Sir William Hamilton, the English Ambassador, whom the Mozarts had met in London. Lady Hamilton was a keen amateur of music and was considered the best pianist in Naples. The travellers were entertained by the Hamiltons, and Wolfgang had the usual success both in private and public performances. At one of the latter his powers were attributed to the " magic " of a ring he wore. So he took it off and, to the surprise of the superstitious Neapolitans, played just as well.

On 26th June they were back in Rome, tired and hungry, having consumed on the journey of twenty-seven hours " only " four cold chickens. Wolfgang wrote a note to his sister complimenting her on a composition she had sent, and ending formally, " Mademoiselle, j'ai l'honneur d'être votre très humble serviteur et frère, Chevalier

61

de Mozart ". The Pope had bestowed on the boy the cross of the Order of the Golden Spur, which Gluck also had received. For a while Wolfgang, at his father's instance, signed his compositions " Del Sign Cavaliere W. A. Mozart ". But he soon abandoned this amiable vanity.

A greater honour was conferred on him, when the travellers returned to Bologna, where he was elected after a severe examination to membership of the Philharmonic Society. The event was celebrated in a picture, which has recently been discovered at a sale of old canvases belonging to the Municipality of Bologna, which came from the collection of the Philharmonic Society and probably belonged originally to Padre Martini.[1] The picture represents Mozart handing a piece of music to a gentleman in sumptuous dress, who is paying more attention to the painter than to the young composer. M. Henri Prunières conjectures that this personage is Count Baldassare Carrati, the founder of the Society, and that the figure in the clerical habit, who occupies the centre of the picture, is the President, Petronio Lanzi. The figure on the right certainly bears a strong resemblance to the other portraits of Mozart at the period, with the sensual mouth, small chin, sloping forehead and prominent nose,

In October the Mozarts were back in Milan, Wolfgang being engaged on the composition of

---

[1] The picture is described and reproduced in the *Revue Musicale* of October, 1925. It is not accepted as genuine by all the critics.

his opera, *Mitridate, Rè di Ponto*, while the father struggled with the singers and prepared the ground for a favourable reception. The libretto, which was adapted from Racine's tragedy by Cigna-Santi of Turin, had reached the composer some time before, but he could not begin work on it seriously until the cast was engaged, and the requirements and abilities of the various singers could be considered. For it must not be supposed that the eighteenth-century opera-composer just sat down and wrote his work according to his own ideas and to please himself in the take-it-or-leave-it manner of Wagner. Popular taste had to be taken into account and the singers given ample opportunities of displaying their various individual gifts.

There was a preliminary rehearsal with skeleton orchestra on the 12th December, so that the opera must have taken about eight weeks to write. A few days later Leopold records a full rehearsal with an orchestra of sixty, consisting of fourteen first violins, the same number of second violins, six altos, two violoncellos, six double-basses, two flutes, two oboes, two bassoons, four *corni di caccia* and two *clarini* (the old natural trumpet). " Before the first rehearsal ", continues Leopold, " there was no lack of people to run down the music and pronounce it beforehand in satirical language to be something poor and childish, alleging that so young a boy, and a German into the bargain, could not possibly write an Italian

63

opera, and that, though they acknowledged him to be a great executant, he could not understand or feel the *chiaroscuro* required in the theatre. All these people have been reduced to silence since the evening of the first rehearsal with small orchestra, and say not a word more. The copyist is completely satisfied, which is a good sign in Italy, for when the music is a success, he gets more money from the distribution and sale of the airs than the composer receives for his work. The singers, male and female, are very pleased and quite happy, especially the *prima donna* and the *primo uomo* on account of their duet, which suits them down to the ground. The *primo uomo* said that if the duet didn't take, he would have himself cut again. Bah! It all depends on the caprice of the public. Apart from a little pride, we have no great interest in the matter. We have already undertaken a good many things in this comic world and God has always helped us ".

Notwithstanding this haughty and sententious attitude, Leopold was highly indignant at the various difficulties and intrigues which seem to be inseparable from opera-production in any country and any period of history. However, they were all overcome, and the first performance of *Mitridate* was given on December 26, 1770. The production was most successful, and a Milan newspaper informed its readers that the young composer had " studied beauty from nature and represents it adorned with the rarest musical grace ". Leopold writes home with great enthusiasm that, contrary to all precedent, one of the soprano airs had been encored on the first night, while on the second two airs had to be repeated. " It was Thursday, however," he continues, " and consequently, as the performance could not continue into Friday, they had to make cuts, which prevented the repetition of the duet, for they began to call for it again. The opera, with its three ballets, lasted fully six hours. . . . They now call our son *Il Cavaliere Filarmonico*, just as they call Hasse *Il Sassone* and Galuppi *Il Buranello* ". Leopold writes also to Padre Martini to inform him of his young friend's success. He was quite convinced that this performance was the real beginning of a glorious future for his son.

Leopold no doubt exaggerated the effect produced by this juvenile work, which has nothing in it to make its revival nowadays anything more than a matter of curiosity. However, the fact remains that Wolfgang was promptly elected to membership of the Philharmonic Society of Verona, and was commissioned to compose a *serenata* in honour of the marriage of the Archduke Ferdinand to Maria Beatrice of Medina, which was to take place in October, 1771. *Mitridate* reached the respectable number of twenty performances, but was not given outside Milan.

After the production of the opera, the Mozarts

sought distraction in visits to Venice, Padua, and other Italian cities. They returned to Salzburg in March. The most valuable experience which Wolfgang brought back was his lessons with Padre Martini. His compositions written after his stay in Bologna bear the marks of his contact with the learned man, who combined an interest in new developments with an adherence to the old traditions of Italian Church music. Martini realized the boy's bent towards opera and taught him the rudiments of the dramatic style. Wolfgang learnt from him his first lessons in *ensemble*, which were to bear such wonderful fruit in the *finales* of the later operas, and began to perceive the peculiar capabilities and limitations of the human voice. It is to be noted that, in his earlier vocal works, Mozart attaches rather too much importance to the individual word, one of the few characteristics which may be traced to the influence of his literal-minded father, and it was not until much later that he freed himself from this tendency to piecemeal illustration. Reference has already been made to another important influence, that of Hasse, a number of whose operas he heard during the tour. The *caro Sassone* was among those who appreciated the boy, and he wrote to his friend, Giovanni Ortes at Venice, a shrewd note on the father and son, which is worth quoting :

" Young Mozart is certainly a prodigy for his age and I am really extremely fond of him. The father, so far as I can see, is unceasingly discontented with all that I myself complain of here. He adores his son a little overmuch, and does all he can to spoil him ; but I have so good an opinion of the innate goodness of the young man that I hope that, despite the adulation of his father, he will not allow himself to be spoilt but will turn out an honourable man."

CHAPTER IV

THE period from Mozart's return to Salzburg in March, 1771, until the end of the following year is one of the important crises in Mozart's development. For quite apart from such external and accidental occurrences as the death of Archbishop Sigismund in December of 1771 and the failure of his second opera, *Lucio Silla*, at Milan, Wolfgang passed during this time from boyhood to the half-awakened stage of adolescence, during which even the most insignificant events may have a vital effect upon the mental development. We know very little at first hand of the six months which were spent in Salzburg before father and son set out once more for Italy, except that during that time, Wolfgang fell in love with a girl at Salzburg, to whom he subsequently sent messages in his letters to Maria Anna. It has been conjectured that the girl, who was the daughter of the Archbishop's doctor, was older than Wolfgang, since she was married during his absence in Italy. This love affair cannot have been a very serious matter, but from this time onward it may be said that Wolfgang was never out of love. This is not to say that he was a debauchee. On the contrary, his heart seems to have been absorbed rather in the fact of being in love than in the object of his affection. Like his own Cherubino, he was set in a flutter by the sight of a petticoat, and, were none by to hear him, he would still sing of love ; but his passion, for all its sensuality, seems to have remained, at least until after his marriage and to some extent right to the end, naïve and boyish. It is clear that he never met the woman who could appreciate to the full his exquisite sensibilities, nor the depths of a passion which was far from being merely physical. It is by no means unnatural that such a man should have been able to glorify, in the person of Don Juan, the sensual side of love and the powers of masculine seduction. Arthur Schurig puts the point admirably when he says that, if we wish to find in Mozart " some link with the hero of his finest creation, we can only regard *Don Juan* as the great adventure of an amorous life, which was, in fact, devoid of such adventures ".

A good deal has been said of late about some of the coarser expressions in Mozart's letters, which have been made public only in comparatively recent times. It is natural enough that there should have been a reaction against the plaster-cast figure of a goody-goody, who was translated to Heaven at an early age as being too pure to live on this earth, which the nineteenth-century biographers of Mozart made by a discreet omission of anything that detracted from their ideas of what a composer ought to be. But the revaluation goes too far, when it denigrates him because he indulged in some jokes which are in bad taste according to our notions, but which were very fashionable in the late eighteenth century, especially in Salzburg. After all, we do not turn up our noses at our stockbroker friends because a certain kind of story is labelled " Stock Exchange ", and there is no more necessity to condemn Mozart on the same grounds because he happened to be a very distinguished man. The chief count against him seems to be that these expressions occur in letters to women, notably a cousin, with whom he was on very intimate terms, and his wife. I shall have more to say about the cousin later on. His references to sexual matters in his letters to his wife can hardly be called reprehensible, since they are the most natural thing in the world, especially at a time when physical indulgence was frankly discussed as a matter of course. On the general count it may be said that the reading and conversation of young ladies was not what the stricter morality of the succeeding century imposed upon them, a fact which will be better appreciated nowadays when ideas on these matters have reverted to a somewhat more liberal view.

The months spent in Salzburg were occupied in the composition of several symphonies and a quantity of Church music, including an oratorio on the subject of Judith and Holofernes, called *Betulia Liberata*, which appears to have been begun during the return journey from Italy. This oratorio is Italian in style. It was the custom during Lent to substitute for opera works in this form, which differed hardly at all from the *opera seria* except in the matter of their being performed without costumes and scenery. Such works had nothing in common with the oratorios of Handel and his successors in this country, although the fact that their subjects were taken from the Bible and the circumstances in which they were performed naturally gave them a more serious and " sacred " air than appears in the operas. The symphonies and the organ sonatas, which are in fact symphonic movements for orchestra with an accompaniment of sustained chords on the organ, also show the effects of the composer's contact with Italian music. The inclusion of the minuet in the symphonies is, however, an indication of German influence, which also appears in the greater strength of the music as compared with the works of contemporary Italians.

In the middle of August, Leopold and his son returned to Italy for the production in Milan of the *serenata*, *Ascanio in Alba*, which had been commissioned for the wedding festivities of the Archduke Ferdinand. This was a kind of ballet with vocal music, in which mythological characters gave utterance to sentiments designed to flatter surreptitiously the persons in whose honour it was given. It has something in common, therefore, with the English masque of the sixteenth and seventeenth centuries. The composition of this work was a much simpler task than the production of a full-dress opera like *Mitridate*, for the music had merely to be tuneful and pleasant, and there was no need for characterization or dramatic power. The *serenata* was successful, though the music contains nothing of interest to us. Leopold presumed upon it to request the Archduke to take Wolfgang into his service, but the Empress Maria Theresa wrote to her son, telling him that, while he could, of course, please himself, she advised him not to hamper himself with useless personnel nor to " give titles or employment to these people, who will only dishonour them by running about the world like beggars ". A caustic comment, which readjusts Leopold's disproportionate view of his own actions and of his son's success.

However, the *serenata* proved useful, for it resulted in a commission to write a second opera for Milan to be produced in December, 1772. A similar offer came from Venice and was accepted by Leopold, although it would have been quite impossible to fulfil both these engagements. Possibly Leopold thought he could cancel the contract with Milan and go to Venice, which was at that time the more important city from the operatic point of view. In the end the contract with Venice fell through, for reasons which we do not know.

The Mozarts returned to Salzburg on December 16th, on which day Archbishop Sigismund died. After a lapse of three months the see was filled by the translation of Count Hieronymus von Colloredo, Bishop of Gurk. This personage has always been regarded as the evil genius of Mozart's career, and, like so many other historical villains, his name has probably been excessively blackened. Like them, too, he has in late years found a champion to whitewash him. It will be interesting to quote Arthur Schurig's view, even though we may not wholly accept it. Hieronymus, he says, was " an active and energetic man, forty-five years old in March, 1772. The picture of him derived from the letters of Leopold Mozart is entirely false. Colloredo was by nature independent, enlightened, perspicacious, and execrated bigotry and hypocrisy. His pastoral letter of 1782, a *rara avis* of religious tolerance, is famous. From the beginning of his reign he set himself to fight and to destroy all the routine beloved by the people of Salzburg, which did not make him popular with his subjects who were accustomed to indolence. He set in order the finances of his little State and gradually appointed competent men to the various offices. Personally he was fond of society and an engaging man. He held the sciences in honour and was a musician, perhaps above the average, and one can hardly reproach him, as a man of his time, for preferring Italian to German music ".

Schurig might have added "of his origin" to "of his time", for, as his name suggests, Colloredo came of Italian stock, though his family had for many generations been in the service of the Austrian Court. The accepted view of the Archbishop's treatment of the Mozarts certainly needs modification, since it is based chiefly upon the splenetic outbursts of Leopold, whose most notable characteristic is his readiness to impute the worst possible motives to anyone who did not fall in with his own wishes. It must be remembered, too, that Leopold was disappointed of his expected preferment. Like his predecessor, Hieronymus appointed a new Italian *Kapellmeister* over Leopold's head, when the position fell vacant. He saw that a man so insolent towards his inferiors, and possessed of such overweening vanity was unlikely to make a good head of the musical establishment, a position requiring sympathy and tact. For reasons of economy, too, he was naturally unwilling to appoint a man who spent most of his time abroad and who happened also to be a third-rate musician. However, when Schurig almost goes so far as to give the Archbishop credit for the results of his harshness to Wolfgang, as if he had only punished to be kind, one can hardly follow him. It is true that the narrow limits of Salzburg itself were not suited to bring the boy's genius into full bloom, but there were other ways of leaving it than on the toe of a Chamberlain's boot.

The effect of the new Archbishop's appointment on Wolfgang's music is also a matter for argument. Sigismund had, as we have seen, been conservative in his tastes and insisted on the retention of the old style of Church music at Salzburg. Hieronymus liked the new Italian style. It is arguable that had Sigismund lived longer, Wolfgang would have developed immediately the serious style of his later years, and that we should have thereby been the richer. As it was, the tastes of the new Archbishop intensified the influence of the fashions of the time and induced the young composer to try his hand at the frivolous and ornate manner. In the end this phase undoubtedly enriched the composer's art both in ornament and in technical methods, and it is at least doubtful whether the full development could have been reached until age and experience had matured his mind.

The Mozarts regarded their stay in Salzburg, which lasted this time for ten months until October, 1772, as something in the nature of a rest between two important engagements. For, as we have seen, they were due to be back in Milan at Christmas for the production of Wolfgang's second opera, *Lucio Silla*. During this period the boy produced a number of symphonies and other works, including a cantata, *Il Sogno di Scipione*, which was performed at the festivities accompanying the enthronement of the new Archbishop in April. The work is insignificant and shows signs of hasty composition. In the symphonies, on the other hand, there is a steady improvement in his style and a development of his individuality, which lead to the first full expression of the Mozartian temperament in the A major Symphony (K. 134) composed in August.

These symphonies all show in their form, and sometimes in the details of expression, the influence of Joseph Haydn, though not yet of his three great symphonies (the "Passion", the "Funeral", and the "Farewell") which belong to this same year. In an article in the *Revue des deux Mondes* of June, 1909, M. de Wyzewa suggests that these three symphonies, so unlike in their passionate emotion anything else that Haydn wrote either before or after that date, were the outcome of some private grief, of which we otherwise know nothing beyond a vague tradition. The best-known of them is the "Farewell", which has retained its place on the repertory, mainly on account of the legends which grew up around the curious *finale*, where one instrument after another ceases playing until only two violins are left to sing its poignant theme. If Haydn really composed this work by way of a joke, there is nothing to move the listeners to mirth—unless indeed the double-bass stumbles over his instrument as he walks out. Schumann records a performance in which, according to custom, the musicians put out their candles and left the hall, but adds "no one laughed", for the fact is the music contains nothing to laugh at. The slow movement of this symphony with its sobbing melody, which seems to express the most passionate sorrow, is certainly one of the most moving things in music.

Apart from the possibility of a private grief to inspire this extraordinary outburst in so happy a musician as Haydn, we may see in this and its fellow works the influence of the wave of romanticism which was at this time spreading over Europe, and was to have a profound influence upon Mozart. The movement began in Paris, with Rousseau as its chief prophet; but it found its most complete expression in more sentimental Germany, and its most typical fruits are Burger's *Leonore* and Goethe's *Werther*, both published in 1774. In Germany this revolution in thought, which in the city of its origin was to be transformed into an actual and political upheaval, quickly found expression in music, the most popular of the arts. There is an absolute equivalent to the literary fashion of this period of *Sturm und Drang* in the music of Joseph Haydn, of Gluck and of Mozart. It must not be understood that deep emotion of a romantic nature had never been expressed in music hitherto: but a slow movement by Domenico Scarlatti or a tragic passage in Bach, have not that touch of what critics of painting call *morbidezza*, which now began to appear.

In Mozart, the new ideas are to be seen for the first time in the opera *Lucio Silla*, and may have been precipitated by some personal crisis, such as M. de Wyzewa suggests in the case of Haydn. The new opera was composed to a libretto by Giovanni da Camera, who uses all the machinery of Metastasio, without bringing to its working any genuine inspiration. However, this collection of sentimental persons, dressed up in eighteenth-century ideas of ancient Rome, ridiculous and senseless as it appears to us, was very much to the taste of the day, and there was no cause for failure on that score. *Silla* suffered from a series of misfortunes on the first night : the performance began two hours late to suit the Archduke who had some letters to write, and the *prima donna* was upset both by the behaviour of the tenor, who overacted his part to the amusement of the audience, and by the enthusiastic reception given to Rauzzini, the *primo uomo.* But these accidents alone do not account for its failure. The opera is, in fact, a poor work with flashes of inspiration here and there. It is not so even in quality as *Mitridate*, and the reason is not hard to find. In the earlier work Mozart was applying his imitative abilities to the production of an Italian *opera seria*, and succeeded in turning out a passable piece of work. In *Silla* there are signs that he regarded his work as a piece of drudgery, while at the same time he was every now and then spurred to the expression of his own individuality, which did not fit in with the general style of the work. So we get those passionate arias sung by Giunia, notably " Fra i pensier più funeste di morte ", which forecasts the dramatic and characteristic airs of Donna Anna and Pamina. We may fairly attribute these romantic outbursts to the influence of the literary movement upon a boy, who had reached the restless and impressionable stage of adolescence, and we find in the instrumental works of the period a similar combination of Italian grace and romantic, introspective sadness.

The failure of *Lucio Silla*, which had the practical result that Mozart received no more commissions from Italy, was an important turning-point in his career, for it closed the possibility of his becoming, like so many of his countrymen, an Italian composer just at the time when he was beginning to show a real aptitude for and appreciation of the Italian style. The romantic phase checked him, and the ambition of Leopold to set up his son as a successful composer in the southern land was thwarted.[1] We owe to these circumstances the subsequent development of Mozart as a German composer, and, through that, the first impetus towards the growth of the magnificent movement in the succeeding generation, which is associated with the names of Weber, Beethoven,

[1] Romanticism gained no ground in Italy until the days of Byron and Shelley, whose influences fostered the beginnings of the *risorgimento*.

Schubert, and Schumann, and, finally, of Richard Wagner.

The Mozarts returned to Salzburg in March, 1773, and Wolfgang remained there until August, 1777. The resumption of his duties in the uncongenial atmosphere of Salzburg combined with the disappointment of his Italian ambitions acted upon the youth's fervent state of mind like a douche of cold water, and cooled his romantic ardour. The effect of this shock produced a reaction which appears in his work. The symphonies, *divertimenti*, and quartets belonging to this period retain the Italian formulas, the use of which was probably dictated by the tastes of the patrons for whom they were written, but the inspiration behind them differs more and more from that which appears in his previous compositions. They are informed with the sweeter spirit of German ideals. At the same time disillusionment had robbed him of the romantic feeling, which might have been expected to accompany a reversion to German ideals, and we find the young composer preoccupied with the learned problems of counterpoint and with experiments in the use of orchestral colour, which were to be of vast importance in the full development not only of his own genius but also of symphonic music generally. The *concertino* for two violins (K. 190) composed in May, 1773, is typical of the blending of the Italian manner with a new interest in counterpoint and instrumentation.

During the summer of this year the Archbishop paid a visit to Vienna, and the ambitious Leopold seized the opportunity of taking his son to the capital, in order, so the Salzburg gossips said, to be at hand in the event of the death of Kapellmeister Florian Gassmann, who was ill, but did not actually die until the following year. Leopold denied the slander, but there is no question that he was anxious to obtain for Wolfgang a post at the Viennese Court. There is little of interest in the letters written during this visit, Wolfgang's being a series of boyish ebullitions written sometimes in a jumble of Italian, Latin, French, and German, which results in phrases like "Hodie nous avons begegnet per strada Dominum Edelbach". (This morning we met Herr Edelbach in the street). Such epistolary methods, tiresome though they are to the modern reader, at least show that Wolfgang was in good spirits.

For more serious information about the condition of music in Vienna at this time, we must go once more to Burney, who had visited the city in the previous year. From a long account, to which it will be well worth the reader's while to refer, the following passages may be quoted as throwing light upon our particular studies :

"Party runs as high among poets, musicians and their adherents at Vienna as elsewhere. Metastasio and Hasse may be said to be at the head of one of the principal sects ; and Calzabigi and Gluck of another.

The first, regarding all innovations as quackery, adhere to the ancient form of musical drama, in which the poet and musician claim equal attention from an audience; the bard in the recitatives and narrative parts; and the composer in the airs, duos and choruses. The second party depend more upon theatrical effects, propriety of character, simplicity of diction, and of musical execution, than on, what *they* style, flowery descriptions, superfluous similes, sententious and cold morality . . .

" The merit of Signor Hasse has so long and so universally been established on the Continent, that I have never yet conversed with a single professor on the subject, who has not allowed him to be the most natural, elegant, and judicious composer of vocal music . . . When the voice was more respected than the servile herd of imitative instruments, and at a time when a different degree, and better judged kind of study rendered it perhaps more worthy of attention than at present, the airs of Signor Hasse, particularly those of the pathetic kind, were such as charmed every hearer, and fixed the reputation of the first singers in Europe . . .

" The chevalier Gluck is simplifying music; and, with unbounded invention and powers for creating capricious difficulties, and decking his melodies with meretricious ornaments, he tries all he can to keep his music chaste and sober. His three operas of *Orfeo*, *Alceste*, and *Paride*, are proofs of this, as they contain few difficulties of execution though many of expression."

Although the worthy Doctor disclaims any intention to " take sides, or to determine which of these parties is right ", it is not difficult to see where his sympathies lie, especially as, in another passage, he proclaims Hasse to be "as superior to all other lyric composers, as Metastasio is to all other lyric poets". Yet it is Hasse who is dead, while Gluck yet lives. But the interest of Burney's criticism rests not in the rightness or wrongness of his personal tastes, but in the sure way he hits upon the difference between the old school and the new. He saw that Gluck was perfectly capable of writing Italian operas in the old style, although, as a fact, he was not one of those Germans who could excel the Italian at his own game. He saw, too, that the essential revolution, which was in progress, consisted in the dethronement of the voice from its supreme place in music.

This change was the inevitable result of the gradual northward advance of musical supremacy in Europe. For, as Mr E. J. Dent pointed out in an article published in *Music & Letters*, whereas the instinct of the Italian is to express himself in song, the Central European is born with a fiddle under his chin. In other words, the German turns to instrumental music when he wishes to express himself. The difference of temperament may be attributed, at least in part, to the difference of language. Italian is a quick-moving tongue and very simple in its sounds, both vowels and consonants. German is slow, heavy, and complex. This is not to repeat the old fallacy that German is "unsingable", but the opponents of German

83

had this much right on their side, that it is certainly not singable after the methods and to the music of the Italians. I think that the delay of a century which occurred before Sebastian Bach was generally recognized, was due simply to the fact of the supremacy of the vocal attitude towards music, which prevailed until the end of the eighteenth century. For the music of Bach, a thorough German if ever there was one, is always instrumental, no less when he employs voices than when he writes for an orchestra.

Mozart comes, historically, just at the turning-point, and holds the balance evenly between the two ideals. In the words which Burney applies to Hasse, " equally a friend to poetry and to the voice, he discovers as much judgment as genius in expressing words, as well as in accompanying those sweet and tender melodies which he gives to the singer ", while he does not disdain the " servile herd of imitative instruments ", but puts them to a use which must have won over even the prejudiced mind of the Oxford musicologist.

The summary which Burney makes of his Viennese experience is also worth quoting for the picture it gives of the musical activities of the capital. " Vienna ", he says, " is so rich in composers, and incloses within its walls such a number of musicians of superior merit, that it is but just to allow it to be, among German cities, the imperial seat of music, as well as of power. . . . I shall only mention the names of

Hasse, Gluck, Gassmann, Wagenseil, Salieri, Hofman, Haydn, Ditters, Vanhall, and Huber, who have all greatly distinguished themselves as composers ; and the symphonies and quartets of the five last-mentioned authors, are perhaps amongst the first full pieces and compositions, for violins, that ever have been composed ".

Unfortunately Burney did not come into personal contact with Haydn, whose music was rapidly growing in popularity with the Viennese public. At the time of the Mozarts' visit in 1773, it was being played everywhere, and the theatregoer could hear works by the distinguished composer in the entr'actes, where now he is given the *Valse Triste* or Luigini's *Ballet Egyptien*. Of the other composers mentioned, the elderly Wagenseil belonged to the conservative party headed by Hasse, while Gassmann and Salieri were disciples of Gluck. None of them exercised over the mind of Wolfgang the fascination of Haydn, who became henceforth his only master, until the day when the elder man in turn became the pupil. Mozart had frequently come into contact with Haydn's work, not least through the brother Michael at Salzburg, but it was not until this visit to Vienna that he fully appreciated its quality.

This revelation resulted in a sudden outburst of creative effort on his return to Salzburg in October. The effect was already apparent in the Serenade in D (K. 185) written for Andretter, and the

85

six string quartets (K. 168–173) composed in Vienna, which show an astonishing advance on the chamber-works of the Italian journey. Now at Salzburg he produced a series of four symphonies, which are the highest mark reached by his creative effort until the period of his full maturity. The earliest of these, according to the latest authorities, is the symphony in C major (K. 200), though Köchel places it at a later date in his catalogue. This symphony has an amplitude of form and a breadth of feeling which have not hitherto appeared in Mozart's work. The most striking movement is the Minuet, which distinctly forecasts the idea of the corresponding movement in the " Jupiter " symphony, which is in the same key. The beautiful instrumentation of the slow movement is the fruit of his experiments earlier in the year, while the peculiar metre of the *finale* is only one more sign of the composer's individuality in a work, which superficially is as like the average symphony of the time as one pea is to another.

The two symphonies in G minor (K. 183) and A (K. 201) show the same seriousness of outlook, and are an advance upon the C major both in mastery of construction and in emotional feeling. In these works we find once more unmistakable signs of the romantic influence, of which I have already spoken and which was momentarily crushed on the composer's return to Salzburg from Italy. It appears here in a thoroughly

German guise and the style is utterly different
from that of the works written during the crisis
in Italy under the influence of men like Sammar-
tini and Tartini. It is not impossible to suppose
that Mozart was acquainted with the symphonies
written by Haydn in 1772, to which reference
has been made above (p. 76). At all events we
find in the symphonies in G minor and A, the
same sense of tragic nobility. Then suddenly in
the D major symphony (K. 202), written in May,
1774, there is a falling-off. This symphony is
brilliant and delightful in its elegance, but the
serious outlook, if not wholly absent, is dis-
appearing.

This is not just a casual falling-off as between
one work and another, but persists over a long
period and is the first symptom of an important
change in Mozart's musical development. Up
to the spring of 1774 he shows a decided tendency
to develop at once the manner of his latest works.
But various circumstances, some of which we
have already noted, intervened to turn him aside
from his serious purpose and to tempt him to an
indulgence in a more meretricious exhibition of
his gifts. In the first place, the tastes of his
master, the Archbishop Hieronymus, inclined
towards the latest Viennese style, while Michael
Haydn, the most important composer at his
court, was an exponent of this highly ornate
music. Although Leopold Mozart bore no love
for his colleague, he did not conceal his admiration

87

for his compositions, and there is no doubt that Wolfgang was captivated by the " modern " developments, which had been held in check by the late Archbishop, and, since they also pleased his new master, he naturally wished to produce works in the same style.

Moreover, Joseph Haydn himself had lately adopted the new fashion, and if it was good enough for the great master, whom young Wolfgang admired above all others, it was surely for him to follow his example. What then, are the marks of the new style? In the older symphonies of Haydn, those which we have just discussed, we may note a concision and preciseness of manner, a close relation between one subject and another and even between the various movements, which give to these works their compactness of form. They are vigorous and skilful productions, but not wanting in emotional significance, as witness especially the slow movements.

The works written in the new " gallant " style show more striving after effect, a desire for contrast at the expense of unity in mood, and a profusion of elaborate detail comparable with the fantasies of baroque architecture. The composer seems concerned rather to amuse his audience with novel effects, or to ravish their ears with lovely sound than to move them by the expression of his inmost feelings. So we find Haydn adopting in the symphonies of this period the brief slow introduction, which was to throw the succeeding *allegro* into higher relief, and was incidentally to be developed in the succeeding century by Beethoven into those magnificent prefaces to the Fourth and Seventh symphonies, where they appear as an integral part of the poetic scheme and not as a mere dramatic effect to excite the listener's interest. So, also, we find that the aria-form of slow movement gives place to variations on a theme with alternations of the key between major and minor ; while the finale in sonata-form is superseded by the looser and more elegant *rondo*, where again the composer can amuse us with variations, with unexpected episodes and novel transformations of his themes. The content of the music is also altered. The subjects are deliberately unrelated one to another, for the sake of effect. Sometimes a third subsidiary theme is added to the usual two, and the tightness both of the form and the contrapuntal writing is considerably relaxed. In so far as this meant greater freedom and an escape from dryness of style, the change is all to the good ; but it led also to superficiality and a lack of significance, which make the music of this period, for all its perfect workmanship and the graceful poetry of its ideas, rather tiresome to listen to in large quantities. Music had become a butterfly—and the life of butterflies is brief.

It is significant, too, that after his submission to the new style, Mozart temporarily abandoned the symphony altogether, and after the work in

D, the first of his essays in the baroque, the form does not appear again until June, 1778. A period of four years is a long space in the life of a composer who was developing so rapidly and who was to be so short-lived. During these years his orchestral output consists, apart from concertos, which again serve for the exhibition of a rather empty virtuosity, entirely of *divertimenti*, serenades and other occasional pieces, which provided a better vehicle than the noble symphonic form for the exploitation of the free and brilliant new style.

It is, one thinks, rather absurd to deplore, as do the French critics, this stage in the composer's development. After all, great geniuses are the children of their time; they are the men most fitted to express the best in current thought in the finest possible way. The men, who are " not of their time ", who write for a circumscribed band of connoisseurs, are, for all their excellence in their own field and for all the admiration they may provoke in their disciples, but secondary men. Mozart was most certainly the child of his age. He reflected even the lesser eddies in the general stream of thought, and since the society which he knew delighted above all things in elegant frivolity, it is not surprising that much of his music is trivial, especially when it was composed for social functions or fashionable concerts at which brilliant execution carried more favour than depth of thought. But were Mozart nothing more than an elegant trifler, he would, even with his fine workmanship, not hold the high place he has won in the affections of musical people. The music of his nineteenth and twentieth years is only important to us from the point of view of what it contributed to his mature development. In performance, most of it can serve no more than as a pleasant sweetmeat to contrast with the heavier dishes of the musical banquet.

The tendency towards the baroque was given a further impetus by a visit to Munich, where the musical fashions were mainly of French origin. For the " gallant " style was compounded of a mixture of French and Italian influences upon Austrian music. The Elector of Bavaria, whose palace, the Nymphenburg, close to the capital, is a magnificent example of the baroque style in architecture, was himself a good musician, and as a player on the *viola da gamba* came, according to Burney, second only to Abel. Through the influence of the Archbishop of Chiemsee, Wolfgang Mozart had been commissioned to write an *opera buffa* for Munich. The libretto of the work, called *La Finta Giardiniera*, was sent to Mozart at Salzburg during the autumn, and he wrote most of the music before going to Munich in December. The libretto had been used the year before by Pasquale Anfossi, whose opera was produced in Rome with great success and quickly won a European reputation. Like *La Finta Semplice*, it is a conventional *opera buffa* story cut

91

to the accepted pattern. Mozart's original score does not exist, for the opera was revised for a performance in German five years later and it is very likely that it was further revised for a performance at Frankfurt in 1789. As these revisions were by no means thorough, there is a considerable diversity of styles in the opera as we possess it.

Mozart undoubtedly had Anfossi's score before him when he composed his music, for he follows the general lines of the Italian's treatment of the work. His music, however, is in most respects very different. Anfossi gives all the interest to the voices, and his accompaniments have no intrinsic interest of their own. He thoroughly understood his task, which was to turn out an amusing work that would tickle his audience without arousing any deep emotion. Mozart, for the first time in his operas, paid little attention to the requirements of the individual singers and his airs are written in a symphonic style, the voice being given a part comparable to that of the solo instrument in a concerto—again, the distinguishing trait of German as opposed to Italian music. Moreover, while Anfossi had no thought beyond amusing his audience, Mozart approached his work primarily as a musician. Even his comic airs do not entirely conform to the accepted *buffo* style, but are written with an ingenuity and point which is really out of keeping with the broad humours of the librettist. When, on the

92

other hand, any idea of sadness or love comes to the fore, his poetic imagination leads him to compose music of a passionate sincerity which is incongruous with the pasteboard figures who sing them. Mozart's opera is musically superior to Anfossi's, and though his music is symphonic while the Italian's is vocal, we have the impression, as MM. de Wyzewa and de Saint-Foix put it, "that in both voices and orchestra everything in Anfossi is spoken, often very agreeably and very wittily, while in Mozart everything sings ". But, as an *opera buffa*, Anfossi's is the better work, because there is a greater unity of style, and the European public cannot be blamed for preferring the skilled workmanship of the Italian to the budding of the young Austrian's genius, as yet unable to express itself fully and hampered by an unsuitable medium.

Mozart's opera was, however, received with favour at Munich, so that Leopold was able to recount to his wife, with his usual gleeful malice, how annoyed the Archbishop Hieronymus, who visited the Bavarian capital at the time of the production, was at the compliments which were showered upon him on account of the brilliant young composer attached to his court.

Leopold was evidently already at loggerheads with his master, and one may be permitted to doubt whether the Archbishop was really so pusillanimous. Leopold was offended that his master did not attend the first performance of *La Finta Giardiniera*, but he seems to have forgotten, on this occasion as elsewhere, that he was, after all, an Archbishop and the reigning sovereign of a large state with other concerns to occupy him than the activities of one of the junior members of his musical staff. Hieronymus, nevertheless, so far appreciated Wolfgang's powers as to commission him to write a *serenata* for performance during the visit to Salzburg of Maria Theresa's youngest son, the Archduke Maximilian, who was later to be one of Beethoven's earliest patrons. For this occasion Mozart set to music Metastasio's *Il Rè Pastore*, which was produced in April, 1775. The work is now remembered only on account of the *bravura* air " L'amerò, sarò constante ", which still serves to show off the abilities and the failings of high sopranos. The *serenata* is, indeed, no more than a series of florid airs, which are nothing but concertos for voice and orchestra with no pretensions to dramatic expression.

During this period Mozart had also developed his ideas of pianoforte-writing, and before he left Munich had composed six sonatas for the instrument. The last of these is the Sonata in D major (K. 284) which was written for Baron Dürnitz, a *dilettante* whom he encountered in the Bavarian capital. This work shows the full efflorescence of the " gallant " style, with its " Rondeau en polonaise " in the French manner, its twelve variations on a theme, which replace the usual minuet or sonata-form *finale*, and the general brilliance of the writing. The Sonata in D shows a distinct advance upon the other five, in addition to the stylistic differences, which prove how strong was the French influence on Mozart during his visit to Munich. It must not be supposed, however, that these sonatas are, in any sense, comparable in value with those of Beethoven or with Mozart's own later works in other forms. The pianoforte had only just been invented and it was Beethoven who first discovered its great possibilities and thereby diverted the development of music into a new channel. In Mozart's day it had a thin, tinkling tone and all he was concerned to get from it was a glittering brilliance.

To read into these works a high significance and to play them with all the subtlety of which modern instruments and modern technique are capable, is simply ridiculous. Edward Mac-Dowell has thrown a well-merited cold douche upon the facile praise of Mozart's " sublimity " in the pianoforte works. " If one had occasion ", he says, " to read over some of the clavichord music of the period, possibly it might seem strange [in view of the praise bestowed on them by musical historians] that Mozart's sonatas did not impress with their magnificence. One might even harbour a lurking doubt as to the value of many seemingly bare runs and unmeaning passages ". After quoting from Rockstro's *History of Music* a page, which compares these sonatas to cathedrals, MacDowell continues, " This is all very fine, but it is nonsense, for Mozart's sonatas are anything but cathedrals. . . . It is a fact that they are compositions entirely unworthy of the composer of *The Magic Flute* or of any composer with pretensions beyond mediocrity. They are written in a style of flashy harpsichord virtuosity such as Liszt never descended to, even in those of his works at which so many persons are accustomed to sneer ".

For Dürnitz, too, Mozart composed two concertos for the bassoon. These have unfortunately been lost, but there exists another work for the same instrument in B flat (K. 191), which belongs to June of the previous year, 1774. This concerto shows the mastery which the young composer had reached in the treatment of wind-instruments, thanks to his experiments after the return from Italy. The solo part is full of understanding of the capabilities of the bassoon, which up to this time had been put to little use in the orchestra beyond doubling the string-bass. There is much of Mozart's characteristically whimsical humour in the writing of the solo, obtained from the combination of agility and dignity of which the bassoon is capable, and in the slow movement the *cantabile* powers of the instrument are fully revealed. But he never demands of this noble instrument the music-hall clowning to which it has often been degraded, and which we might, indeed, expect after reading the letter written by Mozart to his cousin on 5th November, 1777.

To the year 1775 also belong five of the series of six violin concertos composed by Mozart. The sixth, which is of little importance, was written two years later and only three of the others need detain us. These are the concertos in G major (K. 216), D major (K. 218), and A major (K. 219). It has already been mentioned that the new direction taken by Mozart toward the gallant style made the form of the concerto more congenial than that of the symphony. These three works are magnificent examples of his work at this period. They are not free from the faults of the style, notably the routinier working-out, full of " bare runs and unmeaning passages ", of the first movements, the subjects of which are always enchanting. On the other hand the delicate grace of the slow movements and the delightful inventions of the *Rondeaux* (he uses always the French spelling, which indicates also the French form and style of the music) fully compensate us for the rather banal decorations of the solo parts. His prodigality of ideas finds full scope in these final movements, where one delightful melody follows another and nothing comes amiss.[1] The *finale* of the con-

[1] It may be noted that Mozart's prodigality of invention, which so delights us, did not escape criticism from his contemporaries. Dittersdorf, for instance, after stating that Mozart is unquestionably a great original genius and that he knows no other composer who possesses such a wealth of ideas, says : " He gives his hearers no time to breathe : as soon as one beautiful idea is grasped, it is succeeded by another, which drives the first from the mind : and so it goes on, until at the end, not one of these beauties remains in the memory."

certo in A major, the one most frequently played,
though headed *tempo di minuetto*, is more akin
to the *rondo* than the minuet, and is very characteristic of Mozart's free treatment of his
themes. An episode in the " Turkish " style,
similar to the *Rondo alla Turca* of the A major
pianoforte sonata (K. 331), is inserted in the middle
of the movement and produces a gay effect.
Exotic touches of this nature were very popular
in Paris and appear frequently in opera. Gluck's
Les Pélerins de Mecque is an example of this
fashion for the outlandish, which is not peculiar
to the eighteenth century, but has lately sought
for local colour in Russia and Spain. That
Mozart knew Gluck's comic opera is certain, for
he wrote a set of pianoforte variations on one
of its airs, and its style had an influence on the
Turkish music of *Die Entführung aus dem Serail*.
He may also have known Joseph Haydn's *opera
buffa*, *Lo Speziale*, which was produced in Vienna
for Prince Nicholas Esterhazy in 1789. In it
Haydn's librettist provides an opportunity for
the introduction of the fashionable " Turkish "
idiom by disguising one of the characters as
a Pasha. The music has in reality rather less
relation to the genuine music of the East than
most " Spanish " rhapsodies, even sometimes
when composed by Spaniards, have to the music
of Spain.

The works of the following year, 1776, when
Mozart had reached the age of twenty, differ

very little at first sight from those which we have just discussed. But there is a subtle change, in the direction of a more tender poetry and a greater refinement. We may find the cause partly in the fact that during this year Mozart, who had up to now associated mainly with the good honest bourgeois citizens of Salzburg like Hagenauer and Haffner, for whose daughter's marriage he composed the delightful Serenade in D (K. 250), entered more and more into the society of the nobility. He had begun to take pupils, among whom were the two daughters of the Countess Lodron. For them he composed a number of works during this and the following year, including a concerto for three pianofortes (K. 242), which is more curious than interesting. It was to be played by the Countess and her two girls and the third pianoforte part is of a simplicity adapted to a very unskilled performer. There is, however, one interesting feature of the score in that the *cadenzas* are written out in full, since three pianists could not be expected to improvise. These passages are a precious document showing us the kind of thing that Mozart himself played in his concertos. The main characteristic is that, contrary to the practice of later days, virtuosity is less conspicuous than poetical fancy in the variation of phrases from the main movement.

Contact with the nobility, however much it may account for the increased refinement of Mozart's music, does not explain the tender idealism which grows more marked in the compositions of this year. We should expect rather from that influence a more frivolous attitude. Yet what we find is a calm and sunny lyricism, which the troubles of the coming years were to cloud over. He never recaptured the free and amorous disposition of this period, and, when in the last year of his life he composed *The Magic Flute*, he turned to the music of his twenty-first year to find phrases appropriate to express the ideal love of Tamino and Pamina and the boyish sensuality of the " natural " Papageno.

In spite of the sunny carelessness of his music, Mozart was dissatisfied at Salzburg. He hated his shallow Italian colleagues on the Archbishop's musical staff and relations with his master were becoming more strained, no doubt owing to the indiscretions of the young man's sarcastic tongue. In September of this year he sent out a last feeler in the direction of Italy. Probably at the dictation of his father, he wrote a long letter to the Padre Martini at Bologna, in which he tells his old friend the news about himself, dwelling especially upon the success of *La Finta Giardiniera*. He encloses an Offertory in D minor, " hurriedly composed " he assures the learned musician, and asks for an opinion of it. Then he grumbles at the conditions under which he lives—a bad theatre and no *castrati* " because those fellows demand good pay, and there is no chance of that in Salzburg ". Finally he sends his respects to the members of the Philharmonic Society and his regrets that he is so far away from his revered master. A postscript gives directions as to the addressing of the reply. There is no question that this letter is a " kite " flown by Leopold to see whether he could not obtain for his son some more honourable and lucrative position than Salzburg afforded, but Wolfgang was no longer a prodigy to astonish the public with his powers and amuse them with his pretty ways, and even Padre Martini could not gain him a commission from an Italian opera-house nor an appointment at one of the South German Courts, which was perhaps Leopold's true object.

This move having failed, Leopold secretly prepared during the winter of 1776–77 for another tour northwards through Germany to Paris. When, however, he asked the Archbishop for leave of absence, it was refused—not without reason from the master's point of view, since Leopold proposed a long tour. Leopold was, however, determined that Wolfgang should not stay in Salzburg and arranged that he should travel with his mother. He did not trust his son to go alone and, though his wife was a mere woman, she had a more practical head than the boy. It was to be one of the handicaps to the development of Mozart's character that during these important years of his growth he was never allowed off the apron-strings. Had he been gradually inured to responsibility in the ordinary affairs of life, he might have been saved a part, at least, of the sufferings which resulted from his fecklessness and lack of common sense. His artistic temperament would in any case have made life difficult for him, but a more rational treatment during his youth might have disciplined him to a less care-free attitude to the ordinary responsibilities of man. However that may be, Wolfgang wrote to the Archbishop a long and humble petition for leave, in which, among other things, he quoted the parable of the talents in favour of his going abroad instead of hiding his light under the bushel of Salzburg. This flowery epistle, and especially its allusion to the Gospel, irritated the Archbishop beyond measure, and his secretary endorsed it with a caustic comment to the effect that father and son might go and seek their fortune elsewhere.

This decision was, however, not put into effect ; for Wolfgang departed with his mother late in September, leaving the disconsolate father behind.

Chapter V

THE YOUNG MASTER

DURING this new journey, which occupied the whole of the year 1778, father and son kept up a long correspondence, and these letters are the main source of our information about the events of this period. Certain biographers of Mozart have made fun of Leopold's anxious and minute directions to his son and to his wife concerning the youth's conduct and the practical details of the journey. His solicitude for their welfare in the least particular appears to me rather infinitely pathetic, and reveals the pleasanter side of a character which has faults enough without deserving blame for a touching interest in everything the young man did. There is no doubt of the depth and genuineness of Leopold's affection. In his first letter, after describing with pathological details his own and Nannerl's grief at the departure of the mother and son, he gives them all kinds of advice about the price to pay for lunch, the use of boot-trees, the re-direction of letters, the packing of luggage, and so forth. It may seem tiresome, but it brings us at the same time into a more intimate contact with the correspondents and their mode of life than any description can achieve. Leopold's advice was

not always good. He told Wolfgang not to wear
the Star of his Order when at Court, but that he
must pin it on his coat at Augsburg. The ever-
obedient youth was laughed at for his vanity
by an unkind person and suffered therefrom
a mortification such as only the young and sensitive can experience, when touched nearly on
some trivial point of personal pride.

The first important town visited by the travellers was Munich, where they attempted at once
to get an audience with the Elector of Bavaria.
Small hopes were held out to Wolfgang of obtaining any post at Munich, even by those who worked
on his behalf, and, when at last the desired interview took place, the Elector Maximilian regretted
that there was no vacancy for him to fill. Mozart
was too young and not yet famous enough for
a vacancy to be created for him. The father, of
course, leaped at once to the conclusion that secret
enemies were at work to thwart his son and advised
that he should continue on his journey. The
youth, however, at first proposed to remain in
Munich and try his fortune there, on the grounds
that some friends had promised to provide him
with funds until a suitable employment could be
found. Leopold disapproved of the idea, seeing
how precarious such a plan would be and that,
to save expense, it would involve his wife's return
to Salzburg, and leave Wolfgang to face the world
alone. "That you could support yourself in
Munich, is no doubt true," he writes, " but what

honour could there be in that? How the Archbishop would laugh! You can do that any-
where. . . . But you must not belittle yourself
or throw yourself away at any cost. There is no
necessity for it as yet ".

So the two repaired to Augsburg, where they
were hospitably received by Franz Anton Mozart,
Leopold's brother, who carried on the family
business of book-binding. Wolfgang's uncle took
him at once to call upon Burgomaster von
Langenmantl (whom the youth characteristically
dubs *Langotabarro* in his letters), and had to
wait " like any lacquey " in the hall, while the
nephew had with the magistrate a long interview,
which Wolfgang describes with a naughty
humour. Finally he was taken upstairs and gave
a recital to the Burgomaster and his family
while the uncle " had the honour to await me
in the hall ". After dinner Langenmantl's
son-in-law, " bursting with pride ", took Wolfgang to see J. Andreas Stein,[1] the famous maker
of organs and pianofortes, who was delighted
to meet the young virtuoso. Stein had made
great improvements in pianoforte mechanism,

[1] Stein's eight-year-old daughter, Maria Anna (Nanette), was at the time
the musical prodigy of Augsburg. Mozart was critical of her performances
and especially of her affected manner of playing. He gave her credit for
talent, but says that she had no idea of time and that her touch was heavy.
His criticisms, by which the father was impressed, evidently took effect, for
the girl subsequently became a famous pianist. She married Johann Andreas
Streicher, a friend of Schiller's, who eventually succeeded to the business
of his father-in-law and transferred it to Vienna, where Frau Streicher
became the kindly adviser of Beethoven in his domestic troubles.

and Wolfgang writes with great enthusiasm
about his instruments :

"Before I had seen something of Stein's methods,
I liked Spath's pianofortes best, but now I prefer
Stein's : for they damp off the resonance much better
than those of Regensburg. When I strike hard, I can let
my finger remain on the key or lift it, and the sound
ceases the moment I have made it heard. I can do
anything I like with the keys, and the sound is always
equal; it does not jangle disagreeably; it has not
[the fault] of being either too loud or too weak ; in a
word it is equal all through . . . The instruments have
this advantage above all others, that they are made
with an escapement . . . Without an escapement, it
is absolutely impossible to avoid jangling and vibration
after the note is struck. The hammers . . . fall
back immediately they strike the strings placed
above them, whether one holds the key down or
releases it."

If we may judge from the lively humour of
his letters Mozart at first enjoyed his visit to
Augsburg, which was in the nature of a holiday,
but soon he began to wish for a less provincial
atmosphere. A concert at Augsburg, though
successful, brought little financial reward. His
only reason for desiring to remain there was the
presence of his coquettish cousin, Maria Anna,
with whom he had quickly fallen in love. He
writes about her to his father rapturously but
with a touch of mockery, which is both characteristic and charming. He knew his own weakness

for malicious fun at the expense of others, for in one letter he says : " We (i.e. he and Maria Anna) suit one another very well, for like me she is rather naughty (*schlimm*) ; we laugh at everybody and have great fun ! " It was therefore not without regrets that Wolfgang left with his mother for Mannheim late in October.

Mannheim was the seat of Prince Karl Theodor, to whom Leopold hoped that his son would be presented by Anton Raaff, the tenor. Karl Theodor's character has been so admirably summed up by Arthur Schurig, that I cannot do better than quote him :

> " He was a prince typical of his time : an amiable man, though without any striking personality, he showed no profound interest in his subjects, and when, in 1778, he became Elector of Bavaria and transferred his court from Mannheim to Munich, he took no further interest in his old palatine residence. From 1769 to 1792 he spent, they say, thirty-five million florins on the encouragement of the arts and sciences. That may be : Louis XIV spent quite a hundred times as much on the same objects : yet true love of Art was never in reality the *leitmotiv* either at Versailles or at Mannheim, where the sovereign as at so many other German courts, made every effort to play the part of ' roi Soleil.' It was a mere ostentatious show, prompted partly by the desire to interrupt with an intellectual epicureanism the daily pleasures of the table and the harem. Karl Theodor was nothing but a vain fop in the power of his confessors, his mistresses and his favourites."

It is not surprising that the manners of his subjects reflected the morals of their Prince, Gallantry was the fashion and, says Riesbeck, " a tailor's wife thought herself dishonoured, if she remained true to her husband ". Given this atmosphere, the surprising thing is not that the impressionable Wolfgang had one or two love affairs, which have subjected him to the accusation of fickleness, but that he had apparently so few. Indeed, the more one learns of his times, the more respect one gains for the character of this sensitive young man. The occasional bawdiness of his letters is a mere reflection of the manners of his day, and there seems no cause for condemning him for a looseness of language, just because he was a man of genius. His conduct towards women generally appears to have been honourable, the only exception being, as we shall see, the development of his affair with Maria Anna, his " dear little Bäsle " of Augsburg. But even here, he can hardly be accused of anything worse than a want of *savoir faire ;* he forgot to be off with the old love before he put on the new. In fact, his behaviour shows a touch of human weakness which is pathetic and even attractive, rather than disgraceful.

Leopold's first letter to his son at Mannheim points out, among other pieces of paternal advice, that the city provides a good opportunity of writing for the German theatre. Mannheim certainly offered more favourable chances to a

non-Italian composer than most other German
cities at that time. For both in the theatre and
the opera a national consciousness was making
itself felt. In the theatre the foundations were
being laid for the drama of Schiller, while at the
opera was staged the first work on a German
subject which glorifies the Fatherland, Holzbauer's *Günther von Schwarzburg*. This opera
was produced in January, 1777, and Mozart saw
a performance of it during his visit. " Holzbauer's
music ", he tells his father, " is fine ; the libretto
is unworthy of such music. What astonishes
me most is that a man so old as Holzbauer
[he was sixty-six] should still have so much
vigour ; for it is unbelievable how much divine
fire there is in his music ". In the same letter,
he notes that the singers in the German operas
were " pitiable ". During his stay in Munich
Mozart had been attracted by the idea of German
opera, and one of his " castles in Spain " had
been a proposal that he should settle there and
write four operas a year. So far German opera,
though in the air, had not achieved a more
concrete form in the Bavarian capital than the
adaptation of a work by Piccini. In Mannheim
the circumstances were more favourable, especially as the city had served as the cradle of German
symphonic music. German opera began to gain
ground in Mannheim, and *Günther von Schwarzburg* was followed by Schweitzer's *Alcestis*
composed to a libretto by Wieland. Schweitzer

took himself very seriously, and did not shrink from comparing himself with Euripides which brought upon him the mockery of Goethe. His operas did not, in fact, depart from the Italian model. Mozart says that Schweitzer was " a fine and worthy man, dry and quite simple like our Haydn [Michael], though his talk has more distinction ". " *Alcestis* ", he continues, " was a great success, and that although it is not half so beautiful as *Rosamund*. It is true that its success was much abetted by the fact that it was the first German opera. That impression, however, has long been effaced, *N.B.* in those minds which are attracted only by novelty ". Mozart revised his opinion of Schweitzer's *Rosamund*, for in a later letter he says with characteristically involved humour : " This opera is—good, that's all there is to it. For, if it were bad, they could not put it on—just as you cannot sleep without going to bed ! But there is no rule without exceptions —and I have just seen an example. So, good night ! "

Had Mozart, therefore, been able to obtain an appointment in Mannheim, he might well have started on his career as a writer of German opera, the repertory of which he was later, and in a more casual way, to enrich with *Die Entführung aus dem Serail* and *Die Zauberflöte*. However, no post was forthcoming, and the young man spent his time falling in love with various singers and pianists, for whom he composed airs and sonatas

—Augusta Wendling, a mistress of the Prince Elector and the daughter of another singer, Dorothea Wendling, Rosa Cannabich, and Aloysia Weber. Aloysia was the second of the four daughters of Fridolin Weber, a copyist, who was employed by Mozart to copy the airs written for the Wendlings. This Weber, it may be mentioned, was the uncle of Karl Maria von Weber, the composer of *Der Freischütz*. The Webers are first mentioned in a letter to Leopold dated January 7, 1778, in which Aloysia's singing and education are praised with discreet enthusiasm. The references to her become frequent from this time onwards, and, though Wolfgang does not reveal his passion to his father, it is easy to see that the young singer was the chief preoccupation of his thoughts. The lively and occasionally salacious correspondence, which he had been carrying on with his " dear little cousin " at Augsburg, was broken off until nearly two months later he wrote to her, penitent for his neglect and with a forced sprightliness that was intended to conceal his infidelity. At the end of this letter he makes a desperate effort to say he still loves her, but after a long rigmarole he cannot bring himself to it. In his last letter, written in November, he had been " your very affectionate cousin " and had smothered her with kisses ; now he ends " Adieu, ma chère cousine, I am your same true cousin ". To his father he proposes a plan whereby he and Aloysia should go on tour in

Italy. " You know my greatest preoccupation :
to write operas. I would gladly write the opera
for Verona for thirty sequins. . . . I think we
will go on to Switzerland, and perhaps also to Holland. Write to me soon on this matter. If we
make arrangements for this tour the eldest
daughter will be most useful ; we shall be able
to have a proper establishment for she knows also
how to cook.[1] I cannot journey with some people,
with a man whose manner of life would make the
youngest blush. But the thought of helping
an unhappy family, without doing myself any
harm, fills my heart with joy ". His last specious
argument, with its parenthetic assurance to the
father that it will be also for his own good, sheds
a light on one of Wolfgang's true motives. His
sensitive nature was always ready to answer an
appeal for pity, and it was no doubt the impoverished condition of the Webers which first stirred
his emotions and led him into his first real passion.
Schurig aptly calls attention to the fact that the
words of the air which Mozart wrote at this time
for Aloysia[2] deals with the ideas of love and pity.

Leopold naturally showed no enthusiasm for
his son's extravagant schemes. He had already
advised him to go to Paris—hence the reference
to undesirable companions in the letter just
quoted. Now he redoubled his efforts to get

---

[1] Josepha, who sang the Queen of the Night in *Die Zauberflöte*.
[2] " Non sô d'onde vieni quel tenero affetto " (K. 294) from Metastasio's
Olimpiade.

Wolfgang out of Mannheim, but the young man procrastinated for another month. His letters are full of excuses for his delay. In Paris he could only earn a living by taking pupils, which is " a kind of work for which I am not made ". He has tried it in Mannheim. He does not know for certain whether Grimm is in Paris. His mother dislikes the idea of going to Paris, and so on through every excuse save the real one, Aloysia's presence in Mannheim. In one of these letters occurs the first sign of a revolt against Leopold's oppressive guardianship. " The time has gone when I used to stand on a chair and sing *Oragna fiagata fà*, and when at the end I kissed the tip of your nose ; but have my respect, my love, my obedience become less on that account ? " They had not, perhaps ; but youth was becoming impatient. In the same letter Wolfgang writes : " your biting remarks about my happy relations with your brother's daughter offend me deeply. But, as they are inexact, I have no answer to make to them ". He replies in a similar vein to other reproaches regarding his conduct, and in the next letter, *à propos* Aloysia, says : " There are some people who think it is impossible to love a poor girl without evil designs, and this pretty word *mistress* is truly a fine one ! . . . I am not a Brunetti or a Misliweczek ! I am a Mozart, though young . . . so you will excuse me if sometimes in my ardour I become extravagant ". Such dignified and patently honest defences of his conduct make me shrink from believing those who, like Leopold Mozart himself, always attribute the worst possible motives to the young man. In the end, of course, the father had his way, and Wolfgang regretfully set out for Paris with his mother in the second week of March. The journey took nine and a half days, nine and a half days of boredom and melancholy with no one to talk to, and all the more dreary in contrast with the jolly friendships and love-affairs of Mannheim. Wolfgang seems to have found little consolation in the companionship of his mother. Paris, too, was disappointing, not merely on account of Aloysia's absence, but because he himself was no longer a pretty little boy. The Parisians did not accord to the young genius the attention which had been accorded to the infant prodigy. They knew little if anything of Wolfgang's " conquest of Italy ", which was indeed mainly a figment of his father's sanguine imagination. Grimm, to whom the young man at once turned for assistance, had ceased to be the influential figure he had been at the time of the previous visits to Paris. He was as cordial as his frigid temperament permitted, but his word no longer carried weight, and he took no great pains to aid his protégé. For Grimm genius consisted in the art of being successful, in catching the public ear ; and, in common with most men of the time who had not before them the catalogue of

Mozart's works, he failed to perceive anything extraordinary in this young man, who was continually on his doorstep seeking for advice or financial assistance, and whose father wrote him tedious screeds about his marvellous gifts.

However, Wolfgang obtained an introduction to Le Gros, the director of the Concert Spirituel, who commissioned him to supply alternative numbers for a *Miserere* by Holzbauer, the Mannheim composer, whose work was not considered up to Parisian standards of choral singing. He wrote also a *Symphonie Concertante* for flute (Wendling), oboe (Ramm), horn (Punto), and bassoon (Ritter), which to the fury of composer and executants was laid on one side by Le Gros and was never performed. Like father, like son. Wolfgang attributed the non-performance of the work to the jealousy of an Italian composer Cambini, whom he had " quite innocently " put in his place. It is far more likely that the incident was due to carelessness or laziness on the part of Le Gros. Neither of these compositions has survived, but we have a concerto for flute and harp in C major (K. 299), which was written early during the stay in Paris for two amateurs, the Duc de Guines and his daughter, to whom Mozart gave lessons. There is an amusing letter in which he recounts his desperate efforts to teach the girl composition. The Duke was convinced that she could compose, but Mozart found that she had not one idea in her head.

However she was a good harpist, and the concerto is delightful enough to have survived in the concert hall. The writing for the harp differs in no way from that used for keyboard instruments, which is hardly surprising, since Mozart can have had no experience with the instrument and, even if he had, the true harp technique was not discovered until after the invention by Sebastian Erard of the double-action harp early in the next century.

Wolfgang also mentions that he has in contemplation an opera on the subject of *Alexandre et Roxane*, and Leopold in reply urges him to study French tastes before setting to work on it. However, nothing came of the scheme and Wolfgang wrote nothing for the Parisian stage, except a part of the music for a ballet called *Les Petits Riens*, which was given with Piccini's opera *Le Finte Gemelle*. In the meantime, a definite offer of the post of organist at Versailles was made to Mozart, which his father encouraged him to accept. At Versailles, he would be " at court " and in the way of advancing himself to some more important place, when vacancies occurred. Wolfgang, however, could not bear the separation from Aloysia which acceptance involved, and eventually he refused the appointment.

In the midst of his indecision on this matter a greater trouble came upon him. His mother fell ill and on July 3rd she died. Wolfgang's lack of *savoir faire* has often been criticized, but on this occasion he acted with admirable discretion, and with the greatest forethought and tenderness. He wrote to his father a long letter saying that his mother was very ill and recounting his various activities, notably the performance of a new symphony which, in spite of anxieties at the rehearsal, had won much applause. To the Abbé Bullinger, one of his father's cronies at Salzburg, he wrote the truth and begged him to break the news to his family. This behaviour was extraordinarily courageous in a sensitive young man suddenly faced with death, of which, as he says in a second letter to his father, this was his first experience, and with death in connection with his mother and in a strange city far removed from his real friends. The bitterness of his spirit, which was for the most part concealed in the assumption of a natural anxiety for his mother and of his usual lively interest in music, appears for a moment in his savage reference to the death of the " atheist impostor Voltaire, who has died like a dog . . .[1] that is his reward ! "

Wolfgang remained in Paris until the end of September, though there seems to have been little to detain him except a disinclination to do anything at all, which may well have been the form taken by the reaction after his recent experience. Paris was at the moment the battleground of the followers of Gluck and Piccini, that is to say

[1] That is, without being fortified by the rites of the Church.

of the struggle between the dawning ideals of German opera and the old Italian tradition. Mozart, however, seems to have taken little interest in the fight. Grimm was a keen Piccinist, and Mozart, who was still inclined to accept the prejudices of others, had not the courage of his convictions, which should have led him into a fervent support of the opposite party. None the less, if he did not take sides, he could not escape the influence of Gluck, as we shall see, when *Idomeneo* comes under our consideration.

During this period, besides the Symphony in D (K. 297) mentioned in his letter of the 3rd July, Mozart composed a quartet and a number of sonatas, including the familiar one in A major for pianoforte with the *Allegretto alla Turca* (K. 331). By the middle of August, Grimm was getting tired of having the young man continually on his hands and wrote to Leopold that " Wolfgang is too confident, too little a man of action, much too ready to succumb to his own illusions, too little *au courant* with the ways that lead to success. To attain that one must be captivating, enterprising, and daring. If only he had half his talent, and twice his ability for that, I should have no trouble with him ". Grimm goes on to say that Mozart's sole means of getting on would be to give lessons, but he is not sufficient of a charlatan for that, even if his health would stand it. He can have no success in other directions if he stands apart from the " ridiculous divisions " of the Gluckists and Piccinists. Finally, it is unfortunate that the death of the Elector of Bavaria (who was succeeded, as I have already related, by Karl Theodor) has prevented Wolfgang from returning to Mannheim. In short, Grimm wanted to be rid of his responsibilities. Leopold, who accepted everything Grimm said as absolute wisdom, thereupon ordered his son back to Salzburg. By way of inducement, he retails a long list of obituaries and retirements in the musical world of the Austrian city, and holds out hopes of an appointment. He even suggests, as the most tempting bait, that Aloysia may be engaged by the Archbishop to sing at Salzburg.

There is something pitiful in the father's desperate efforts to get back his son, who was becoming more and more estranged from him now that his mother was dead and he was leading an independent life in a distant city. Wolfgang loathed the idea of returning to Salzburg and was by no means inclined, after his spell of freedom, to submit once more to the oppressive tutelage of his father. The tale about Aloysia did not take him in. He had more accurate news of the Webers with whom he kept up a correspondence, most of which has been lost. He wrote submissively to his father, excusing his delay on the ground that J. C. Bach had just arrived from London, and so on. To his friend the Abbé Bullinger, he poured forth his scorn. Why,

he asks, should they want a *prima donna* at
Salzburg when they have got Ceccarelli (the male
soprano) ? His exasperation with life in general
leads him even into making disagreeable jokes
at the expense of the unfortunate Misliweczeck.
whose immoral conduct had been punished by
Nature in a disgusting, but not unusual, manner.
Our gentle hero is by way of developing into a
savage Swift, snapping and snarling at anyone
who happens to cross his path.

Wolfgang left Paris at the end of September,
furious with Grimm, who had deceived him about
the length of time taken by the particular coach
by which he travelled. Grimm told him he would
be in Salzburg in five days, but the day before
leaving Wolfgang found out that it would take
twelve. His anger, which he dissimulated before
his protector—from whom he took leave politely
after paying a debt of fifteen *louis d'or*—would be
more convincing, if he had reached Salzburg
before the following January. However, his
annoyance with Grimm had some basis in fact ;
for, as he says in a letter dated September 11,
1778, Grimm had done nothing for him.[1] His
mother had perceived that Grimm's attitude
had become colder, but Wolfgang, " though convinced of the fact in his own heart ", had defended
him. Such was his haste to reach Salzburg, where
he had now been promised an appointment with

---

[1] The reader must not allow himself to be misled by M. Sacha Guitry's
charming and sentimental, but almost wholly imaginary play, *Mozart*.

a salary of 450 florins (Leopold added fifty more to the sum, to make it a more attractive figure !), that he spent a month in Nancy and Strassburg, and then made his way to—Mannheim !

The Webers had gone, when Karl Theodor's Court was transferred, to Munich, where their condition had been greatly improved. Aloysia was getting a salary of 600 florins and her father 400. But Mannheim, the scene of his first real passion, had an irresistible attraction for the romantic youth who was always more in love with love than with the individual object of his affection. He stayed with Frau Cannabich, whose husband[1] had also gone to Munich. Perhaps he hoped that further delay would exasperate the Archbishop and that his appointment would be cancelled. He certainly had hopes of a post at Munich. His father cajoled and threatened in vain. At the end of November he ordered Wolfgang to return by the first coach and by way of consolation added that he had never opposed a match with Aloysia when she was poor and now——. Wolfgang obeyed so far as to leave Mannheim on December 9th. He arrived in Munich on Christmas Day.

He presented himself before Aloysia in his red coat with black buttons—the livery of a Court musician. But she laughed at her awkward lover. Absence had not made her heart grow fonder and the prosperous *prima donna* no longer

---

[1] The conductor of the famous Mannheim orchestra.

thought the out-of-work composer a good match. She preferred to marry a singer named Lange, who made her thoroughly unhappy, and in after years she confessed that she had not appreciated Wolfgang Mozart. He, for his part, took his dismissal with a good grace, and sat down at the pianoforte and sang " Ich lass das Mädel gern, das mich nicht will ". He remained on good terms with the Webers and, even at this moment, completed for Aloysia the famous *coloratura* air, " Io non chiedo eterni " (K. 316), whose enormous difficulties are in themselves a tribute to the singer's technique. That he was deeply affected by the incident cannot be doubted, and three years later he wrote to his father : " I was a fool about Lange's wife, but who is not when he is in love ? I loved her in very truth, and I feel that she is not yet indifferent to me. A good thing for me that her husband is a jealous fool, and never lets her out of his sight so that I seldom see her ! " For the moment, however, he told his father nothing. His first letter from Munich hardly mentions the Webers, and asks for letters to be addressed to the house of his friend Beecké, the pianist, who consoled the young lover and interceded for him with his father.

Beecké was not Wolfgang's only resource in his unhappiness, for on his way to Munich he had addressed to his " very dear cousin " at Augsburg an extraordinary letter, in which he announces his intention of going to Munich. He cannot,

he regrets, go to Augsburg because " the Imperial
Prelate has not allowed me to go, and I cannot
hate him since that would be against the law of
God and Nature, and he who believes not that
is a —— ". He begs her to come to Munich,
where he cannot give her a lodging, " because
I am not staying in an inn, but with—yes, where?
that is what I should like to know ". By which he
means that he will be at the Webers ! " But,
joking apart ", he continues, " that is just why you
must come ; you will perhaps have a great *rôle*
to play ". This *rôle*, it has been suggested, was
to be that of bridesmaid at his wedding to
Aloysia ! Poor little Ophelia ! She had taken
her mad cousin's amorous protestations at their
face value, and regarded his very Elizabethan
coarseness as a symptom of his serious intentions.
Now she was to play the *rôle*, not of bridesmaid
indeed, but of comforter to a heart broken by a
rival. She accepted the part meekly and submitted to the jibes of her cousin, who turned
a blot on a letter, which they wrote jointly to
Leopold, into a " picture of my cousin writing
in her shirt-sleeves " and inserted before her
signature the words, " *votre invariable cochon* ".
On January 8th Leopold replied sternly to this
childish jesting : " *I definitely wish* you to travel
with M. Geschwendtner ", a merchant who was
coming to Salzburg from Munich. " If my
niece ", he added, " wishes to honour me with
her presence, she can come by the post-chaise

123

on the 20th ". For Wolfgang had suggested bringing his cousin home to console him for the dreariness of Salzburg. Leopold would apparently not have opposed a marriage between Wolfgang and his niece. Perhaps he was willing to agree to anything which would sober his feckless son. But the idea never entered Wolfgang's head. However, he did at last obey his father to the extent of returning to Salzburg, but he brought his " dear little Bäsle " with him.[1]

---

[1] Mozart's cousin, Maria Anna Thekla Mozart, was a remarkably plain young woman, if we may judge from the portrait of her in the Mozarteum at Salzburg. The authenticity of this likeness is put beyond doubt by the pen-drawing by Wolfgang himself in a letter to his cousin written in May 1779. Both the drawing, which proves that Mozart had considerable skill in draughtsmanship, and the portrait show the same long hooked nose, receding forehead, long upper lip, and eyes set too wide apart. The drawing is, of course, a caricature, and a cruel and coarse one at that. We may hope that its offensiveness was mitigated by the frequent repetition of the word " Angel " round about it.

CHAPTER VI

WOLFGANG was welcomed by his father quite in the manner which is considered to be correct for the reception of prodigal sons, even though in this instance the prodigality, like the prodigious success of the operas written for Italy, existed mainly in Leopold's imagination. The fatted capons, which were substituted for the conventional calf, may have cheered the young man for the moment, and he had the lively company of his cousin to distract him. But it was a sad and disillusioned youth who took his place at the Archbishop's table, somewhere below the valets, between Ceccarelli, the male soprano, and Brunetti, the violinist. A passage from Wolfgang's letters, which has been quoted in the preceding chapter, gives us an idea of Brunetti's morals, which appear to have been no better than his table manners. Such company must have accentuated the sense of disappointment and failure which Wolfgang felt at the results of his travels. He could hardly see, as we can, how much his experiences both of life and of love had strengthened his moral character. So he settled down disconsolately to his duties as *Konzertmeister* and organist, in which capacity he composed a number of symphonies and *Divertimenti* for the orchestra, and Masses and other music for the Cathedral. These works show a distinct advance in his technical treatment of the orchestra, notably in the development of the wind-instruments as independent voices. For the rest they are conventional in style, and the Church music is superficial and devoid of any deep expression of religious feeling. The only one of these compositions which remains in the ordinary repertory is the *Symphonie Concertante* for violin and viola in E flat (K. 364), a work full of invention and of such passionate and even tragic feeling, that it is worthy to take its place beside the works of Mozart's maturity.

As a distraction from his duties and the distasteful company of the Salzburg musicians, he was glad to seize upon any opportunity of writing dramatic music which presented itself. When a travelling company of players directed by Emmanuel Schickaneder visited Salzburg, and played Gebler's *Thamos, König in Ägypten*, he unearthed, revised and added to the incidental music which he had composed for the play in 1773 after his return from Italy. The play was religious in character and considerable use was made in it of the Egyptian Mysteries, which served to cloak the expression of the new religious ideas that were permeating Central Europe under the influence of Freemasonry. Mozart's incidental music, most of which seems to follow the earlier version closely, is of little importance ; but the choruses, which the dramatist had intended for Gluck, express a religious feeling, which is absent from the Masses of this period, probably because in them the composer did not feel at liberty to break away from the conventions. It would perhaps be an exaggeration to say that the music to *Thamos* bears the same relation in Mozart's works to *Die Zauberflöte* as *Lohengrin* bears to *Parsifal*, but it does serve to show that the ideas which were expressed so fully in his last opera were already attractive to Mozart in his early youth and evoked a keen emotional response. He himself valued the music highly, for in 1783 he expresses his regret that, owing to the failure of the play to attract the public, there was little likelihood of its further performance.

A second dramatic experiment, which forecasts the nearer future, was the setting of a German libretto by his friend the horn-player, Schachtner. This work, which is unfinished and unnamed, was published after Mozart's death under the title of *Zaïde* after its heroine. Its story resembles somewhat that of *Die Entführung aus dem Serail*, the scene being laid in Turkey and the plot being concerned with the escape from the harem of one of the Sultan's ladies with an European captive. The work is chiefly important as being the first essay made by the composer in setting a German text. Schachtner's book is exceedingly clumsy and the music is clearly written for singers, probably amateurs, from whom little could be expected. It is interesting also as containing Mozart's only experiment in writing melodrama, that is a musical accompaniment to spoken dialogue. The result is not satisfactory, as the composer himself evidently saw. He is no exception in his failure to deal with this unsatisfactory form.

The composition of *Zaïde* was interrupted by a commission to write the *opera seria* for the Carnival at Munich in January of 1781. Here at last was the great opportunity for which he had been waiting. There were, however, one or two flies in the ointment. One was the librettist, the Abbé Varesco, chaplain to Archbishop Hieronymus. Varesco was a worthy poetaster with little sense of the theatre. He produced a libretto modelled on Metastasio. But, whereas Metastasio was always concise in his exposition of the dramatic situation and had regard to what was possible and effective on the stage, Varesco is long-winded, pompous and, from inexperience of the theatre, ineffective. The opera deals with the return from Troy of Idomeneo, King of Crete, and is a variant on the story of Jephthah and his daughter, the victim in this case being Idomeneo's son, Idamante. There is also a sub-plot dealing with the loves for Idamante of Ilia, daughter of Priam now a captive, and of Electra, who has taken refuge in Crete after the murder of Clytemnestra, and the consequent jealousy of the Greek princess produces a situation parallel to that in *Aïda*. The plot is admirably suited for musical treatment and only needed a skilled hand to make a first-rate libretto. Varesco based his work on a French libretto, which in turn was derived from Crébillon's tragedy, but gave it a happy ending by using the familiar Euripidean knife of the *deus ex machina* to cut his Gordian knot.

Mozart's second difficulty was with his singers or rather with three of them. There was Raaf, the elderly tenor who sang the part of Idomeneo. He had been a fine singer a generation before, but his voice was now worn and allowance had to be made for this fact in the composition of his airs. Moreover, he was a poor actor, and was only too willing to put at the composer's service " the benefit of his long experience ", that is to say to oppose any idea which did not conform with the operatic conventions of his youth. " You can't do that, me boy ", one can hear him say ! Dal Prato, the singer cast for Idamante—" my molto amato castrato dal Prato ", Mozart calls him in his fondness for a jingle—was handicapped neither by age nor by experience. He was a boy of sixteen, had never been on the stage, and showed no ability either for acting or for singing. " He is incapable of beginning an air in a way that sounds like anything ", writes the despairing composer, " and his voice is uneven ". And again : " His voice would not be so bad, if he would not force it out from the back of his throat; for the rest, he has no intonation, no method, no sentiment, but sings like the best of a batch of young boys at an audition for an appointment to a choir ". Panzacchi, who sang the part of Idomeneo's confidant, Arbace, was, on the other hand, a good actor, though rather old, and opportunities for the display of his gifts had to be found, to the detriment of the drama, just as certain important scenes had to be curtailed on account of the incompetence of Raaf and Dal Prato. Mozart showed infinite tact and good humour in dealing with both Raaf's experience and Dal Prato's ignorance. He coached the latter in his part with the utmost patience and managed to get his own way when Raaf's suggestions interfered with important details of construction. He skilfully provided airs which the old tenor could sing with effect and bolstered up his weak voice with the accompaniments; on the other hand, when Raaf suggested that another air for himself would be more effective than the quartet, which in Mozart's opinion and our own is the best thing in the opera, he stood his ground. The women singers, Dorothea and Elizabeth Wendling, happily gave the composer no trouble. Dorothea, who sang Ilia, was " archi-contentissima " with her music.

Mozart's instinctive genius for the theatre is nowhere more clearly displayed than in the letters which he wrote to his father from Munich, where the greater part of the music was composed.

He saw at once the faults of Varesco's book, the
verbosity of the dialogue, the failure to make
the most of the dramatic situations, and the small
technical errors, like the insertion of an aside in
one air and the use of a string of awkward words
with the same unvocal vowel-sound in the last
line of another. Varesco was annoyed at the
composer's excisions and at the alterations,
which he was asked to make and for which he
expected to be paid extra, but was pacified by
an assurance that his drama would be printed as
it stood. There was another momentary anxiety
caused by the death of the Empress Maria Theresa
on November 29, 1780. But the mourning in
Munich was decreed for six weeks only and the
production of the opera was not due until the
end of January. Moreover the Munich theatres
were not closed.

As usual Mozart left the completion of the
opera until the last possible moment and was
still at work on the third act on January 3rd.
" My head and hands are so busy with the third
act ", he writes, " that it would not be surprising
if I turned into a third act myself ". He had
trouble with Count Seeau, the Intendant of the
Munich opera, even at this late stage about his
proposal to use trombones to accompany the
speech of the oracle, which disentangles the
dramatic complex at the end of the opera. Again
he had his way. The oracle's speech was one of
the passages which was severely cut down. He

wrote three versions of it, each shorter than the last, and comments in an earlier letter : " Tell me, do you not find that the speech . . . is too long ? . . . Imagine yourself in the theatre : the voice must be terrifying, it must penetrate into the depths of the soul, one must believe in it. So how can this effect be produced . . . if the length (of the speech) allows the audience to be convinced that it is only an illusion ? If, in *Hamlet*, the ghost's speech was shorter, its effect would be improved ". That is a very fair sample of Mozart's dramatic insight, and his care for the smallest details which would intensify the effect of his work in the theatre.

The music of *Idomeneo* shows, like its libretto, a mixture of French and Italian influences. Professor Dent sums it up admirably when he says that Mozart " was French by deliberate intention, but Italian by natural instinct ". By " French " is meant Gluck, whose *Alceste* provides the model for the choruses and the big dramatic scenes, such as the storm. The recitatives and the airs are entirely Italian in feeling. The airs have none of Gluck's straightforward simplicity, but are complex movements full of detail. The German in Mozart comes out in the use of elaborate instrumental *obbligati*, which necessitate the development of his airs into long concerted movements so that the *concertante* instruments may be properly exploited. To modern ears accustomed to the Wagnerian music-drama, the method may seem undramatic. But in studying any work of art, we must accept the conventions which govern it, and the air must be regarded as a point of repose during which the dramatic situation is summed up in terms of music. The action is carried on in recitative, whether *secco* or accompanied, and no better means for the purpose has yet been devised by operatic composers, at any rate when dealing with the Italian language. We are accustomed in England to regard *recitativo secco* as an unmitigated nuisance, because we rarely hear it properly sung. We judge either by the recitatives in the oratorios of Handel, who was none too familiar with the English language or the Italian style, or from performances at Covent Garden by cosmopolitan singers, who may or may not have acted together before and who have often very little notion of what the words mean. Those, however, who heard the performances in 1925 of Rossini's *Barber of Seville* will have a good idea of the thoroughly dramatic quality of Italian recitative when it is properly sung.

The airs in *Idomeneo*, it must be confessed, are too like concertos for voice and orchestra to be absolutely suited to the stage. There is among them nothing that sums up the dramatic situations as do the Countess's airs or "Deh! vieni, non tardar" in *Le Nozze di Figaro*. This is one of the respects in which Mozart developed his sense of the theatre as his genius

matured, although even in *Don Giovanni* some
of the airs seem to hang up the action rather than
hold it poised for our discernment of its full
significance. The quartet in *Idomeneo*, for which
Raaf wished another air for himself to be substituted, does fulfil this function of summing
up the situation and its occurrence in an *opera
seria* was, if not novel, sufficiently unusual to
make the conservative old singer's criticisms
intelligible. In the old Italian opera, it was
considered improper for one character to interrupt
another and even duets were confined to persons
whose sentiments were in harmony. In *opera
buffa*, however, quarrel-scenes and the like inevitably led to the writing of concerted music for
several voices, which developed gradually into the
concerted *finale*, Mozart's treatment of which is
the crowning glory of the operas. The quartet in
Idomeneo is not, however, a *finale*. Like the airs,
it is a formal movement designed to bring out the
full significance of the scene and the contrasting
emotions of the four characters. It is this last
element, the clash of personalities, which makes
movements of this nature intensely dramatic.
The great quartet in the last act of *Rigoletto* is
a superb and familiar example of the dramatic
effect which can be obtained by this means. This
kind of concerted movement originated with
Alessandro Scarlatti, but was not developed
fully until the nineteenth century, mainly because
singers who dominated operatic fashions naturally

showed little enthusiasm for music which gave them far more trouble to learn than an *aria* and far less personal glory in its execution. This quartet is, therefore, apart from its intrinsic merits a considerable landmark in operatic history and one of the first signs of Mozart's instinctive feeling for what was right in the theatre.

It has already been mentioned that Mozart had difficulties with the Intendant about the trombones which he required to accompany the oracle's speech. At the time trombones were not normally used in the orchestra, so that to a contemporary audience they must have produced a startling effect. The instruments were used in Church music which gave them an additional association of solemnity, such as we connect with the organ.[1] Mozart never wrote for the trombones, except when he wished to produce an imposing supernatural atmosphere, as in the statue-scenes in *Don Giovanni*, in the solemn ritual of *Die Zauberflöte* and in the tragic Requiem Mass. Gluck had used the trombones for similar purposes, notably in the accompaniment to the Oracle's speech in *Alceste*, and it was probably

---

[1] This association of the trombone with solemnity persisted in the works of Beethoven, who used it only when he wished to produce an unusually noble and exalted effect, for instance in the *finale* of the C minor symphony. Brahms followed his practice of reserving the instrument for a similar purpose in his first symphony, but in the second the trombones with a tuba have taken their place in the normal orchestra. Berlioz, who always used his colossal forces with economy, keeps his trombones for the horrors of the " March to the Gallows " and the " Witches' Sabbath " in the *Symphonie Fantastique*, and in the *Messe des Morts* he is equally sparing in his employment of the lower brass.

his example that prompted Mozart to associate them with the oracle in *Idomeneo*. The speech is punctuated with chords for two horns and three trombones played behind the scenes, each chord being marked with a *crescendo* and a *diminuendo*. Professor Dent aptly suggests that these chords, swelling out and dying down again, portray " the miraculous animation of Poseidon's statue, as its huge breast of bronze begins to heave, and then, after the climax of its utterance, lapses once more into rigidity when the god no longer breathes into its nostrils the breath of life ". Such devices may have lost some of their power for us, who are accustomed to hear the trombone in every normal orchestra. Yet even now Mozart's trombones can make us shudder when the Commendatore's statue interrupts Don Giovanni's boastings about his amours in the churchyard scene.

Idomeneo had a momentary success, in spite of the handicaps of an aged tenor and an unmusical male soprano in the principal parts, and Mozart had hopes of a performance in German at Vienna later in the same year. For this occasion he intended to re-write the part of Idomeneo for a bass and that of Idamante for a tenor. However, the opera was not accepted and remained unperformed until 1786, when it was sung by an amateur company, Idamante being taken by a tenor. The part of Idomeneo was not transposed, though it was shortened and simplified. For this performance Mozart wrote an additional air for Idamante with violin *obbligato*, " Non temer amato bene " (K. 490). This vocal *rondo*, although little suited to the original work, justly remains in our concert programmes.

In the spring of 1781 the Archbishop of Salzburg went to Vienna and took with him a part of his musical staff, Leopold Mozart not being among them. Wolfgang, who was still at Munich, was summoned to the capital, and had once more to assume his servile position and join the company of Brunetti and the only less-detested Ceccarelli, for whom, however, he wrote the fine recitative and air " A questo seno " (K. 374). To his father he writes on March 17th : " I have a charming room in the same house as the Archbishop. Brunetti and Ceccarelli are lodged elsewhere. What a distinction ! . . . We dine at eleven, a little too early for me, alas ! There we sit, the two body-servants (also of his soul), the Comptroller, M. Zetti, the pastry cook, the two cooks, Ceccarelli, Brunetti—and My Littleness. *N.B.* the two valets are placed at the head of the table. I have, at least, the honour to sit above the cooks. Good ! . . . I really believe I am at Salzburg ! At table they make gross and stupid jokes, but not with me for I say not a word, and when I must speak it is with the utmost seriousness. . . . In the evening no meal is provided but we get three ducats—with that one can do a lot ! The Archbishop is glad enough to get credit from his people ; he takes their services and does not pay for them ".

The storm was brewing and Leopold vainly counselled his son to be patient. The Archbishop's meanness culminated in refusing Wolfgang permission to play at a charity concert on behalf of a musician's pension fund. The Archbishop was persuaded by influential persons to give way, but Wolfgang was allowed no opportunity of supplementing his small salary. The Archbishop regarded his *Konzertmeister* as a conceited young puppy, while the youth, confident of his own genius, considered the Archbishop's conduct mean and "grossly impertinent". The impending return of his master to Salzburg further convinced Mozart that a complete rupture was the only possible course. He had as usual fine plans for his future, which were, alas ! as ill-founded as Leopold feared. He sent in his resignation on May 9th but it was returned to him. Early in June he again applied for his dismissal, but the letter was apparently not handed to the Archbishop. On the 8th he sought an interview with Count Arco, Grand Chamberlain to the Archbishop, and according to his own account spoke to him with such insolence that that dignitary kicked him out of the room. Wolfgang was furious at this added indignity and, in a letter to his father, threatened to return the compliment if ever he met the Count in the street. He hoped, incidentally, that his disgrace

with the Archbishop would lend him favour
in the eyes of the Emperor, who bore no love to
the Prince of Salzburg.

Leopold was furious at the inevitable event,
which finally put his son beyond his control. He
could not understand that Wolfgang must now
walk on his own feet, and only relinquished with
the greatest reluctance his dream of basking in
the glory of a famous son. He loved Wolfgang
according to his lights, and was ambitious for his
success. But it was to be a success for which he
was to share the credit, as the guide and ruler of
his son's career. He was therefore horrified at
the idea of an independent Wolfgang living in
Vienna, and went so far as to reproach his son
with the wholly imaginary grievance that he
would soon leave his father in the same straits as
Aloysia Weber had left hers. Wolfgang was
deeply distressed by Leopold's references to the
debts he had incurred on his son's behalf, but he
dealt firmly with this ridiculous comparison of
himself with Aloysia and with the rumours about
his dissipations in Vienna and his relaxation of
religious belief, which had reached Leopold's
ears. " Your comparison of me to Madame
Lange astounds me ", he says. " This girl lived
at her parents' charge so long as she could earn
nothing herself. As soon as she could have shown
them some gratitude (*N.B.* her father died
before she had received a single kreutzer here),
she abandoned her poor mother, took up with

an actor and married him—and her mother has not received from her the slightest help. Good God ! my one aim, as God knows, is to help you and all of us ! Must I then write to you a hundred times, that I can do that better here than in Salzburg ? I beg you, my very dear and excellent father, to write me no more letters of that kind ! " In his autobiography, Lange puts his wife's conduct in a more favourable light, and it is probable that Wolfgang, still sore about Aloysia's conduct to himself, was retailing the grievances of old Frau Weber, who proved in other matters to be an untrustworthy informant. But that does not affect the genuineness of Mozart's retort.

Before his dismissal by the Archbishop, Wolfgang had gone to lodge with the Webers. The family had moved from Munich to Vienna, when Aloysia procured an appointment at the National Theatre. Soon after the move, Fridolin Weber died, and Aloysia married Lange. So Frau Weber was left with three unmarried daughters, Josepha, Constanze, and Sophia. Josepha had a remarkable voice—she created the part of the Queen of the Night in *Die Zauberflöte*—and could earn a living. The two others were less accomplished, but they were at least women, and therefore marriageable. The mother was not scrupulous and she had consented to the match between Aloysia and Lange on the condition that her son-in-law paid off a debt of 900 florins. Constanze was not beautiful. The best that Wolfgang himself could say of her in a letter to his father was, " She is not ugly, but certainly is anything but beautiful—her entire beauty consists of two black eyes and a good figure. She is not clever, but has enough common sense to fulfil her duties as wife and mother. She is not extravagant . . . on the contrary, she usually dresses simply. For the little that the mother could do for her children, she has done for the others. . . . She knows how to make for herself all the things which a woman needs, and she dresses her own hair every day and can manage a household. . . . She loves me and I love her— tell me, could I wish for a better wife ? "

Frau Weber was quite pleased to rid herself of the liability of an ugly girl, even if the prospects of the suitor were not bright. After marriage that would be his affair. Wolfgang seems to have fallen in love partly out of pity and partly because Constanze happened to be the nearest object on which he could lavish his susceptible affection. The love-affair developed this time into a genuine and lasting passion whose growth was assisted partly by the obstacles placed in its way by Leopold and by the difficulties of another kind raised by Frau Weber. This woman who, as Mozart had to confess, took more liquor than a lady should (though " he had never yet seen her drunk "), put the worst possible construction on Mozart's love-making. Abetted by Johann Thorwart, an accountant at the National Theatre, who had been appointed guardian to Weber's

141

daughters, she made Wolfgang sign a bond under the terms of which he must marry Constanze within three years or pay her 300 florins a year. In his relation of the incident to his father, Wolfgang says lightly—and we can see the creator of Figaro in the jest and its semi-serious qualification—" to sign it was the easiest thing in the world for I knew I should never have three hundred florins to pay . . . supposing I would ever abandon her ". Constanze was, however, too proud to allow herself to be sold in this way, and, directly Thorwart left the house, she asked her mother for the bond and tore it up. " I have no need of a written engagement from you ", she said to Wolfgang. " I believe your word ".

I think we may believe it too. After all, it matters very little at this time of day whether Mozart did or did not seduce Constanze before he married her. His father chose to think the worst of him. He accepted as truth the gossip of one Peter von Winter, a pupil of the Abbé Vogler, who had had a grudge against Wolfgang Mozart ever since the visit to Mannheim where Wolfgang had been disrespectful to his master. Wolfgang again defended his character with dignity and with a frankness which involved the exclusion of his letter from the English translation of Jahn's *Life*. As there is nothing offensive in this letter and as its obvious sincerity is the best answer that can be made to Mozart's

detractors—there are some even to-day—I quote
the essential passages :

> " I have discovered to you my desire [to marry],
> permit me now also to discover my reasons, very well
> founded reasons. Nature speaks in me as strongly as
> in any other, and perhaps more strongly than in a
> great many big and vigorous louts. I cannot live like
> most of the young men of to-day. In the first place
> I have too much respect for my religion, and in the
> second I love my neighbour and honest ideals too
> much to be able to seduce an innocent girl, and thirdly
> I have too great a disgust, a horror, a repulsion and a
> fear of disease and too much regard for my health to
> be able to amuse myself with whores. So that I can
> swear that I have never had anything to do with
> persons of that kind."

Mozart was, in fact, a decent, self-respecting
man. We may admire these qualities in him all
the more in that they were not encouraged by
the general standard of morality in his day and
in that he was himself, as he confesses, of an
unusually passionate nature. In his attitude
towards sex, as in other things, he was the fore-
runner of the Romantic Ideal. Yet alongside
this restraint there was in him an ebullient spirit
which took an almost primitive delight in things
which are not considered mentionable in the
drawing-room. He comprised in his character
the lofty ideals of Tamino and the naïve sensuality of Papageno. Those who know anything
about their fellow-men will realize very well

that the co-existence of these two traits is not inconsistent with an adherence to the first of them in practice.

Wolfgang could on occasion be prudish. He rebuked his *fiancée* for allowing her leg to be measured by a young man in a game of forfeits. Constanze sulked under his reproaches and he wrote her a dignified lecture on the conduct proper to young women in general, and *fiancées* in particular. On the whole, however, the obstacles to the course of love came from without and not from any mutual disagreements. Leopold ordered his son to leave the house of the disreputable Frau Weber, and it was certainly unwise for his reputation's sake that Wolfgang should be living under the same roof as Constanze. Matters were not improved when Constanze, for some reason, left her mother and went to stay with the Baroness von Waldstätten, an elderly lady with a kind heart but of a very doubtful character. Leopold steadfastly refused to consent to a marriage, and his dutiful son persisted in denying himself and in resisting the importunities of Constanze's mother and guardian, until his father gave way.

During this period of emotional turmoil he composed his first German opera, *Die Entführung aus dem Serail*, which is better known in England under the more manageable title of *Il Seraglio*. The Emperor Joseph II had, like the Elector of Bavaria, adopted the idea of encouraging

German opera and drama. He took over as a national institution the management of the imperial theatre, which had previously been let to commercial managers, and substituted for the Italian opera the " *National-Singspiel* ", whose repertory consisted, however, mainly of translations from the Italian or the French. The moment was, therefore, favourable for any composer who could write a German opera. Mozart seized it. He proposed in the first instance a revised version of *Idomeneo* with a German text, but the work was refused. He then suggested the production of *Zaïde*, the unfinished opera on which he had been working at Salzburg before he received the commission to write an opera for Munich. This plan was also turned down, probably on account of the badness of Schachtner's libretto. However, Gottlieb Stephanie, the inspector of the opera, was sufficiently impressed by Mozart's work to propose writing a libretto for him on the lines of *Zaïde*, and evidently intended that he should make use of the music he had written.

Stephanie adapted his libretto from one written by Bretzner which was produced in the same year with music by André at Leipsic. Bretzner was not unnaturally furious at this plagiarism and, still more, the alterations made by Stephanie. The incident is typical of the lack of protection from which authors, and musicians too, suffered at this time. Beethoven continually complains in his letters of the pirating of his work by unscrupulous publishers. Bretzner himself had less cause for complaint, for he owed a good deal of his plot to various English plays dealing with the rescue of a lady from a Turkish harem, a subject which is ever dear to feuilleton-writers and their public. The sole trace of its English origin in Mozart's opera is the nationality of Blöndchen, the heroine's English maid. The heroine herself was called after the composer's *fiancée*, Constanze, his love for whom is generally supposed to have inspired the work. As Professor Dent suggests, however, it is probable that the opera would have been a better one, if Mozart had not been distracted by his personal worries. Excepting Osmin, none of the characters have any individuality, and are not always even types. Constanze sinks into insignificance beside Mme Cavalieri, the *prima donna* who sang the part, and her big air is a concerto for voice and orchestra without dramatic meaning. Belmonte, her lover and rescuer, is the most colourless of Mozart's tenor heroes, while his servant Pedrillo is a conventional figure from *opera buffa* hardly worthy to be named with Figaro and Leporello. Yet Pedrillo's serenade is one of the finest gems in the opera, and it is unfortunate that this lovely melody is usually subjected to stupid buffoonery in English performances of the work. The soubrette Blöndchen has more character ; her vivacity and her spitfire wit are well portrayed in the scenes with

Osmin. She is the first of the sisterhood, which includes in its membership Susanna, Zerlina, and Despina. Osmin is a droll creation of the most complete originality. He is not a mere buffoon, but a living character, with whom as well as at whom we may laugh. His rage, his stupidity, and his grossness are admirably drawn in the music, and the scenes in which he appears are consequently the best in the opera.

The greatest flaw in the work is the fact that one of the principal characters, the Pasha Selim, has nothing to sing—simply because there was no singer available to take the part. The scenes between him and Constanze are, therefore, singularly ineffective, since they are musically one-sided. For in opera, in which the music takes up the situations where the spoken words leave them, and intensifies them emotionally, a character who does not express himself in music is almost non-existent. The effect is similar to that which would be produced by an oil-painting of a group in which one of the principal figures was merely sketched in with a crayon. · Nevertheless, in spite of these faults, *Die Entführung* remains in the popular repertory, on account of its comic subject and its delightful music, while the finer tragedy of *Idomeneo* is only brought out on rare occasions in Germany, where the historical interest in music is strong.

Die Entführung was begun in August, 1782, and was intended for immediate production.

Various obstacles, however, delayed its performance until July 16th of the following year. The Emperor himself intervened on Mozart's behalf, though he does not appear to have been wholly satisfied with the opera. For it was of this work that he made the often quoted remark that there were too many notes in Mozart's music. This may seem a silly piece of criticism, but in so far as he meant that the music was not simple enough to be truly German in style and was rather over-elaborate for the subject, there is some justification for it. The work was, however, favourably received both by the general public and by the musicians, among whom Gluck complimented the composer. It was given fourteen performances in 1782 and remained in the repertory at Vienna until 1787, when the Emperor, discouraged by the failure of his patronage to produce masterpieces of German opera by the dozen (as if any new style in art could be brought to immediate fruition!), restored the Italian opera, which in his heart he much preferred.

Mozart was encouraged by his success to press his father more persistently for his consent to the marriage with Constanze Weber. Leopold remained obdurate and on August 3, 1782, Wolfgang, having at last decided to ignore his father's objections, signed a contract of marriage with Constanze. The ceremony took place on the following day, and the Baroness von Waldstätten gave a supper for the young couple, which the bridegroom described as " more worthy of a prince than of a mere baron ". On the day after the wedding Wolfgang received his father's reluctant consent coupled with the announcement that he must not look to Leopold for further assistance.

Chapter VII

THE MARRIAGE OF FIGARO

At the time of her marriage Constanze was only eighteen—eight years younger than her husband. This was a good augury for their happiness, but a bad one for the management of their affairs. Wolfgang had been closely looked after by his father and had rarely been allowed to manage his own affairs until he had long passed what are supposed to be the years of discretion. He was naturally feckless and of a sanguine temperament which expected success to be lurking just out of sight round the next corner, and it is doubtful if he would under any circumstances have been a " good manager ". If, however, he had had to assume responsibilities gradually at an earlier age, his story would not have been such a pitiable one—the more pitiable, because his faults were lovable ones, the faults of a generous and careless nature. It must not be imagined that he was the immoral artist of convention, bound up selfishly in his own dreams and caring not a jot for the rights and feelings of other people. He was, indeed, thanks to Leopold's influence, easily prejudiced against people he did not know well—the Abbé Vogler's is a case in point ; but the general affection, in which he was held by a large number of friends, shows that he was not a " difficult " person. Constanze, on her side, was not the woman to make a home for a man of genius. She came from a house, where if one can judge from her mother's character, untidiness always reigned, and notwithstanding Mozart's tribute to her abilities as a housewife, expressed before his marriage, she did little to enhance the comforts of their poor lodgings. She was capricious and easily put out. She was at once coquettish with other men and jealous of her husband. She was, in short, an empty-headed girl, who for all that she came of a family connected with the drama and with music, showed no real appreciation of her husband's worth. Wolfgang was infinitely patient in giving way to her whims and did his best to check her less amiable characteristics. His letters prove that he was very much in love with her and the records of his friends show that the *ménage* was a happy one. We may imagine them as a gay young couple taking little notice of their cares except when these thrust themselves to the fore, chattering happily like Papageno and Papagena.

More than this happy companionship in everyday things Wolfgang did not get from his wife. What we may well call the Tamino side of his dual personality, his idealistic and spiritual side, can have found no outlet in the company of Constanze. Like most men of great genius, he was very lonely. It is possible that this personal loneliness, the inability to find a kindred spirit to whom may be revealed the intimate thoughts of the soul, is one of the chief driving forces which compel the artist to create. He cannot find the ideal sharer of his mind in any one person, and he therefore takes into his confidence the whole world, or such part of it as will listen to his message. Whatever faults, then, genius may have, it is always deserving of reverence, if not of blind hero-worship, and of all the affection that gratitude for its creations can give.

We must not be too hard on Constanze. It is very easy to criticize her conduct, but it is a difficult thing to be the wife of genius, even of one so lovable in character as Mozart. She was only a girl when she married; her home life had been sordid and unhappy, for she was the least favoured of her sisters; and when her husband died she had barely reached womanhood. In the face of the poverty in which she was left she showed courage, and an ability to manage her affairs, which was unfortunately developed too late to benefit her husband. She became eventually the mistress and afterwards the wife of Nikolaus von Nissen, a Danish diplomat on service in Vienna, and found in him a worthy husband and protector of her children. That he was unworthy to write his predecessor's life and an untrustworthy editor of his letters, is another matter.

Mozart started upon his married life in his usual sanguine mood. His first musical action of importance was the composition of a Mass, which he had vowed as a thank-offering for the successful issue of his suit. This is the Great Mass in C minor (K. 427), which stands high above all his other Church music, with the exception of the *Requiem*. In each case the composer was faced with one of the great crises of human life, in the first with the happy one of marriage, in the second with that of death. Mozart approached his task with the most sincere feelings, as witness his letter of August 17th, in which he says, " We go always together, not only to Mass, but to Confession and Communion, and I find that I have never prayed so earnestly, nor confessed and received communion so reverently as by her side ".

The Mass is planned on a large scale, which makes it comparable with those of Bach and Beethoven, rather than with Mozart's smaller works intended for actual use as accompaniments to the Church service. It cannot be placed on an equality with the great Masses in B minor and in D composed by the two other masters. These works were the products of their composers' maturity and had behind them all that deeper philosophy, which experience of life twice as long as Mozart's at this period, brought to these two profound thinkers. None the less, Mozart's extraordinary intuition enabled him to set the

153

Liturgy to music worthy of the tremendous subject. One of the most extraordinary things about the Mass is its entire difference in spirit from the other music upon which he was engaged at the time. He owes a great deal to the giants of the North German school J. S. Bach and Handel, with whose music he was at this time becoming more closely acquainted. The Baron van Swieten, a rich amateur of Dutch origin settled in Vienna, who was naturally in sympathy with the music of North Germany, invited Mozart to his house every Sunday to join in the performance of works by Bach and Handel. Although Mozart had been on intimate terms with J. C. Bach and knew the music of his brothers, his knowledge of their father's music was until now slight. " Old " Bach was very much out of fashion, especially in gay Vienna. Encouraged by van Swieten, Mozart like every composer fell under the spell of Bach and Handel. He arranged some of Bach's fugues for string-quartet and at a later date supplied those additional accompaniments to Handel's oratorios, including *The Messiah*, about which there has been and ever will be so much controversy. It is sufficient to say that Mozart's arrangements were made for performances, which could otherwise not have taken place, and that, though he sometimes mistook Handel's intentional bleakness—for instance, in the chorus, " The people that walked in darkness "—for barrenness and inserted the

ideas of a mind that was not in tune with that of
the creator, no permanent injury has been done
to Handel's masterpiece (which is not a picture
from which re-painting cannot be removed) and
conductors can always, and sometimes do, revert
to the original score.

. The result of his contact with North German
music is immediately apparent in the tendency
towards archaism, which is evident in his music
at this time. His strong passion for fugues, the
musical expression of the mathematical side of
his mind, was strengthened by his admiration for
the works of the earlier masters. He composed
a suite for pianoforte in their manner and the
fugue in C minor for two pianofortes (K. 426),
which is remarkable for the extraordinary freedom
of its polyphony. But the new influence is, not
unnaturally, most conspicuous in the C minor
Mass. The Mass is laid out for four solo voices,
chorus (sometimes divided into five and eight
parts), and full orchestra (including four trombones and timpani) with organ. But like the
Requiem it was destined to remain unfinished.
The score as Mozart left it consists of the *Kyrie,*
the *Gloria,* the *Credo* down to the words " et
homo factus est ", the *Sanctus,* and the *Benedictus.*
The Mass was actually performed at Salzburg
during the Mozarts' visit to Leopold in 1783, and
Constanze sang the soprano part. It then remained
neglected (though it was of course published in the
collected edition of Mozarts' works by Breitkopf

and Härtel), until Alois Schmidt published an edition for a performance by the Mozartsverein at Dresden in 1901. Schmidt supplied the missing sections from other Masses by Mozart, the *Agnus Dei* being set to the music of the *Kyrie*, an expedient which was also resorted to by Süssmayer when he completed the *Requiem* Mass. There is naturally a decided drop in the interest when the sections from the smaller Masses intervene, the Fugue " Et in vitam venturi saeculi " from the Mass in C major (K. 262) composed in 1776 being in particular an empty piece of learned counterpoint. But on the whole the patching is well done and is at least defensible on the ground that it has made possible the performance of this fine work. Less defensible is Schmidt's curtailment of some of the fine *bravura* in the airs "Laudamus te" and "Et incarnatus est".

The four-part *Kyrie* is introduced by a descending figure on the violins very similar to the sobbing *motifs* which occur so frequently in the works of Sebastian Bach. The chorus, however, introduces a dramatic element, which is enhanced by the entry of the soprano solo on the words " Christe Eleison ". We are at once at a far remove from the calm and restrained sorrow of the opening of the B minor Mass. The solo has *coloratura* passages to sing, which might be called rococo if they were not so full of meaning. The *Gloria*, on the other hand, opens with a reminiscence of Handel's "Hallelujah Chorus ", and then proceeds through a lively fugue to a quiet ending on the words " Et in terra pax hominibus bonae voluntatis ". The florid mezzo-soprano air, *Laudamus te*, takes us back to Vienna again. Again the *coloratura* is justified by its effect and the movement is a beautiful expression of adoration. The *Gratias Agimus*, a short and dignified movement for five-part chorus, is followed by a duet for soprano and mezzo-soprano (*Domine Deus*), which is characteristically Mozartian, with its syncopation at the end of the second bar. The voices do not fall over one another in the lovely manner of Bach's duet on the same words, which is like the antiphonal singing of two angels answering each other in imitation ; but there are some beautiful moments in Mozart's version, notably at the end where the two voices cross one another, singing alternately high and low over a range of nearly two octaves.

The *Qui Tollis* is certainly the finest movement of all. It is written for a double chorus in eight parts and is accompanied throughout on the strings by a broken figure in dotted rhythm, which suggests vividly the heaviness of the load borne by mankind, while the wind-instruments (oboes, bassoons, horns, and trombones) support the voices. Once more the dramatic genius of Mozart is felt at the word " miserere ", which is wailed on a chromatic sequence by the sopranos of one choir and answered in imitation a tone higher by the whole of the other choir. The same effect is used again at the words " suscipe deprecationem nostram ". This noble and poignant movement is alone sufficient to refute the idea that Mozart's was a light and elegant mind incapable of rivalling the great composers of Northern Germany in the expression of deep religious feeling. The *Quoniam* is a florid and difficult fugue for three solo voices (soprano, mezzo-soprano, and tenor). It is worked out with consummate skill, but with no emphasis on the mathematics of fugue-writing. We can hardly hope to hear it adequately performed in these days, when singers have mostly lost the art of singing with the purity and flexibility of instruments. The *Cum Sancto Spiritu*, which is preceded by a noble *adagio* of five bars sung on the words " Jesu Christe ", is a slow fugue, the subject being announced by the basses with a unison accompaniment for bassoon and bass trombone. The effect of this opening is startling in its grandeur. The movement is very different from the exhilarating music of Bach's setting, but it is none the less exultant if sung with spirit. The swinging figures, to which the word " gloria " is set, maintain a fine rhythm and the accompaniment of the three trombones, which play throughout in unison with the altos, tenors, and basses respectively, is very striking in its effect. It must be confessed, however, that in practice this polyphonic use of the trombones, both here and in the *Osanna*, is sometimes more bold than happy. The trombones are, as Berlioz pointed out, best confined to harmonic effects and to sustained or slow-moving chords. In passage work of the kind written by Mozart for them they are apt to sound clumsy. The unfinished *Credo* consists of two movements, the first of which takes us down to the words " descendit de coelis ". Mozart has not attempted to make the doctrinal statements into an elaborate musical composition. He has written a declamatory five-part chorus, for the most part free of contrapuntal effects. It is an emphatic affirmation of faith. The idea of the Incarnation, on the other hand, provides a subject for more poetical and extended treatment, and Mozart has written a long and elaborate solo for soprano with *obbligato* accompaniment for flute, oboe, and bassoon. This movement is similar, at least in form, to the great concerted airs in *Idomeneo* and Constanze's air in *Die Entführung*. At times it is difficult for a modern audience not to hear the voice of the Queen of the Night, when in the *cadenza* the voice runs up to repeated high B flats with the three *obbligato* instruments in attendance. But that is mainly because a modern audience is familiar with this kind of music only through such works as *Die Zauberflöte*. To Mozart's contemporaries, these devices were the natural and appropriate adornments of worship. Although, therefore, this air smacks at first something too much of the opera-house, an unbiassed examination will discover its real beauty and the aptness of its decorations. It is unfortunate that circumstances have deprived us of Mozart's settings of the *Crucifixus* and *Et resurrexit* on the grand scale. He must have paused at this point, waiting for the inspiration which was never to come. The dramatic movements, which he would surely have written, must have thrown into a better perspective the lovely *roulades* of the *Et incarnatus est.*

The remaining movements are the *Sanctus*, the *Osanna*, and the *Benedictus.* The *Sanctus* is a quick-moving chorus in five parts ; for although it is marked *largo*, the intention is that it should be broad in feeling, not slow in pace. It opens with a shout of joy, thrice repeated. Then the violins enter with a persistent figure in thirds, two semiquavers followed by a triplet of three demi-semiquavers with a semiquaver rest before each beat of the bar. It sounds like the quick ringing of joy-bells. When the excitement has been worked up to a climax, there is a pause, and the basses, again supported by bassoon and trombone, state the subject of the fugal *Osanna.* In this elaborate movement the brass take independent parts in the working-out of the fugue, so that the effect is even richer and more complex than in the *Cum Sancto Spiritu.* The *Benedictus* takes us from the brilliant key of C major into the relative minor. The contrast is further emphasized by the use of a solo-quartet with small orchestra for this movement, whose quiet melody comes nearer than anything else in the Mass to the spirit of Bach. The *Benedictus* is followed without a break by a repetition in shortened form of the *Osanna*.

Cynics will no doubt seize upon the fact that Mozart did not finish this Mass, which was to celebrate his marriage, and failed to complete every one of the works which he wrote for dedication to his wife. The explanation is less unpleasant. In the first place, Mozart was incapable of working without the stimulus of a definite performance in view, and he usually waited until the last possible moment before he put pen to paper. He had not the *cacoethes scribendi* which urges some people to write, whether or no they are likely to secure the publication or performance of their effusions. Secondly, in the case of the Mass, before he had time to complete a work on such a large scale, a profound change in his religious convictions made it impossible for him to continue it in the same spirit of faith in which it had been begun. The fate of the Mass was finally sealed by this event, and the music was adapted rather inappropriately for the setting of an oratorio, *Davidde Penitente*, which he was commissioned to write at short notice in 1785.

Mozart had shown up to this time a child-like faith in the religion of his fathers, but at Vienna

he came into contact with numerous musicians
and literary men, who belonged to the secret
Society of Freemasons, which increased its
membership with great rapidity in Germany
towards the end of the eighteenth century, and
had a considerable influence in social, political,
and artistic matters. Freemasonry was dis-
countenanced, like all other secret societies, by
the Roman Catholic Church, and to be a Freemason was, in the eyes of the orthodox, as heinous
an offence as a century later it was to be a free-
thinker. In Vienna, however, the Freemasons
were to some extent encouraged and protected
by the Emperor. Ignaz von Born was a leading
spirit in the Society, which soon became fashionable with other elements in Viennese society than
the intellectuals, so that abuses crept in and
had to be suppressed by an Imperial decree. At
its best, however, Freemasonry included in its
membership men like Frederick the Great,
Goethe, Herder, and Wieland, while among its
Viennese associates were Gluck and Haydn.
Mozart joined the Society a year after his marriage and took a keen interest in its activities.
He even thought of founding a lodge of his own
and drew up the rules for it. He wrote a number
of works inspired by the ideals of the Society, the
most familiar of which is the Masonic Funeral
March (K. 477), composed for the funeral of
one of the Esterhazys. The other works are
choruses and cantatas to words supplied by

brother Masons. But the most important outcome of his interest in Freemasonry is his last opera *Die Zauberflöte*, which must be reserved for subsequent discussion. It is worthy of note that, during a visit to Vienna in 1785, the bigoted Leopold was persuaded to become a Mason.

The months immediately following Mozart's marriage were not prolific in musical composition. There were few opportunities to provide a stimulus and it was natural that Wolfgang should be absorbed in his newly found domesticity. However, his output was by no means negligible, since to the period immediately after his marriage belongs the first of the six string quartets, which the composer dedicated to Joseph Haydn. Mozart had not tried his hand at the string quartet since 1773, nearly ten years earlier, and this group comprises the first of the wonderful series of chamber-works which many people regard as his highest achievement. It is not unlikely that his passion for counterpoint, the outcome of his study of Bach and Handel, may have influenced him as much as the example of Haydn's own quartets towards resorting to a form of composition in which it can be turned to such wonderful account in the interweaving of the four voices. It is certain, at any rate, that his preoccupation with this side of his art accounts in part for the peculiarities of the quartets, which caused one princely amateur to tear up the parts in fury at the outrage committed upon his ears, and resulted in the return to Mozart's publishers of some copies sent to Italy as being full of printer's errors. It is difficult for us nowadays to understand how astonishing these quartets sounded to contemporary ears. They were the subject at once of the violent criticism and the no less violent enthusiasm which original work always arouses. To-day they are generally regarded as works of consummate beauty, though the famous opening of the C major quartet (K. 465) is still the subject of controversy.

The first of these quarters, the G major (K. 387) was composed in December, 1782. In it Mozart shows a seriousness of purpose which is very far removed from the elegant frivolities of his " gallant " style, although the accomplishment, which he had gained from his practice in that style, is everywhere apparent in these quartets, and gives them a surface-finish which may be compared, in the art of painting, with the perfection of Vermeer or the Van Eycks—different though the subjects were, in everything except a certain melancholy, to which these artists applied their marvellous technique. The slow movement of the G major quartet is written in a mood of extraordinary exaltation such as we find, outside Mozart, only in the later works of Beethoven. Even the *finale*, which obviously owes something to the gaiety of Haydn's last movements—his " Russian " quartets had recently been published—is unusually severe in its counterpoint, a fact which makes its humour the more subtle. This work definitely marks the composer's entrance upon the period of his full maturity. The D minor quartet (K. 421) is even more serious in mood. It was written in June, 1783, during the anxious days of Constanze's first confinement. The first movement, like that of the later quartet in D major (K. 499), is thoroughly romantic and has been said to foreshadow the style of Schubert. Instead of a fugal *finale*, such as ends the first quartet of the series, Mozart wrote a set of variations, the theme of which is in the metre of a *Siciliano*, a dance-form with which his recent studies of Bach must have made him familiar. The final variation, in which clever use is made of the counter-subject in the third and fourth bars of the movement, brings the quartet to a tragic, almost gloomy, ending.

The third quartet of the series, in E flat major (K. 428), is comparatively gay and light-hearted, but the romantic warmth of feeling remains in the first and second movements, while it is not far-fetched to see in the brusque opening of the minuet the beginnings of the development of the graceful dance into a serious movement more in keeping with the general mood of an extended work, whose four movements represent a musical idea approached from different points of view— a development which was completed in the *scherzi* of Beethoven. The *Trio* is highly original with its long flowing melody over a drone bass.

Even in the Haydnesque *finale* the *coda* takes on a melancholy mood, which reminds one for a moment of Pamina. But it must not be forgotten that Haydn himself, even in his sprightliest moments, could suddenly become serious. The variations at the end of his G major quartet (Op. 76, No. 1) provide an obvious example, though one in which the influence of Mozart upon his senior may be recognized. In the music of Mozart's C minor Mass we can trace the composer's debt to Bach and Handel undisguised ; in these quartets Mozart turned their learning entirely to his own account.

Another series of compositions, the first of which dates to 1782, deserves mention. These are the concertos for horn and orchestra (K. 412, 417, 447, and 495). The first is in D major, the other three are in E flat. They were composed for Joseph Leutgeb, a horn-player from Salzburg, who had settled in Vienna. Leutgeb was an excellent performer, but something of a boor. Mozart used him as a butt for his high spirits, and even made a running commentary on his manuscript at the expense of his friend. The second concerto was inscribed : " Wolfgang Amadé Mozart takes pity on Leutgeb, ass, ox, and simpleton, at Vienna, March 27th, 1783." The last, which was composed in 1786, is written alternately in black, red, blue, and green inks. In the *Rondo* he marked the horn part *adagio* and the accompaniment *allegro*, a reference to Leutgeb's tendency to drag the time. As might be expected, works written in this mood are light and gay ; but anyone who has heard Mr Aubrey Brain play the second of these concertos, will know how delightful Mozart's humour is, and that his frivolity is not inconsistent with beauty. The *Rondo* of this work provides a typical instance of the kind of musical wit which delighted the eighteenth century, when the melody suddenly pauses and is resumed again by the repetition of the note on which it was broken off—perhaps yet another jest at poor Leutgeb's expense, suggesting that he had to stop and fetch a breath. The quintet for horn and strings (K. 407), which was also written for Leutgeb, is a more extended and important work nearer in style to the quartets.

On June 17, 1783, Constanze gave birth to a son, Raimund Leopold, who lived only for a few months, and in August the young couple went to pay a visit to old Leopold at Salzburg, where they stayed for three months. Constanze was faced with the difficult position in which every bride is placed in regard to her husband's relatives, but in her case the situation was made more than usually unenviable by the prejudice entertained against her by her father-in-law. She was not the person to charm away his preconceived notions, which were shared also by Nannerl. Wolfgang did his best to win his family over, but without success. He hoped in vain that his father would give his wife some of the presents which he had collected during his early tours. The long visit must have been an unpleasant one, especially as Wolfgang hated Salzburg, and he parted coldly from his family, if we may judge from the formal language in which he expresses his thanks for his father's hospitality and his regret at having to put him to so much trouble.

On the way back to Vienna, the Mozarts made a short stay at Linz, where Wolfgang composed the symphony in C major (K. 425), which is known as the "Linz Symphony". The work shows no signs, unless it be at the end of the *finale*, of having been composed in four days in order that it should be ready for the concert at which it was performed. It is written for a small orchestra, and the instruments are treated in the chamber-music style. The result is a little masterpiece, full of poetic ideas, sometimes happy, sometimes of that tender melancholy which Mozart's contemporaries regarded as his most characteristic trait. This sensuous melancholy is too often overlooked nowadays by interpreters of Mozart's music, who regard it as melodious and elegant, but empty. It is true, of course, that he turned out a certain amount of music whose content is not profound in thought or feeling, but the more we listen to his quartets and his symphonies, the more we realize that beneath their gay exterior lies the spirit of a sad and disillusioned man.

The great pianoforte concertos, which belong

to the years immediately following his marriage, certainly provide some examples of empty virtuosity. Most of these works were composed for performance by Mozart himself at the series of concerts he gave in Vienna. He was no exception among pianist-composers in making up for a lack of ideas with a show of manual dexterity. But this display is usually confined to the first movements. The slow movements nearly always glow with warm and tender feeling. One has only to recall the lovely melody of the D minor concerto (K. 466), the most popular of all, to realize that the composer used some of his finest inspirations for these works. The finales, usually in rondo-form, are no less delightful in their charm and gaiety. Unfortunately the nineteenth-century style of pianism, inaugurated by Beethoven, was too violent to do justice to their frail beauty. It burst them asunder with torrents of tone which, by over-emphasis, made the music seem more empty than it is. Yet Beethoven, as his C minor concerto bears witness, made a profitable study of his predecessor's works in this form and paid him the sincerest compliment of taking them as his models. Fortunately pianists are beginning once more to realize the beauty of these works and to play them with a true understanding of their style. Busoni, a great exponent of the D minor concerto, must be honourably mentioned as one of those who fully appreciated Mozart, in spite of his leanings towards a more leonine style of pianoforte playing.

During the years immediately after his marriage Mozart managed to support himself by taking pupils and giving concerts. Like most composers of genius, he hated the drudgery of teaching; but when his pupils were worthy of his pains, he took infinite trouble and wrote music for them. For instance, he dedicated to Frau von Trattnern the C minor Fantasia (K. 475), which is the noblest of his works for pianoforte solo, and composed the concertos in E flat and G major (K. 482 and 453) for Barbara Ployer. The concerts were given in Lent, when the theatres were closed, at the Augarten, which was built by the Emperor Joseph II as a place of public entertainment. The programmes were, according to modern notions, excessively long, and the results were very meagre in comparison with the sums earned by popular executants to-day. But they were successful at least from the social and artistic points of view. Mozart describes proudly how Gluck praised his music and " invited us all to dinner on Sunday, while the Emperor stayed to the very end until the *encores were finished* ".

At one of the concerts given in March, 1783, the programme opened with the symphony in D (K. 385) which Mozart had composed in the previous summer for his Salzburg friend, Haffner. The symphony is in reality four movements taken from a serenade, not to be confused with the earlier " Haffner Serenade " (K. 250), which was written to celebrate the wedding of Elizabeth Haffner in 1776. This second serenade was hurriedly written for some festive occasion at Haffner's house just after the completion of *Die Entführung*. The work is, indeed, dated internally by the identity of the theme of the *finale* with that of Osmin's second song in the opera. The emphatic opening of the first movement, on the other hand, looks forward to the Count's air in *Figaro*. This forceful theme occupies in varying forms the whole of the first movement, which is a masterpiece of ingenious workmanship. The slow movement is light in character, as befits music written for such an occasion, but the playful second subject is followed by a sudden outburst of the characteristic Mozartian melancholy in a passage, marked *forte*, whose harsh harmonies must have sounded very strange and dramatic to the composer's contemporaries. The minuet opens with a figure similar to that employed in the later E flat symphony (K. 543), but continues in a lighter vein. The construction of the *finale* is, like that of the first movement, unusual. The development-section makes use of the principal and subsidiary themes in such a way as to suggest that it is the recapitulation, while the recapitulation is delayed and preceded by a linking passage similar in character to that in the *Figaro* overture. This delightful and effective little work is a worthy companion to the Linz symphony in C major.

On his return to Vienna after the visit to Salzburg, Mozart continued the writing of the six quartets which he subsequently dedicated to Haydn. The fourth of the series, that in B flat (K. 458) is similar in character to the E flat written eighteen months earlier. It is known as the " Hunt " quartet on account of the resemblance of the first theme to a hunting-call, an idea which may have come into the composer's mind on account of his recent preoccupation with the horn-concertos for Leutgeb. The quartet in A major (K. 464) is more serious in mood and may be paired with the D minor. As in the earlier work there is a movement in variation-form, in this case the slow movement. Like Beethoven, Mozart used the variation as a means of expressing some of his finest thoughts. At least this is true of these two quartet movements, which are infinitely superior to the facile variations for pianoforte. Again like Beethoven, Mozart used the quartet at this period for the expression of his most serious musical ideas, and these works are both on a far higher level of musical achievement than the brilliant concertoes on which he was engaged at the same time, and far more profound than the two symphonies (the " Haffner " and the " Linz "), delightful though they are.

It was after a performance of the third, fourth,

and fifth of this series that Haydn made his famous remark, with its strangely bathetic ending, to Leopold Mozart : " In the face of God and as an honest man, I tell you that your son is the greatest composer known to me either personally or by reputation. He has taste and also a very great knowledge of composition ". When one has heard such enchanting passages as that in the slow movement of the " Hunt " quartet, where the first violin and the violoncello play in alternation a lovely phrase against a *staccato* accompaniment, one feels inclined to echo Haydn's estimate.

But greater was to follow. Four days after the A major quartet was written, Mozart composed the last work of the series, that in C major (K. 465). It can hardly be an accident that the greatest of Mozart's quartets and of his symphonies are in the same key. Even the earlier symphony in C major (K. 200), stands out, as we have already remarked, from among the other works of its time, while the so-called " Jupiter " symphony, the last he wrote, is, notwithstanding the claims of the symphonies in E flat and G minor (K. 543 and 550), his finest work in this form. It is, therefore, not unnatural to suppose that the key had some particular significance to Mozart, who was more susceptible than perhaps any other to the meaning of tonality, just as the key of C minor had for Beethoven its own poetic meaning. What that significance was cannot be put into vords ; all we can say is that it was the key in

which he expressed his most exalted mood, just
as he chose the key of G minor as the most
suitable vehicle for his peculiar melancholy, for
example, in the symphony just mentioned and in
the string quintet (K. 516).

The C major quartet is not light-hearted and
gay. "The frame of mind expressed", says
Jahn, "is a noble, manly cheerfulness rising in
the *Andante* to an almost supernatural serenity
—the kind of cheerfulness which, in life or
in art, appears only as the result of previous
pain and strife". This quartet is the only one of
the set which has a slow introduction to the first
movement. In it the composer establishes the
gloomy mood, over which cheerfulness is to
triumph. It is an example of the poetic use of
the introductory passage, which had been used in
the first instance by Haydn as a facile manner of
exciting interest by contrast (see p. 88). As in
Beethoven's symphonies, the introduction has
here become an integral part of the poetic idea.
The dissonant harmonies, with which the quartet
begins, have been explained grammatically as an
"anticipation", and we may find in them one
more example of the influence of Mozart's
study of the North German masters of the contrapuntal style, in whose music such anticipations
frequently occur. There is no question that the
passage still sounds strange and harsh, and at
least one distinguished modern critic has con-
demned it as bad writing. Mozart's contemporaries

criticized it severely. Haydn, being under some obligation in the matter, hedged with the remark that if Mozart wrote it, he must have had his reasons for doing so. The Italian composer, Sarti, talked without ambiguity about " music going to the dogs ". But, as Abert points out, that may only show how far the average Italian musician had lost touch with the new developments of German music. However, the grammar or logic of the music may be left to the theorists. The ordinary man must judge for himself whether the discords are ugly in the sense of being æsthetically bad, or whether their " ugliness " is of the kind which is a part of beauty and, therefore, æsthetically right. Whatever his opinion on this point may be, he will probably agree that the quartet as a whole sets the coping-stone upon the finest monument which one composer has ever erected to the honour of another.

At about this time Mozart encountered the man who was to be the collaborator in three of his greatest masterpieces, the librettist Lorenzo da Ponte. Da Ponte was by birth a Jew, by profession a priest, and by inclination a poet. He was born in 1749 at Ceneda, near Venice. When he was fourteen years of age, his widowed father re-married with a Catholic and was baptized together with his three sons. The eldest, Emmanuel, was given the name of Lorenzo after the Bishop, Lorenzo da Ponte, who performed the ceremony and whose surname was also adopted by the converted family. The boy was sent to a seminary and turned into a priest. But the most valuable thing which he brought away from school was a love and an appreciation of poetry, Latin and Italian. His clever brains gained him the appointment of professor of rhetoric; but six months after his ordination, he quarrelled with his superiors.

He went to Venice, which was then—even as it has become once more in recent years—one of the great pleasure-cities of Europe. Here young Lorenzo became involved in a number of amazing adventures, in character not unworthy of Casanova himself.[1] After another short period of work as an instructor of youth, he found it advisable to leave Italy, not indeed on account of his undoubted moral delinquency, but because his opinions did not coincide by a large margin with those who had authority in the Church and State. He went to Dresden, with the prospect of becoming theatre-poet in that city; but the letter, which held out this promise to him, turned out to be a forgery. Da Ponte was not the man to take a practical joke with too much seriousness—he had played too many upon others. He consoled himself by falling in love with the two daughters of an Italian painter. The mother of the girls, whom he also found not unattractive, had in the end to tell him that this state of affairs could not continue.

[1] A brief account of Da Ponte's life will be found in the *London Mercury* of August, 1926.

So the handsome young priest repaired to Vienna and, after four years of poverty, his luck turned in 1783. In that year the Emperor, tired of his experiments in German opera, restored the theatre to the Italians and acknowledged his preference for Salieri. Salieri needed a librettist to counterbalance the fame of Gianbattista Casti, who was working for Paisiello. Salieri and Da Ponte therefore collaborated in the comic opera, *Il ricco d'un giorno*, a tale of Venetian intrigue in which the librettist was an expert. The opera failed, mainly on account of Salieri's inability to write comic opera, but partly also owing to Da Ponte's inexperience. For this was his first *libretto*. His next effort, an adaptation of a play by Goldoni for Martini,[1] met with more success.

After the failure of his opera, Salieri vowed he would not set another line by Da Ponte, and the poet approached Mozart, who proposed an adaptation of Beaumarchais's comedy, *Les Noces de Figaro*. Two motives, independent of the admirable plot, influenced Mozart in making this suggestion : Paisiello had scored a success with a setting of *Le Barbier de Seville*, and the sequel to that first part of Figaro's story had been banned in Vienna on account of its political references. Da Ponte approached the Emperor and obtained permission for its production as an opera.

[1] Vincente Martin y Solar, a Spaniard, generally known as Martini. He must not be confused with the Padre Martini of Bologna or with the other Martini, who wrote the still popular song, " *Plaisir d'amour.*"

Mozart had written nothing important for the theatre since *Die Entführung*. There exist sketches for two operas, *L'Oca del Cairo* and *Lo Sposo Deluso*, neither of which is sufficiently important to detain us, and a short German *singspiel*, or comedy with music, called *Der Schauspieldirektor* (*The Impresario*). This amusing little work deals with the difficulties of a theatrical director in handling his company of singers, who rejoice in the characteristic names of Mmes Herz (dramatic soprano) and Silberklan~ (*coloratura* soprano), and MM. Vogelsang (teno⸲ and Buff (bass). The piece was produced by command of the Emperor in the Orangery at Schönbrunn in February, 1786. The play is by Stephanie the younger, who wrote the libretto of *Die Entführung*. Slight though the work is, there is a great deal of charm in the music, especially in the lively overture, which is sometimes played at orchestral concerts. The results of the experience gained in the composition of the string quartet show themselves in the contrapuntal style of the writing and in the individuality of the accompaniments to the air, which creates, more than anything, the dramatic feeling in Mozart's later operas.

This technical method is developed at once to its full strength in *Le Nozze de Figaro*, in which Mozart's genius as a writer of opera suddenly blossoms forth in all its glory. It is not my purpose in this book to enter upon a detailed analysis of this or the succeeding operas. For one thing space forbids it ; and for another it would merely involve going over ground which has already been fully explored in Professor Dent's book on the operas. There are, however, some general questions which it may be interesting to consider. In the first place the English opera-goer must be warned that the version of *Figaro* produced by Sir Thomas Beecham during the war and retained in their repertory by the British National Opera Company, departs very considerably from the original. Apart from the interpolation of one or two instrumental movements and the excision of some airs, which are as a matter of fact rarely heard at any performance, the whole of the recitatives have been supplanted by spoken dialogue adapted from the original play by Beaumarchais. The work of revision has been admirably done and I should be the last to deny that this version makes an excellent play with music, especially for production in English. Modern audiences in this country are notoriously impatient of *recitativo secco*, and so far as we have any national style of opera, it seems to be in the direction of works in which spoken dialogue is interspersed with songs and *ensemble* movements, as, for example, in the comic operas of Sullivan. The modification in the case of *Figaro* is none the less a real one. It makes the opera more *dramatic* —I use the word as an adjective for the ordinary spoken play—and less *musical*. If we accept this fundamental alteration in the balance, there is only one important fault in the Beecham version, namely the introduction of the Countess into the first act. She has nothing to sing, because in the original she does not appear until Act II, and her short scene is dramatically not very effective. The real objection to this alteration is that it takes the edge off the effect of her first appearance proper, that is as a singing character. For, as I have already pointed out in connection with the Pasha Selim in *Die Entführung*, a person in opera who has nothing to sing is practically non-existent.

Now the Countess's *cavatina*, " Porgi amor ", which opens the second act, is one of the crucial moments of the opera. The whole of the first act is occupied with the frivolous intrigues of Count Almaviva and the light-hearted love-making of Figaro and Susanna—not to mention Cherubino. If the work proceeded in that style, it would be a very light opera indeed—a delightful entertainment, perhaps, but not the profoundly moving comedy which has endeared it to nearly all men of sensibility, whether they are musicians or not. Did this light mood persist, there might be some justification for the view, commonly held in the earnest years of early nineteenth-century romanticism and by Beethoven[1] among

---

[1] For a discussion of Beethoven's attitude towards Mozart, the reader may be referred to an article by the present author in the Beethoven Centenary number of *Music and Letters*. (March, 1927.)

others, that both *Figaro* and *Don Giovanni* are frivolous trivialities unworthy of a " great " (how pompously they used the adjective !) composer. But the Countess introduces a new atmosphere into the opera, an atmosphere of genuine comedy, which has tears also in its laughter, as opposed to the mere amusingness of the intrigues. It is that note of melancholy and disillusionment, which appears also in Strauss's *Der Rosenkavalier* and, in precisely the same way, sheds a warm and human beauty over that cruel and, at times, almost disgusting farce. This note of seriousness is sounded again even more significantly in Susanna's air (" Deh ! vieni non tardar ") in the last act, which exhibits her character in an entirely new light. Like Mozart himself, Susanna can be as frivolous and high-spirited as it is possible to imagine, but, when she is alone and confronted with a serious situation, she shows a deep and passionately tender feeling in the most lovely bridal song which has ever been composed. The mood continues, even during the misunderstandings of that mad evening, and appears as strongly as ever in the duet of reconciliation between Figaro and his bride. Anything which detracts from the carefully arranged emphasis upon this serious vein of thought in the opera is an artistic mistake of real importance.

Mozart and Da Ponte have often been accused of turning a fine comedy with an almost Shavian touch of political propaganda in it, into a sordid farce. It is difficult to say how far this criticism is just, as regards Da Ponte. He has certainly omitted, no doubt in deference to Imperial susceptibilities, the more stinging social references of his original. But it must be remembered that he was writing an opera-book and that his business was to supply material suitable for music. He has done that with consummate skill. The *finales* are models of construction, the climax being gradually built up and new interests introduced to heighten the dramatic excitement at exactly the right places. We cannot, indeed, judge Da Ponte's book apart from Mozart's music ; the two are so inextricably associated in the mind. Against Mozart the accusation fails except in so far as concerns the justifiable omission of the political satire, which is unsuitable for music and would, unlike the social satire, probably be lost upon a modern audience. For, even if the intention is not present in the book, the music raises the opera from that of farce into the realm of true comedy. It has always astonished me that anyone could regard as vicious an opera which glorifies, almost to the verge of sentimentality, the genuine love of Susanna and Figaro, pours out the deepest compassion upon the unhappy Countess, and whips the Count's licentiousness with a stinging scorn, which is tempered a little for the youthful back of Cherubino.

That Mozart himself took a similar view of the work may be seen in the letter written from Prague in October, 1787, when *Figaro* was given at a gala in honour of Prince Anton von Saxe and his bride. *Don Giovanni* was to have been produced on this occasion, but was not ready, and some busybody had attempted to prevent the performance of *Figaro*, on account of its "immorality". "Some of the first ladies here (and in particular one of the highest rank) deigned to think it very ridiculous and improper and I know not what else, that it should be proposed to play *Figaro* before the Princess—*La Folle Journée*, as they are pleased to call it. It never occurred to them that no opera in the world was better suited to the occasion ". In another letter to the same correspondent, Gottfried von Jacquin, dated a few days later, there occurs a passage which throws a light on Mozart's views on morality : " Dear friend, you cannot but be happy, now that you have all you can desire at your age and in your station—the more so, since you now appear to have resumed your former mode of living, one more free from agitation. Are you not every day more convinced of the truth of my little sermons ? Is not the pleasure of a passing and capricious love-affair as far removed as the sky from a sincere and rational affection ? Often you must have thanked me in your heart for my good advice ! You make me quite proud ! But, joking apart, you owe me some gratitude if, owing to the change, you have become worthy of Miss N——, since I have certainly played no insignificant part in your amendment or conversion ". Are these the sentiments of a light-hearted profligate ?

On the musical side, *Figaro* shows as prodigious an advance upon Mozart's previous operatic works as it does on the intellectual side, not that the two aspects can in reality be separated. The most notable feature is a tendency towards a breaking down of the hard and fast conventions of the day. To us, who know Wagner, *Figaro* must seem, at first sight, conventional enough with its division into formal airs and *ensembles* linked together by the recitatives. In comparison with the operas of the time, however, there is a very decided advance towards the continuous music-drama. For one thing there are, as Professor Dent shows by a statistical table, fewer airs in proportion to the total number of musical pieces than in the average operas of the day. More important still, the airs themselves are far more dramatic. They do not merely sum up the emotion of the situation where the recitative has left it, as we saw they did in *Idomeneo*. In many of them, the action is actually carried a step farther. The most notable instance of this is Susanna's air, " Venite, inginocchiatevi ", in the second act, which is sung while she is dressing Cherubino in female costume. This number is so full of action and in outward appearance so

little like a formal air, that if one spoke of
Susanna's first air to ninety-nine people out of a
hundred who had just come away from the
opera, they would be puzzled to remember
what air she had sung besides " Deh! vieni ".
" Deh! vieni " itself, though it cannot be said
to carry on the drama, takes the psychological
action an important step further, because it
throws a new light on Susanna's character, or
rather clinches the implication already made
throughout the previous scenes of Susanna's
genuine love for Figaro.

The question of characterization in music is a
very difficult one to write about. We cannot
explain on paper why it is that certain musical
phrases give us an insight into the psychology
of the character to whom they are attached. The
problem is the more difficult in the case of Mozart,
because different characters often have the same
music to sing, and yet somehow are distinctly
individualized by it. The opening duet provides
a simple enough instance, indeed, in the contrast
of the short business-like phrases of Figaro, who
is occupied upon the practical matter of measuring
up his new bedroom, and the seductive melody
given to Susanna, who is busy in the feminine
pursuit of trying on a hat and of wanting to be
admired in it. But in the second duet, where the
two discuss the possibility of the Count's designs
upon the bride, both sing much the same music.
Yet Susanna's nimbleness of mind is distinctly

contrasted with Figaro's obtuseness. It may, in this instance as in others, be due partly to the difference in the *timbres* of the voices and of the accompaniments—Figaro is supported by the bassoons, Susanna by the oboes. There is also the complicated question of tonality, in which the solution of the problem is most likely to be found. The simple Figaro states his view in the tonic key, while his more acute partner takes up the melody, varies it, and ranges through a number of keys. Yet no amount of technical explanation can diminish one's astonishment at the composer's power of expressing exactly, and in the smallest number of notes, any given idea. Could the sly and fawning nature of Basilio be more aptly summed up than in the sleek tune which is his first musical utterance? Or could the rustic stupidity and annoyance of Antonio, the gardener, be better " hit off " than in his reiteration of one rhythmical phrase consisting of repetitions of a single note and the next above it in the scale?

Figaro was completed on April 29, 1786, and was first performed on the 1st May. The legend that the whole opera was written in six weeks must be consigned to limbo, together with a number of other fairy tales about the composer, who has so fascinated romantic inventors of anecdotes. Six months is probably nearer the mark, and the achievement is no less remarkable. There were the usual intrigues about the production, of which Michael Kelly, who, under the Italianized name of Signor Ochelly, created the tenor parts of Basilio and Don Curzio, has left an amusing account in his *Reminiscences.* "Mozart", he says, " was as touchy as gunpowder and swore that he would put the score into the fire, if it was not produced first ", i.e. before the operas of the rival composers. The Emperor himself apparently intervened and ordered *Figaro* to be put into rehearsal, and saved the world from this potential disaster.

The performance was received with great favour and Kelly describes how " the little man acknowledged by repeated obeisances his thanks for the distinguished mark of enthusiastic applause bestowed upon him ". Leopold had come to Vienna and wrote accounts of the performances to Nannerl, who had married Johann Berchtold von Sonnenburg in August, 1784. He enumerates the encores, which were demanded and which were subsequently prohibited by the Emperor. This action has been attributed to the intrigues of Mozart's rivals, but those who have endured the stupid enthusiasm of our Gilbert-and-Sullivan audiences, who continually hold up the action with their greedy demands for more, will applaud the prohibition, which was excused on the reasonable grounds of sparing the singers. The original cast included Nancy Storace, the most popular singer of *soubrette* parts of the day (Susanna); Benucchi, whose singing

of Figaro's air, " Non piu andrai ", brought
the house down on the first night ; and
Nannina Gottlieb, (Barberina), who was in later
years to create the part of Pamina in *The Magic
Flute*.

CHAPTER VIII

A PROPHET WITHOUT HONOUR

In spite of its favourable reception *Figaro* proved to be, so far as Vienna was concerned, a mere *succès de scandale*. Smart society, having tasted with the sauce of music the fruit that was not allowed to be eaten alone, mistook an eternal classic for a fashionable piece, and passed on to the next sensation. Moralists might point to this result as the just reward of a meretricious attempt to catch the public ear. However that may be, Mozart found himself no better off after the production of *Figaro* than before it. Whether as a direct result of this disappointment or not, a profound moral change seems to have come over him during the later part of 1786. He turned his back once for all upon the superficial virtuosity which appears in much of the music, especially the pianoforte concertos, of the previous year. His writing for the pianoforte becomes from this time more serious ; it is made the vehicle of the composer's thoughts rather than of the executant's skill.

The familiar string-quartet in D major (K. 499), which was written in August of this year, seems to be almost a final bid for popularity. The quartets, which he had dedicated to Haydn, had been received with favour only by the elect. In this new quartet he attempts, says Jahn, " to meet the public taste without sacrificing the dignity of the quartet style ". He made no concession to vulgarity but maintained and even surpassed the mastery with which he had already handled this most difficult medium. Only the ideas are not on the same exalted level as in the C major quartet, nor the emotion so profoundly felt.

In October Constanze bore a third son, Leopold, who died early in the following year[1]. In the following month, weary of the routine of teaching and of public performance as a pianist, Mozart proposed to leave Vienna with his wife in order to visit England. He was encouraged in this plan by Michael Kelly and Nancy Storace, the singers who had appeared in *Figaro,* and above all by Thomas Attwood, who had taken lessons from Mozart during his visit to Vienna three years before. Wolfgang suggested that his father should look after the two children during his absence, but Leopold, whose resentment against Constanze flared up in a letter addressed to Nannerl on this subject, declined to do anything of the sort. So the idea had to be abandoned.

At about this time Mozart received the good news that *Figaro* had been produced with

[1] The second son, Carl, was born in 1784. He adopted a commercial career in the first instance, then attempted the profession of music, and finally obtained a subordinate official appointment at Milan, where he died in 1859. He appears to have been, like his younger brother Wolfgang (born in 1791), a respectable pianist.

enormous success in Prague. The capital of
Bohemia was then, as it is now, one of the most
important centres of musical activity in Europe.
The Bohemians are by nature a musical nation,
and music has always been an essential part in
their education. Burney relates how he visited
a school " full of little children of both sexes,
from six to ten or eleven years old, who were
reading, writing, playing violins, hautbois, bassoons, and other instruments ". The aristocracy
in the capital, though they spent most of their
time in Vienna, encouraged music and supported
an Italian opera. A new national theatre, which
is still in use, had been built in 1783, and at this
time was managed by Pasquale Bondini. *Figaro*
was produced by Bondini, and its success appears
to have saved the situation at a moment of
financial crisis. Mozart gained directly nothing
more tangible from these performances than
honour and glory. Copyright laws did not exist,
and anyone who could get a score, was at liberty
to produce an opera without any obligation to the
composer.

Mozart was, nevertheless, pleased enough to
have the opera performed instead of neglected,
like *Idomeneo*, after its initial production. He
visited Prague in January, 1787, was received with
enthusiasm, and conducted some performances
of his opera. He had good friends at Prague
in Franz Duschek, a pianist, and his wife Josepha,
who was a famous singer. The Duscheks were

unable to offer Mozart their hospitality on this occasion, and he stayed at the house of Count Josef Thun, a great lover of music, whose daughter-in-law was a leader of musical society in Vienna and had done a great deal to further Mozart's interests. In a letter written on January 15th to his friend, Gottfried von Jacquin, Mozart gives a joyous account of his social activities. " At six o'clock I drove with Count Conac to the so-called Breitfeld Ball, where the flower of Prague's beauties are wont to assemble. That would have been the very thing for you, my friend ! I think I can see you—you thought I was going to say running—no, hobbling after all the lovely girls and young women. I did not dance because I was tired, and I did not make love to the ladies on account of my natural bashfulness ; but I watched, with the greatest delight, all these people hopping round in the joy of their hearts to the music of my *Figaro* turned into *contredanses* and *allemandes*. For here, they talk of nothing else but—*Figaro !* They play, they sing, they whistle nothing but— *Figaro !* No other opera draws except *Figaro*, always *Figaro*—truly a great honour that for me ! "

During his visit Mozart gave two highly successful concerts, at which his improvisations on the pianoforte were received with tremendous acclamation.[1]

[1] It was expected of virtuoso pianists that they should extemporize at their concerts, and Mozart was, as we might expect, conspicuous in this type of musical performance, which the complexity of modern music has

At one of these concerts a new symphony in D (K. 504) was performed. It had been written during the previous month in Vienna, and is often called the " Symphony in D without minuet " to distinguish it from the " Haffner " symphony (K. 385), which is in the same key. The " Prague " symphony is more serious in outlook than its predecessor, which was written for a festive occasion, and than the C major symphony, which was hurriedly composed at Linz. Mozart shows already the complete mastery over the symphonic style, which was to find its supreme expression in the three great symphonies written eighteen months later. There is a slow introduction to the first movement, a relic of the methods of the " gallant " period, but this *adagio* is not merely there to throw upon the succeeding *allegro* the showy brilliance of a sudden contrast. Like the introduction to the C major quartet, it sets the mood of the whole movement, which is one of earnest conflict.

Mozart returned to Vienna with a commission from Bondini to write an opera for the following winter. He turned once more to Da Ponte for assistance, and it was decided that the subject of the new opera should be the story of Don Juan.

abolished from our concert halls. Beethoven's improvisations were, we are told, wonderful spontaneous outpourings from that great mind. We can hardly gain any idea of these inspired moments, for the act of writing down the music probably destroys the peculiar charm of extemporization. But, though we may regret the passing of this form of music, there is the compensation in the thought of the boredom we might endure at the hands of lesser men.

The tale of the profligate who invited the statue
of a man he had murdered to take supper with
him, is one of those eternal legends which have
captured the imaginations of great artists in
generation after generation. The legend, like
that of Faust which has exercised a similar
fascination, has been traced back to mediæval
times, and one learned critic has hinted at Diony-
siac origins. One would not be surprised if some
anthropologist labelled it a " sun-myth ". Early
in its historical career, the tale became associated
with Spain, the land of hot blood and bravado,
just as the more philosophical legend of Faust
grew up in a German setting. Before Da
Ponte took it up, it had been used, among others,
by Molière, Goldoni, and Thomas Shadwell as
a subject for plays entitled respectively, *Le Festin
de Pierre*, *Il gran Convitato di Pietra*, and *The
Libertine*. It will be noted that our Restoration
dramatist underlines by his title the profligate
side of the Don's character, while the Frenchman
and the Italian emphasize rather his aspect as
the " fulminated atheist ". The story has, of
course, the double appeal of impropriety and of
the thrill which the superstitious experience
from seeing a blasphemy committed and duly
punished. This latter aspect of the story had,
perhaps, less attraction for Protestant England
under Charles II than for the Catholic countries
of Europe.

Da Ponte was engaged at this time on two other

libretti—one for Martini and the other for Salieri—and it is not improbable that he suggested Don Juan as a subject, because he had to hand a text on which he could base his own book. This was an opera, produced in Venice during the Carnival of 1787, under the title of *Don Giovanni ossia il Convitato di Pietra.* Giuseppe Bertati was responsible for the book, and Giovanni Gazzaniga, a Neapolitan composer, for the music. Da Ponte pulled this somewhat straggling drama, which consists of little else but a series of the hero's amorous exploits, into shape, and gave individuality and dramatic interest to the female characters, who were mere lay-figures in Bertati's book. The first act is a masterpiece of dramatic construction. The exposition is economically devised in scenes of swift action, the characters are clearly defined, and the whole is worked up to a climax, which is only marred by the not very clearly explained escape of Don Giovanni from Don Ottavio's pistol—a difficulty which is sometimes avoided in performance by giving Don Ottavio a sword and by bringing on Don Giovanni's servants to clear the ball-room of the intruders. The second act falls below the level of the first only because there seems to have been a change of plan, which was hastily made and not sufficiently considered by author and composer. Professor Dent suggests that the original intention may have been that the opera should have three acts and that, owing to the necessity of curtailing its length, it was reduced to two. The sextet, " Sola, sola in bujo loco ", would in that case have been the second *finale*.[1]

As it stands, the second act presents great practical difficulties to the producer, who must make some rearrangement of the scenes. In the production at the " Old Vic." Theatre, which adheres as closely as possible to the text, Don Ottavio's air, " Il mio tesoro ", is removed from its place after the sextet to the scene in which Donna Anna sings " Non mi dir, bel idol mio ", the words being modified in Professor Dent's translation to make it fit the situation.

The *libretto* is, even more than that of *Figaro*, a frank and unblushing tale of gallantry. The eighteenth century regarded immorality as a perfectly normal course of behaviour. We must, therefore, divest our minds of all the later aspects of Don Juan as the lover in search of ideal woman-hood, who is portrayed in Strauss's symphonic poem or as the superman seeking his super-mate (Donna Anna)—a view presented first by E. T. A. Hoffmann in his interpretation of Mozart's opera, and more recently by Bernard Shaw in *Man and Superman.* Mozart's Don never for a moment expresses that self-disgust which is so important a feature in Strauss's masterly portrait. He goes from affair to affair with a careless gusto and faces his end with a nonchalant bravado. Repentance and regret are emotions unknown to him. His very

[1] Some interesting new evidence on this scene is discussed in Appendix I.

virtuosity in love-making saves him from being disgusting to us, the audience, and the opera is redeemed by the fierceness with which, in spite of the acceptance of immorality as the norm, his conduct is satirized by Mozart.

It is necessary to emphasize the author's attitude towards the work, because *Don Giovanni*, as we usually see it performed, does not accord with it. The nineteenth century regarded it as an immoral work—which indeed it is, from some points of view—but did not wish to be deprived of so much beautiful music. So it was turned into a romantic tragedy, partly by the omission of the comic *vaudeville* which ends the opera, but chiefly by the style in which it was played. Mozart calls it quite plainly a *dramma giocosa*, a comic opera, and we cannot doubt that both he and Da Ponte regarded it as such. Yet even nowadays there are critics who claim that the opera is more serious than comic in intention. It is true that the music becomes at times intensely serious— for example when Donna Anna finds her father's body, and in the supper scene at the end ; and there is no question that the composer was profoundly moved by certain of the dramatic situations. It has even been suggested that the powerful emotion which is displayed in the first of these two scenes may have been aroused by the recent death of Mozart's own father.

Leopold had been ill for some time. On April 4, 1787, Wolfgang wrote to his father a letter which proves that, on Wolfgang's side at least, affection had not been killed by recent misunderstandings. The letter throws such important light on Wolfgang's character and philosophy that I quote it in full :

MY VERY DEAR FATHER,

It is very annoying that, owing to the stupidity of Storace, my letter did not come into your hands. I expressed therein, among other things, the hope that you had received my last letter ; but as you make no allusion to this letter (the second dated from Prague), I do not know what to think. It is quite possible that some servant of Count Thun's found it profitable to pocket the postage. But in truth I would rather pay double the cost than know my letter to be in hands other than those for which it was intended !

Ramm and the two Fischers[1] from London—the bass singer and the oboist—are spending Lent here. If the oboist played no better than he does now at the time when we met him in Holland, he does not deserve the reputation he enjoys ! That is between ourselves. At my age in those days I was not in a state to pass judgement upon him—all I can remember is that he pleased me, like everyone else, exceedingly. It is true that that will appear natural enough, if it is admitted that tastes have greatly changed—and he plays according to the old school. But no ! to put it in one

---

[1] Ramm was the celebrated oboist of the Mannheim orchestra for whom Mozart had written the delightful oboe quartet (K. 370) in 1781. This work has been made known to modern audiences by Mr Léon Goossens. Ludwig Fischer sang the part of Osmin in the first performance of *Die Entführung*. Johann Christian Fischer was oboist in Queen Charlotte's orchestra in London. Mozart wrote a set of variations (K. 179) on a minuet composed by him. It is to Fischer, not to Ramm, that the criticism in the letter applies.

word he plays like a mere beginner ! Young André, who learnt from Fiala, plays a thousand times better— And then his concertos !—of his own composing !— Each *ritornello* lasts a quarter of an hour ; that is where my hero shows his quality ! He lifts his leaden feet one after the other and lets them sink again to earth. His tone is nasal and his held notes are veritable organ tremulants. Can you imagine it ? Yet it is only the truth—though I tell it to no one but you.

At this moment, I have heard news which has greatly upset me, the more because from your last letter I had supposed that, thanks to God, you were quite well. Now they tell me you are really ill ! I need not tell you with what fervent desire I await from your-self better news. I count upon that with certainty, although I am wont in all things to anticipate the worst. Since death (take my words literally) is the true goal of our lives, I have made myself so well acquainted during the past two years with this true and best friend of mankind that the idea of it not only has no more terror for me but much that is com-forting and tranquillizing. And I thank God that he has granted me the good fortune to obtain the oppor-tunity (you understand my meaning) of regarding death as the *key* that unlocks our true happiness. I never lie down in bed without considering that, young as I am, perhaps I may on the next day be no more. Yet not one of those who know me could say that I am morose or melancholy in my social intercourse; and for this happiness I thank my Creator daily, and wish heartily that the same happiness may be known to every one of my fellow men. In the letter, which Storace packed so carefully, I clearly explained my way of looking at the matter, on the occasion of the sad death of my very dear, my best friend Count von Hatzfeld. He was just thirty-one, like myself. I do not grieve for him !—but I grieve from the bottom of my heart, I and all who knew him as intimately as I did. I hope and wish that you may be in better health at this moment of writing ; but if, contrary to my expectations, you are no better, I beg you by . . . not to conceal it from me, but to write the whole truth or let some one write it for you, that I may be in your arms as soon as is humanly possible. I conjure you by—all that we hold sacred. But I hope to receive a reassuring letter, and in this same hope I kiss your hands a thousand times with my wife and Carl, and I am always your most obedient son,

VIENNA,   W. A. MOZART.
    4th April, 1787.

The cryptic allusions in this letter have reference to the Masonic views, to which both father and son subscribed. It is probably owing to the fact that their letters contained references of this kind, that so little of the correspondence between Wolfgang and his father during the last two years of the latter's life has survived. Intolerance of new religious views not acceptable to the Church made it advisable to destroy such evidence.

Wolfgang never saw his father again, for Leopold died rather suddenly on the 28th May. To his anxiety about his father and the sorrow caused by the other bereavement, of which he speaks, has been attributed the tragic mood of most of the music composed at this time. This includes the two great string quintets in C major (K. 515) and G minor (K. 516) and the song "Abendempfindung", which recalls to Professor Dent M. D'Indy's criticism on Beethoven's second period : " Hitherto he had written only music, now he wrote life ".

The G minor quintet for two violins, two violas, and violoncello, is the high-water mark of Mozart's achievement in chamber-music. The addition of a second viola to the ordinary string quartet was in itself something of a novelty. Boccherini had written innumerable quintets in which his own instrument, the violoncello, was doubled, and the charming minuet from one of these works is in the repertory of every string orchestra. The extra violoncello brings with it the danger of heaviness—a danger of which Boccherini may have been conscious, for in his quintets he continually employs the highest register of the instrument with rather unpleasant results, even when it is played by a first-rate executant. A second viola adds to the subtlety of colouring without overweighting any section of the compass of the four instruments. Moreover, the peculiar veiled tone of the viola has a natural melancholy which is exactly the tint required by Mozart for his palette in this instance. With what mastery Mozart handled the new combination may be seen at once in the first movement of the G minor quintet, where the first subject, announced by the two violins and one viola, is given a deeper significance by its immediate repetition on the violas and violoncello. But these technical matters are of little importance beside the dignity and pathos of this work, which seems to be the musical expression of the calm and noble thoughts embodied in the last part of the letter to Leopold Mozart.

This same anxiety and bereavement and the mental reaction they produced, may account for the somewhat curt way in which young Ludwig van Beethoven, aged seventeen, was received when he called upon Mozart at this time. What happened at the interview is not precisely known. There is the legend that Beethoven's improvisation was received coldly, as though it had been carefully prepared, and that he then asked the older man to give him a theme. Mozart, having listened to Beethoven's treatment of that, is reported to have gone into the next room and said to some friends who were there, " Keep an eye on this young man—the world will hear of him some day ! " Whether this account is true, or whether the prophecy was posthumously credited to Mozart *post eventum* it is impossible to say ; but nothing came of the interview and no great cordiality sprang up between the two men, possibly on account of Mozart's preoccupation with his sorrow.

Not all his compositions at this date are on this plane of lofty tragedy. The two quintets were followed quickly by the *Musical Joke* (K. 522) for string quartet and two horns, in which the vagaries of a village band are amusingly satirized. Less frivolous, but certainly not in the same serious mood of tragedy as the G minor quintet, is the serenade in G major (K. 525) for string quartet with double-bass, usually known as the *Kleine Nachtmusik*. This delightful work, whose slow movement is built up on one of Mozart's loveliest melodies, was probably composed for some evening party, and was possibly intended for a small string band rather than for a solo quintet. But, as the double-bass merely plays the violoncello part an octave lower, it can be played effectively by a string quartet.

This lengthy digression has been necessary in order that we may fully understand the undoubted mixture of comedy and tragedy which appears in *Don Giovanni*. The opera called forth the two opposite moods, to which the composer shows himself alternately subject, or rather the tragic mood asserted itself whenever there was suitable occasion—with remarkable results. For in the scene where Donna Anna finds her father's body she expresses her grief in a passage of declamation, which is a distinct development from the ordinary accompaniment recitative towards the dramatic ideals of Wagner. This passage is as thoroughly German in style as Don Giovanni's serenade ("Deh ! vieni alla finestra") in the next act is Italian. Mozart suddenly arrived by instinct at the same solution of the operatic problem which it took Wagner years of conscious excogitation to reach. The problem is how to treat a scene of great dramatic and emotional significance, which cannot be expressed within the formal limits of an air, but for which ordinary recitative is too dry a medium. The device of writing accompanied recitative had already long been used at such moments with more or less success, but never before—unless it be in the passage which introduces Susanna's air, "Deh! vieni non tardar", in the last act of *Figaro*— had the device been used with such sensibility. Instead of the conventional rising and falling of the voice leading on to the inevitable full-close, Mozart has written a perfect piece of melodic declamation which merges into the duet between Donna Anna and Don Ottavio. The horror of the situation is marvellously depicted in the cruel phrases for wood-wind, which punctuate Donna Anna's breathless sentences.

The scenes between Don Giovanni and the Statue of the Commendatore at the end of the work are not less wonderful examples of Mozart's power of handling a big dramatic situation. Even nowadays, when trombones are no more strange than violins and all manner of fearful monsters are accepted as normal members of an orchestra, the sudden interruption of the Don's conversation with Leporello in the churchyard by the warning voice of Fate, embodied in the

bass voice of the Commendatore and supported
by three trombones, has lost none of its impressiveness. If the scene is well played, it can hardly
fail to send an uncomfortable shiver down the
spine of the listener. In the succeeding duet,
in which the Statue is invited to supper, this eerie
feeling is not dispelled even by Leporello's comic
terror. The same effect of supernatural horror
is produced in the final scene, which is introduced
by an unsurpassed stroke of genius. It will be
remembered that Don Giovanni is at supper.
Like any other nobleman of his period, he has his
own orchestra, which plays selections from the
popular operas of the day. On this particular
evening the programme consists of tunes from
Martin's *Una Cosa Rara* and Sarti's *I Litiganti*,
and Figaro's air, " Non più andrai ", which we
may imagine the errand boys of Prague whistling
in the streets, as to-day they whistle " Valencia "
or whatever the latest favourite may be. The
meal is interrupted by Donna Elvira, who
attempts to persuade the Don to reform his way
of life, but is far too hysterical to make her
meaning clear. He laughs at what he takes to
be renewed advances from the half-demented
lady, and sends her away. This scene has already
tightened the dramatic tension, which is suddenly
stretched to the uttermost, when Elvira, having
left the scene and met the Statue outside, lets
out a shriek on high A flat, which jerks the tonality
of the music into the key of C minor. Even Don

Giovanni's nerves are shaken for a moment. The short duet between the Don and his servant, which leads up to the Commendatore's entrance, reverts to comedy. But the sudden lowering of the dramatic pitch seems to make the arrival of the fearful visitant all the more impressive. He is heralded by the same chords which have been heard before at the beginning of the Overture, but now made more massive by the addition of the trombones.[1] The whole of this scene is indeed a model of musical-dramatic construction, and has rarely, if ever, been equalled in the whole history of opera.

Yet, despite the seriousness with which these scenes are treated, the style of the opera generally is comic. We are apt to overlook, in these days, when the distinction has long been broken down, the fact that *opera seria* differed very materially from *opera buffa* in Mozart's time. *Don Giovanni* might be taken, perhaps, as the first attempt to combine the two styles. But it remains a comedy, in the serious meaning of the word. The characters are all treated with a touch of satire, which does not, however, prevent their being true portraits of real human beings. Even little Zerlina is drawn with perfect seriousness. Her first air, " Batti, batti ", presents her as a coaxing minx, soothing her jealous lover, who has not yet anything really serious to complain of. But

[1] The parts for trumpets, trombones, and drums do not occur in the autograph score of the opera, but there is good reason to believe that they have the authority of Mozart. See Dent, *Mozart's Operas*, p. 259.

when the unfortunate Masetto has been soundly
beaten by Don Giovanni masquerading as Leporello, she soothes his smarting mind and body
with the most tender and genuine sympathy in
" Vedrai, carino ". Donna Anna takes herself
with such intense seriousness, that there is no
other course but to laugh at her, if we are not
to be bored by her. If she is presented as a
tragic figure, she appears merely cold and unsympathetic. There is, however, no more necessity to take her at her own valuation than there
is to accept without a smile the affectations of her
near relation, the Countess Olivia in *Twelfth
Night*. Her lover, Don Ottavio, is, one must
admit, a colourless creature whose ineffectual
conduct can only be forgiven when he can sing
his two lovely airs well—which is an all too rare
occurrence. One can, however, sympathize with
his probable fate, when a year after the end of
the opera, he becomes the husband of that
tigress, the masterful Donna Anna—supposing
that she can support for so long this ninny of
a lover. Donna Elvira is the most wonderful
creation in the whole work, not even excepting
the Don himself. The very inconsistency between her alternating desire to encompass her
seducer's ruin and to save him—with the proviso of a wedding-ring for herself—and her final
acceptance of the veil as an alternative to marriage
with the only man she wants (but cannot have),
is too true to life to need further comment.

Leporello would have become, in less masterful hands, another Figaro. But while Figaro is a manly rascal and a likeable fellow, Leporello is a thorough knave. Compare " Non più andrai " with Leporello's catalogue-air and you will see how much broader is the humour of this pimping valet, who has none of Figaro's wit and refinement. The Don himself is the very embodiment of sensual love. He enters upon every fresh adventure with a tremendous gusto which carries us, too, away and blinds us for the moment to the nature of the proceedings. When confronted with a crisis, he behaves with a cool daring which cannot but rouse sympathy and even liking, and he goes to his doom with a nonchalance, which is all the more splendid because we have seen him visibly shaken. Taken all in all, *Don Giovanni* as Mozart and Da Ponte left it, is unsurpassed as a music-drama. One may doubt the fact from time to time, when the score is read in the study or when some other opera has created a deep impression, but the next time we see " The Don ", the same effect of overwhelming mastery, both in the handling of the drama and in the drawing of the characters, is again produced and we come away from the theatre convinced that this is the greatest of all operas.

The second act has faults of construction, due, as has been suggested, to hurried work, but they can be overcome by a careful producer. The *finales* are not, perhaps, in musical interest quite on a level with the great *finale* in the second act of *Figaro*, where melody succeeds melody in marvellous profusion. But nothing could surpass the assurance with which the complex emotions of the ball-room scene are treated, nor the overwhelming effect of the final catastrophe. Nor does any opera of Mozart's contain such a number of airs which are at once of the greatest melodic beauty and absolutely characteristic of the persons who sing them. There is a possible exception to this last statement in Donna Anna's air, " Non mi dir, bel idol mio ", to which reference has already been made in a previous chapter. This number smacks a little too much of the *prima donna* and too little of the proud lady whom she is supposed to impersonate. But, as Professor Dent remarks, it is a relief when this rather unsympathetic character, who shows from beginning to end no other sign of weakness and consequently very little of humanity, gives way at last to the vanity of indulging in a little *coloratura*.[1]

---

[1] Berlioz, who could never tolerate virtuosity in any form, except in his own orchestration, was of the contrary opinion, and his tirade against this air is worth quoting. " Quand vient l'allegro du dernier air de dona Anna," he says " pas un de ces aristarques si sensibles en apparence sur les convenances dramatiques, n'est choqué des abominables vocalises que Mozart, poussé par quelque démon dont le nom est demeuré un mystère, a eu de malheur de laisser tomber de sa plume. La pauvre fille outragée s'écrie : *Peut-être un jour le ciel encore sentira quelque pitié pour moi*. Et c'est là-dessus que le compositeur a placé une série de notes aiguës, vocalisées, piquées, caquetantes, sautillantes, qui n'ont pas même la mérite de faire applaudir la cantatrice. S'il n'y avait jamais eu quelque part en Europe un public vraiment intelligent et sensible, ce crime (car c'en est un) ne fût pas demeuré impuni, et le coupable allegro ne serait pas resté dans la partition de Mozart."

Numerous legends have grown up about the composition of *Don Giovanni*, the most familiar and most preposterous being to the effect that the Overture was composed on the night before the performance, the while Constanze kept her husband awake by telling him fairy tales. It is quite possible, of course, that Mozart did not consign the music to paper until the last moment and that the copies were made only just in time for the final rehearsal—not, as the legend has it, the actual public performance. That would be quite in keeping with what we know of the composer's methods. He always put off until the last possible moment the labour of writing down his music, and he was gifted with the most extraordinary power of carrying a whole composition in all its details in his head. He did not need to hammer out his ideas by making sketches, revising them and remodelling until they satisfied him, as the slower-witted Beethoven had to do. His manuscripts show very few corrections and those mainly of slips of his pen. The tale about the Overture to *Don Giovanni* is based on a complete misunderstanding of Mozart's mind. He had, I do not doubt, worked out the Overture in his head and with his amazing rapidity transferred to paper in a few hours what must in fact have been the result of many days' hard thinking. Mozart had a very marvellous brain, but we need not credit him with working miracles. And no other word would fit the supposed composition of a masterpiece of musical construction such as this Overture in a single night without preparation.

The Overture is remarkable for the manner in which it sets the mood for the succeeding tragi-comedy. Opening with a slow introduction, it forecasts the awful fate in store for the reckless adventurer who is portrayed in the lively melodies of the succeeding *Allegro*. There is a curious affinity between the first subject of this *Allegro* and that which opens Strauss's tone-poem on the same theme. There is no melodic resemblance, and Strauss's melody leaps as usual, boldly over the whole scale. But both have the same urgent impulse produced by the same effect of an emphasis on some of the weaker beats in the bar. There is no need to suggest that the later composer, for all his admiration of Mozart, has deliberately modelled his idea upon that of his predecessor—though that hypothesis is not impossible. The resemblance is more probably due merely to the fact that here the two composers are presenting us, each in his own way, with the same view of their hero. Strauss, as I have already pointed out, quickly diverges into a more romantic treatment of Don Juan, and his portrait is altogether more complex than Mozart's. But we cannot say that it is more complete ; for Mozart has given us a very full study of the Don, as he saw him, setting beside the impulsive nature of the first subject the humorous gusto of the second with its alternations of pace and sudden leaps from low to high on the violins. The Overture to *Figaro* had been a perfect expression of the light-hearted mood, tinged now and again with melancholy, of the comedy that follows. But the Overture to *Don Giovanni* goes a step further in the direction of definite character-painting and so towards story-telling. We are not so very far from the *Leonore* Overtures of Beethoven and those Preludes of Wagner, in which the whole story is summarized for us.

Don Giovanni was produced, after some delays owing to illness in the cast, on October 29, 1787. It was received with tremendous enthusiasm and Mozart, who conducted, was the hero of the hour. He had been in Prague since September and remained there until the middle of November, staying with the Duscheks at the Villa Bertramka just outside the city. It was during this visit that occurred the often-related incident of the composer's imprisonment in the summer-house by Josepha Duschek. He had promised the singer an air, but had been too lazy to fulfil his promise. So she locked him in on November 3rd and declined to release him until the composition was finished. He wrote the dramatic scena, " Bella mia fiamma " (K. 528), but retaliated by refusing to hand over the manuscript unless Josepha could sing it at sight. He did not put in any exceptional difficulties, but the air requires a wide compass and a big style.

The visit to Prague marks the high-water mark of Mozart's worldly success. On his return to Vienna his attempts to get *Don Giovanni* produced were for a time thwarted by the intrigues of Salieri, whose opera, *Axur Re d'Ormuz*, was due for production in the following January. However, his position in Vienna was made a little more secure by his appointment as Chamber-musician to the Court in succession to Gluck, who died on the 17th November. This post brought him a salary of 800 florins, equivalent to about £80 a year,[1] and his duties included the composition of dances for the Court balls, a task which subsequently fell to the lot of the next great genius in musical history, Beethoven.

In the end *Don Giovanni* was produced, by the command of the Emperor himself, in May, 1788. For this performance there was a fine cast of singers including Aloysia Lange (Donna Anna), La Cavalieri (Donna Elvira), Benucci, who had created Figaro (Leporello) and Francesco Albertarelli (Don Giovanni). Mozart had to make some slight alterations. The tenor cast for Don Ottavio could not manage " Il mio tesoro " and was supplied with the hardly less beautiful air, " Dalla sua pace " which was inserted in the first act after Donna Anna's air, where some expression of Ottavio's personality, such as it is, was certainly needed. La Cavalieri, in her turn, demanded something more difficult to sing than already

1 Gluck had been paid at the rate of 2000 florins a year.

existed in the music written for Elvira. She was given the fine air, " Mi tradi quell' alma ingrata ", which remains an embarrassment to producers of the opera. It was originally spatchcocked into the second act after the sextet. That unfortunate scene became a kind of rag-bag for any odds and ends ; for immediately before " Mi tradi " a new, and quite silly, comic duet for Leporello and Zerlina was inserted at the instance of Benucci. This duet is now invariably omitted, even at complete " festival " performances of the work. But Elvira's air cannot so easily be dropped. It is too good a plum for the singer. Yet it does not fit in well with the emotions of the character at this stage of the drama, and is even less appropriate when it is sung, as often happens, in the first act after Leporello's " Catalogue-air ". It ought in fact to be relegated to the concert platform, where it will always give delight as a piece of vocal music.

The net result of these alterations was that the confusion of the second act became worse confounded, and that, owing to the additions made to the already long score, the final *vaudeville* had to be cut out. Thus was established the precedent, which was followed throughout the world during the nineteenth century, until at Munich in 1896 the original Prague version was restored. The comic ending to the work was not performed in England until the opera was produced in 1923 at the " Old Vic. " with Professor

Dent's translation. Covent Garden followed the example of the less fashionable house three years later.

Although fifteen performances were given, *Don Giovanni* was not a success in Vienna, and it was not revived there until after Mozart's death. Performances at Mannheim, Hamburg (in German), and Berlin also failed to arouse the enthusiasm which Prague had shown for it. In Berlin it was even compared to its disadvantage with the operas of Grétry, Philidor, and Monsigny. In Munich, where it was given in August, 1791, the reception was more favourable. But that may have been due to the interest aroused by the fact that, until that date, the opera had been banned by the censorship. Even so, though the Müncheners were " extraordinarily pleased " with the music, the text was considered to be in bad taste.

The music of *Don Giovanni* was in fact too serious in quality to please the frivolous Viennese society, who wished merely to be amused, not made to think. Perhaps, too, the sting of its satire went a little too far down to the quick to be comfortable. So the production of his second great operatic masterpiece left Mozart no better off than before. He worked to obtain a livelihood, but he was never to reach even a decent competence; and his own fecklessness in practical affairs and the constant illnesses of his wife did not permit him to make the best of his meagre circumstances.

Chapter IX

THE SHADES OF THE PRISON HOUSE

Mozart's unhappy situation in the middle of 1788 is indicated only too clearly in his correspondence with Michael Puchberg. Puchberg was a prosperous Viennese merchant, an amateur of music and a Freemason—three things which qualified him as a suitable person to receive applications for a loan. Mozart shows himself a good hand at writing begging letters. He begins with flattering references to the loyalty and friendship of the addressee and then asks for a loan, in the first instance, of one or two thousand florins to enable him to put his affairs (which are, of course, only temporarily deranged) in order, so that he may be able to work better and in consequence to earn more. At last he comes to the real point, which is that—supposing the larger sum cannot conveniently be lent—the writer *must* have 200 florins at once in order to pay off an impatient creditor. This creditor was Mozart's late landlord. He had just moved from his lodgings in Vienna and had taken others outside the city. This, he explains, will mean a saving in expenditure, and in time which might otherwise be wasted in social amusements. Puchberg sent the 200 florins, and received ten

216

days later a further appeal for help. Mozart confesses that he cannot repay the debt already incurred, and says that he is in urgent need of more money—things will soon be better and then the debt will be repaid. But, alas! a few weeks later a brief note informs the merchant of Mozart's continued insolvency. We do not know what reply was made to these last two letters, but we may hope that Puchberg was moved to alleviate Mozart's distress, which was not entirely due to his own fault. The man who had given to the world *Figaro* and *Don Giovanni* deserved from it in return the reward of a decent livelihood.

Yet at the very time which is covered by these appeals from the desperate family man, he had just finished the composition of his happiest symphony, the one in E flat (K. 543), and was engaged upon the great symphony in G minor (K. 550), while the C major (K. 551), which is the third member of this wonderful group, followed after an interval of three weeks. These three symphonies, Mozart's last essays in this form of music, were written with a definite object in view ; but the concerts for which they were intended did not take place, and they remained for posterity to honour. Nothing is more remarkable in Mozart's career than the production of these three masterpieces, so utterly different from one another in spirit, within the space of three months. The E flat symphony is the swan-song of his youth. In it is summed up all the gaiety and humour of his nature, and the mood is brought to a climax of merriment in the *finale*, which I once heard Herr Bruno Walter direct the orchestra to play " with exaggerated youthfulness ". Even the tender sentiment of the slow movement casts no tragic shadow, and the conductor who sentimentalizes the second subject of the Minuet, does not understand Mozart. Wagner found a " marked relationship " between this symphony and the seventh of Beethoven. " In both," he says, " the clear human consciousness of an existence meant for rejoicing, is beautifully transfigured by the presage of a higher world beyond. The only distinction I would make, is that in Mozart's music the language of the heart is shaped to graceful longing, whereas in Beethoven's conception this longing reaches out a bolder hand to seize the Infinite. In Mozart's symphony the fullness of Feeling predominates, in Beethoven's the manly consciousness of Strength." Personally I feel, however, that this E flat symphony is more closely akin to the eighth, in which the almost boyish humour of Beethoven flows over so joyously and we are allowed to forget for the moment the conflicts in his soul and the capitalized Infinite.

The G minor presents a complete contrast to this blithe and happy work. It is the final expression in " absolute " music of Mozart's

characteristic melancholy. At the same time
it is completely free of the morbidity which
appears here and there in the works of his last
year of life. Still less does it represent a struggle
with Fate, which is the leading motive of so
much nineteenth-century music—in Beethoven,
whose nobility of mind rises above adversity, and,
at the other end of the scale, in Tchaikovsky,
who cries out in hysterical self-pity at his defeat
by circumstance. Mozart did not indulge in
self-dramatization ; all is reflective, contemplative
and lyrical, even when the mood is one of rest-
lessness. We are so accustomed to the more
conscious self-revelations of his successors, that
the poignancy of his music is apt to escape us,
unless we can put ourselves at his point of view.
Nor can we realize, except by a deliberate exercise
of the historical sense, what an extraordinary advance these symphonies represent upon his own
previous achievements and those of Haydn.

It must have been of the earlier symphonies
that Wagner was thinking when he wrote that
Mozart " habitually relapsed into that banal
building-up of phrases which constantly shews
his symphonic movements in the light of so-called
table-music, i.e. a kind of music which offers
between attractive melodies, also an attractive
hubbub for conversation's sake. On myself, at
least, the perpetually recurring and noisily
garrulous half-closes of the Mozartian symphony
make the impression as if I were hearing the

clatter of a prince's plates and dishes set to music."[1] For, in his essay "On Conducting", Wagner admits a kinship between these later symphonies of Mozart and those of Beethoven, and points out that Mozart had already begun to break down the rigid conventions of the symphony and to equalize the interest throughout. The bridge-passages have ceased to be a mere changing of plates between the courses. Indeed Mozart often puts them to a rather curious use, making them the means of casting a mysterious glamour over the music. Instead of going on their even and expected course, these passages suddenly lead us off the track and bewilder us as to the direction we are taking for the moment that passes before they bring us back, as if through some delightful lane, to the high road, whose charm is heightened by this brief excursion into the by-paths that branch off from it. For by seeing in this way what lies on either side, we are able to appreciate more fully the main view. Even the little Haffner Symphony contains several examples of this treatment of the bridge-passages, of which the most delightful occurs towards the end of the witty final movement. But Mozart's manner of bringing mystery into music, that is otherwise as lucid as the air on a sunny day, is better exemplified in the first

[1] Wagner takes no account of Beethoven's prolonged cadences, which seem to many people a mannerism no less wearisome than Mozart's conventional bridge-passages.

movement. This is one of the true Mozartian characteristics, as opposed to those turns of phrase which really belong to all the music of his time, but which are so often labelled " Mozartian."

Elsewhere Wagner says : " Compared with Haydn's, Mozart's symphonies are of significance almost solely through this extraordinarily feeling, *singing* nature of their instrumental themes ; in it lies expressed the thing that makes Mozart great and inventive in this branch of music too." And yet again : " Haydn was the genius who first developed the symphony to a broader compass, and gave it power of deep expression through an inexhaustible play of motives, as also of their traditional links and workings-out. Though the Italian operatic melody had kept to its threadbare formal build, it had received in the mouth of talented and feeling singers, and borne on the breath of the noblest musical organ[1] a graceful sensuous colouring as yet unknown to German musicians—a colouring whose sweet euphony was absent from their instrumental melodies. It was Mozart who became aware of this charm, and, while he brought to Italian opera the richer *development* of the German mode of instrumental composition, he imparted in turn to the orchestral melody the full *euphony* of the Italian mode of song. The ample heritage

[1] And there are still some people who assert that Wagner despised the human voice !

221

and promise of both these masters was taken up by Beethoven."

I have thought it worth while to quote from Wagner's many comments upon Mozart's music, not merely because it is always interesting to hear what one great artist has to say about another; nor because, in this instance, the comments are a very just appreciation of Mozart, made at a time when the world in general hardly understood him at all, by a man whose own music was of a very different kind; but because they do sum up very clearly Mozart's place in the history of music. When he wrote these three symphonies, Mozart had reached the first stage of maturity, which was unfortunately never to be succeeded by a full development. He had already, in two great operas and in the six quartets, far outstripped his contemporaries in the creation of individual works of art, each with its own character. Now he took the symphony, the highest form of musical expression, a step forward in the same direction. Each of the three works composed in 1788 is a complete whole unified by a single basic idea, not a sequence of movements, delightful enough in themselves, but with nothing more potent to bind them together than a conventional relationship of keys. Key-relationship is, of course, an important factor in these new symphonies, as in the operas, but it is now used as a means to giving the whole work a character of its own, and not merely in order that the movements may follow one another smoothly and without jolting the listener suddenly from one plane to another.

There is, moreover, a distinct advance as between the three works in this group. The symphony in E flat is lighter in mood than its successor, the G minor ; it is nearer in style to the " Linz " and " Prague " symphonies. So, too, the C major symphony towers above the G minor by reason both of the more exalted idea it embodies and of its closer reasoning as musical thought. It may be said that the advance is only due to the comparative greatness of the ideas expressed, but the fact remains that the ideas came to the composer in this order ; and we may not unreasonably suppose that he was developing with extraordinary speed both in mental and musical power. The C major symphony is the finest example we possess of *pure thinking* in sound, with the possible exception of Beethoven's later quartets, where the thought is on a very different plane of philosophy. The note of egotistic emotionalism which was introduced into music by Beethoven is entirely absent from Mozart's symphonies, though we may find a foreshadowing of it in the somewhat hysterical mood of the *Requiem*. The passion for labelling pieces of absolute music with names suggestive of a programmatic basis, which gave to one of Beethoven's sonatas the silly title of " Moonlight "

and to another that of " Appassionata ", has
fixed to the C major symphony the title of
" Jupiter ". The word is sufficiently vague in
its associations, for most of us, to do no harm,
and, if we accept it as no more than a synonym
for a divine grandeur and nobility, the cap fits
well enough.

To the same period as the Symphonies belong
three of Mozart's five mature Trios for pianoforte, violin and violoncello, the other two having
been composed two years before. All these
Trios were composed for special occasions, parties
given by his friends, and are consequently light
in character and, though delightful, of no great
importance in comparison with the string
quartets. The best of them is the E major
(K. 542) which is mentioned in a postscript to
the letter to Puchberg of June 17, 1788. Mozart
asks, " When can we have a little music at your
house? I have written a new Trio." We may
take it that the work was presented to Puchberg
in hopeful recognition of favours to come.

In the autumn Mozart re-scored, at the request
of Van Swieten, Handel's *Acis and Galatea* and
The Messiah. In 1790 he performed the same
operation upon *Alexander's Feast* and *The Ode
for St Cecilia's Day*. Some arrangement was
necessary because no organ was available for the
performance of the works. It is unfortunate,
however, that these accretions should have been
blindly accepted by subsequent generations, and

been incorporated in nearly all the editions of *The Messiah*, so that they have become part of the Handel canon. Even Prout, who produced a scholarly edition twenty years ago, had not the courage or, perhaps, the heart to delete all Mozart's additions. It is certainly difficult to resist the beautiful wind-parts supplied to " The people that walked in darkness ", even though we may feel, like Rockstro, that they suggest not darkness, as does the bleak scoring of Handel, but a radiance of golden light. Mozart's mind was not in accord with Handel's. His genius lay in the direction of delicate ornament ; Handel had a giant strength and directness which makes such things seem superfluous and trivial. Nevertheless it is not Mozart's fault that his additions have been perpetuated, and he certainly does not merit the blame laid upon him by the purists, who, after all, cannot tell us what precisely Handel did in the way of filling-in on the organ when *The Messiah* was first performed. At least Mozart shows a profound knowledge of and respect for Handel's music and a good, if misdirected, taste. It may be added that by no means all of the additions usually attributed to Mozart are now admitted to be by him.

In March, 1789, Prince Karl Lichnowsky, the son-in-law of Countess Wilhelmina Thun and the future patron of Beethoven, proposed to Mozart that he should accompany him on a journey to Berlin. Mozart was delighted at the idea of an expedition, which was not to be a mere concert-tour. Moreover there was the possibility of obtaining commissions at the Prussian Court and, perhaps, a more remunerative position than Vienna offered. From Prague, which was reached on April 10, Mozart wrote to Constanze, who had been left behind under the care of the Puchbergs, that the contract for another opera had been discussed and almost concluded. Nothing came of this project, however. The next day the travellers departed for Dresden, where, as he informs Constanze, Wolfgang's first action was to seek out his dear friend, Josepha Duschek, who was visiting the family of Johann Leopold Neumann, the Secretary to the Military Council. Through Neumann Mozart was introduced into the musical world of Dresden, which included Kapellmeister Naumann and Körner, whose sister-in-law, Dora Stock, made an excellent sketch of Mozart, which is one of the more credible portraits. This portrait, which is now in Peters's library at Liepzig, shows Mozart in profile. In spite of a certain amount of conventionalization and a little flattery to the sitter, it faithfully brings out his characteristic traits : the long nose, full mouth, large forehead, flabby chin inclined to doubleness, and the mass of fine hair. The eye is large with signs of a pouch beneath it, which appears more noticeably in Posch's medallion and the portrait by Lange. But Dora Stock has given the eye the very quality of brightness which all observers agree that Mozart's lacked—owing, we may suppose, to his early illnesses which must have affected his sight. For he was short-sighted. However we are told that his eyes became bright and piercing when he was improvising at the pianoforte, and it is evidently one of these passing gleams which shot out occasionally from between the clouds, that the artist has preserved for us.

Naumann and Mozart seem to have inspired one another with mutual dislike. Mozart was contemptuous of Naumann's " mediocre " Mass, while Naumann is reported to have returned the compliment by calling his visitor a " musical *sans-culotte* ". There is more truth in this gibe than Naumann knew—he was evidently referring merely to Mozart's harmonic boldness — for Mozart was always contemptuous of rank as such, and took no pains to conceal the fact. This attitude, adopted alike towards Archbishops, royalty and his superiors in the social world generally, probably goes some way to account for the lack of favour with which he was regarded. The time had not come when ill manners were forgiven as the eccentricity of genius—an allowance which was made for Beethoven, who alternately insulted and flattered the nobility, a decade later when the Revolution was an accomplished fact. We may admire Mozart's consciousness of his own superiority, and his impatience of Philistine stupidity in high places, but we could wish that, for his own sake and ours, he had tempered it with a little tact and a sensible acceptance of the conditions under which he lived. So he might have been spared much suffering and the early death which deprived us of so much that he might have accomplished.

During the stay in Dresden Mozart played before the Court and was rewarded with a snuff-box containing 100 ducats. He also met and vanquished in single combat Johann Hässler of Erfurt, a distinguished player on the clavichord and the organ, who had boasted that " strong as Mozart may be on the pianoforte, he cannot play the clavichord ".

Leipzig was visited next and Mozart hastened to pay his respects to Anton Doles, the pupil of J. S. Bach and his successor as Cantor of the Thomaskirche. Doles was delighted with his performance on the organ and declared that his old master had come to life again. By way of return Doles made the choir sing Bach's motet, " Singet dem Herrn ein neues Lied ", which so astonished and delighted Mozart that he demanded to see more of Bach's works, which, apart from some of the instrumental pieces, were quite unknown to him, as to most musicians outside Leipzig. No scores existed and he surrounded himself with the parts, which Doles produced for him, and so studied these compositions, of which he exclaimed, " That's music to learn something from ! "

The next day Mozart and Lichnowsky left Leipzig and arrived forty-eight hours later at Potsdam, the seat of the Prussian Court. King Frederick William II was a good musician and a capable violoncellist. He already knew something of Mozart's music and received the visitor with favour. Mozart, however, succeeded at once in offending Dupont, the King's violoncellomaster, who addressed him in French, which language he declined to use. "The grinning mounseer," he said, "has been long enough making German money and eating German bread, to be able to speak the German language, or to murder it as best he may with his French grimaces." He likewise annoyed Reichardt, the Kappellmeister, by his outspoken criticisms to the King of the orchestra's performances. The King himself took his remarks in good part, but there is no evidence that he offered Mozart a post at his court with a salary of 3,000 dollars, and it is most unlikely that he would have done so in the face of the opposition of his leading musicians and so have introduced into his *entourage* a discordant personality. So we must dismiss one more legend, to the effect that Mozart declined a lucrative offer from Potsdam out of loyalty to a master who did not appreciate his worth. It may be added that it is unlikely that Mozart's gay and southern temperament would have blossomed happily in the cold and stiff environment of Potsdam. It was left to the less imaginative Ditters von Dittersdorf to achieve success and a fortune in Berlin.

Mozart returned to Leipzig on May 8, in order to give a concert, which was not a financial success, mainly because he allowed the tickets to be given away freely. After the concert he retired with Karl Gottlieb Berger, a violoncellist, and played for him till midnight. Suddenly stopping, he exclaimed : " Now, you have heard Mozart. Others can play as well as I at a concert!" The incident is typical not only of Mozart, but of all true artists. Mozart loved from his childish days to play to men who could fully appreciate his art, and detested appearances before a public, which might applaud enthusiastically, but did not understand what they applauded.

He returned ten days later to Berlin, where he heard a performance of *Die Entführung aus dem Serail*. Sitting near the orchestra, he seems to have made himself conspicuous by his gestures and comments upon the music. When, in Pedrillo's air in D major, the second violin played a D sharp, he could contain himself no longer, but shouted out, " Damn you, play D ! "—or words to that effect. He was recognized and at the end of the act was called upon the stage. Henriette Baranius sang Blonde on this occasion, and she extracted a promise from the composer that he would coach her in the part. This charming young singer enjoyed the royal favour, and tradition has it that Mozart was not less honoured than the King. Jahn reluctantly mentions the tradition, but pronounces it incredible on the naïve grounds of the tone of Mozart's letters to his wife. We know, however, that Mozart confessed to and was forgiven some infidelities in his later years. This may well have been one of them and there is no reason to suppose that they affected his genuine devotion to Constanze.

Another and more pleasing anecdote belongs to this time. Before one of the performances of *Die Entführung*, Ludwig Tieck, the poet and translator of Shakespeare, then aged sixteen, entered the theatre some time before the opera was due to begin and saw a strange man in the orchestral pit. "He was short," says Tieck's biographer, "quick, restless, and weak-eyed— an insignificant figure in a grey overcoat. He went from one desk to another, and seemed to be hurriedly reading through the music placed upon them. Ludwig at once entered into conversation with him. They spoke of the orchestra, the theatre, the opera, the public taste. He expressed his opinions without reserve, and declared his enthusiastic admiration of Mozart's operas.

" 'Do you really hear Mozart's works often and love them?' asked the stranger—'That is very good of you, young sir.'

" The conversation continued for some time longer: the theatre began to fill, and at last the stranger was called away from the stage. His talk had produced a singular effect on Ludwig, who made enquiries about him, and learnt that it was Mozart himself, the great master, who had conversed with him, and expressed his obligation to him."

The picture of the enthusiastic boy and the great but unsuccessful man, who was probably both touched and amused, is a very human one. But its chief value lies in the vivid and accurate description of Mozart's appearance. Scarlet fever and small-pox had harmed his sight, which must have been further strained by constant attention upon musical notation, though his manuscripts are neat and not written large, as might be expected. Illness and the exertions of his early tours, too, had stunted his growth. He cut, indeed, an insignificant figure in the world, and had none of the advantages of a striking appearance, which usually marks out men of genius from their fellows. Beethoven also was short in stature, but he was immensely strong and sturdy of build, and his broad forehead, crowned with wild and unkempt locks, and, above all, his flaming eye proclaimed the genius. Mozart had none of the external aids to success. He could be charming, when he chose, but he was no courtier, and it was only the sympathetic and the intimates who were privileged to see the fire burning clearly within his unprepossessing exterior. Ludwig Tieck caught a glimpse of it, and then saw him no more.

The visit to Berlin brought no material profit to Mozart, and he returned to Vienna no richer then he left it. The King of Prussia did, indeed, commission him to write a set of six string quartets, and his daughter, Princess Frederika, likewise asked for a set of pianoforte sonatas. Of the latter only one was actually composed, that in D major (K. 576, dated July, 1789). Of the quartets the first, also in D major (K. 575), was completed in June immediately after Mozart's return to Vienna. The King was mightily pleased with it, but had to wait until the following summer for two further instalments, the quartets in B flat (K. 589) and F major (K. 590), and the set was never completed.

It is usual to regard these three quartets, the last which Mozart composed, as being definitely below the level of those in the Haydn set. They are written down as elegant and courtly music well adapted to the purpose of pleasing a royal dilettante, but on a comparatively low plane of musical thought. It is true, especially of the first two works, that they are light and graceful, but beneath the superficial triviality one may hear a new note which, if not wholly absent from the works of the preceding years, is sounded here definitely for the first time. Even the lightest of the three quartets, that in B flat, contains a remarkable and exceptionally long minuet, the *Trio* of which forecasts the music of the three Genii in *Die Zauberflöte*.

But this new note is sounded more clearly in the F major quartet, the most serious of the group. Yet this work is usually treated by the critics as being, like its two companions, a pot-boiler " thrown off " to please a royal patron. Superficially there is, perhaps, no conspicuous difference between the F major quartet and those in D major and B flat. But, speaking for myself, every time I hear it I feel that a new spirit, hitherto only hinted at, underlies its polished grace. Mozart had reached the age of thirty-four, the age at which most composers begin to " set ", to enter on what is called their second period. Their individuality is found, their personal idiom becomes crystallized, and, while the youthfulness of their vigour has not lost its strength, they settle down to a more conscious and intellectually directed philosophy of life. It is the age at which Beethoven wrote the Eroica Symphony, and at which Wagner was engaged on *Lohengrin*.

It is, therefore, an age at which, even allowing for the peculiarities of Mozart's case, we might naturally expect to find some change in his style. I may say that this expectation did not in any way suggest the existence of such a change or prompt me to look for it. The process was the other way about, and I merely advance the argument of his age as support for what are, after all, slender indications of a change. For, unhappily, Mozart was cut off before the new development, which I suggest, had time to make itself definitely felt in his music, and from this time onward his health began to fail and illness inevitably hampered the growth of his mind. Had his circumstances been happier and his life been spared, the F major quartet might be now regarded, not as a rather undistinguished composition, but as the first step towards a new development of his music.

Such an elevation of its importance in history would not, of course, affect its absolute value as music; but what I wish to point out is that this quartet is not just a lesser example of the style, which had been brought to perfection in the set dedicated to Haydn, but is a not wholly successful effort to do something different. Mozart seems here to be groping towards the expression of the kind of idea which was to be the basis of Beethoven's work. There is a sense of strenuousness, of struggle in the very first phrase, with its startling *forte*, lowered as suddenly to *piano*. For a few moments the music goes on in the usual elegant manner, but there succeeds a dialogue between the violoncello and first violin, which may have been written thus in order to give prominence to King Frederick William's own instrument, but which nevertheless has a quiet fierceness which we do not normally find in Mozart. The most definite sign occurs in the last movement, which starts off like any other piece of gay Mozartian chatter, but is soon interrupted by dramatic pauses in the manner

235

to be used with such immense effect by Beethoven in nearly every one of his important works. Perhaps these pauses are merely put there to startle the hearer, are no more than a recrudescence of a mannerism frequently applied, as I have noted in an earlier chapter, during the period of Mozart's and Haydn's adherence to the gallant style. I do not think so. Rather I believe that this use of the dramatic pause is a development from a meretricious trick, merely designed to hold the interest, of a significant effect, not imposed upon the music but growing out of it logically, just as the slow introduction, intended originally to set off by contrast the gaiety of the succeeding *allegro*, became, in the C major quartet and in Beethoven's works, a part of the general poetic design. If one were asked to say in a word what it was that Beethoven introduced into music and that made his influence predominant throughout a century, I think the answer would be a sense of struggle, of aspiration. Before Beethoven there had been contrast in music, but rarely the heroic conflict to attain to an ideal. This quartet seems to me an exception, puny enough perhaps and spasmodic in its adoption of the new idea, but sufficiently definite to show that Mozart was moving with his times towards the conception of self-expression in art, which was to dominate the composers of the nineteenth century. The tendency in this direction did not develop in him fully, in part for the reasons I have already stated. But *The Magic Flute* has many characteristics which support the supposition that Mozart was cut off at a new turning-point in his musical career.

Just before he wrote this quartet in F major, he had composed, as if in final leave-taking of his youth, *Cosi fan Tutte* or *The School for Lovers*, the last and most delicious of his Italian comic operas. The success of a revival of *Figaro* soon after his return from Berlin had brought Mozart once more to the notice of his unappreciative master, the Emperor, who ordered a new comic opera and himself suggested the outline of the plot, which is said to be based on an actual incident of recent occurrence in Vienna. Da Ponte was once more and for the last time Mozart's librettist. He produced a piece of fooling so airy and so delicate that for more than a hundred years it has been derided as a mere absurdity. "As if women could not see through the disguises in which their lovers masquerade!" the literal-minded exclaim. But gentlemen of this obtuse nature never can see past a convention to the reality behind. It is true that the stage-trick of a disguise, sometimes consisting of no more than a mask held before the face, has been worn threadbare by abuse in a thousand inane musical comedies. In *Cosi fan Tutte*, however, nothing turns on the impenetrability of the disguise. It is merely assumed to be impenetrable, because it makes things more amusing than the simple and, for the operatic impresario, more costly expedient of hiring two other characters to carry out the plot.[1] But it is, indeed, ridiculous seriously to criticize the artificial and inconsistent plot—for the sham lovers take their false wooing very seriously at times. Either you must accept it as a fine example of fantastic baroque design, or you must admit that that kind of thing does not amuse you, which will be a pity.

With the exception of Don Alfonso, the cynical philosopher who pulls all the strings of the plot—and the strings are never for a moment concealed from the spectator—all the characters in the opera are unreal, mere puppets. Yet they are as subtly differentiated by Mozart's genius as any of the living human beings in his more familiar stage-works. As Professor Dent says, "They are only marionettes; but their machinery is so elaborate that they act better then human beings." All the stock tricks of *opera buffa* are used—the disguise of the maidservant, first as a doctor, then as a notary ; the Oriental disguise of the lovers (though there is no " Turkish " music as in *Die Entführung* and Haydn's *Lo Speziale*) ; the odd operatic marriage

[1] This expedient was actually resorted to in one of the many humourless German attempts to make sense of the airy unreality of the plot. These two accomplices were given a servant, Pedrillo, who replaced the maidservant Despina as the doctor and notary—presumably because members of the legal and medical professions do not generally have high-pitched voices.

before the sham notary.[1] But all these stock situations are treated by Da Ponte with a refreshing ingenuity that almost makes them seem original. It must be confessed, however, that Da Ponte's ingenuity is somewhat exhausted by the end of the first of the two acts, which closes with that superbly funny scene when the lovers pretend to poison themselves and are revived by means of a magnet in the hands of the sham doctor—a gentle dig, this, in the ribs of Dr Mesmer, the expert in animal magnetism, as who should in these days make fun of the late M. Coué or Professor Freud. The second act has nothing in the action to equal that and at times is in danger of dragging. Mozart averts that danger most of the time and a judicious blue pencil will do the rest. Given that, a lively production and a ready acceptance of the conventions, the audience is in for the most delightful evening.

Yet the opera has been called too absurd and, even more absurdly, disgustingly immoral. As if morals had anything to do with these puppet-lovers! So *Cosi fan Tutte* never kept the stage in the nineteenth century ; it was too frivolous. In Germany a bad and humourless translation

[1] I am told that these operatic marriages are perfectly valid in law, since at this period the marriage laws of most countries were similar to that which still holds in Scotland, the parties having merely to attest their consent to marry before witnesses. How this works out with a sham notary and a contract which is not signed by the male contracting parties is a matter for counsel's opinion, not for me.

sufficed to crush its butterfly wings. In England
it was given in Italian in 1811, in English as
Tit for Tat in 1828 and as *The Retaliation* in 1841.
Then an obscure country parson, not a little
inspired by the rhymes of W. S. Gilbert, set
himself to make an able and witty translation
which was submitted to Stanford and performed
by students of the Royal College of Music in
1893. The Reverend Marmaduke Browne's
translation was published by Messrs. Novello in
vocal score, but lay for another generation in their
cellar until, through the enthusiastic efforts of
Dr Napier Miles, it was produced, with an
added polish administered by Professor Dent,
at Bristol in 1926. The production was transferred to London in the Spring of 1927, where at
the moment of writing the opera is at last enjoying
the popularity it always deserved.

Mr W. Johnstone Douglas, who was responsible
for this production, has given the piece a decided
English twist. The action is supposed to take
place in Naples, but its real site is Vienna. In
this English version, it is transferred to one of
our Cathedral towns half a century after the
original date. The spirit of Jane Austen is
abroad, and the two sisters are surely the daughters
of a deceased canon with a red-brick Georgian
house in the Close. Their lovers are subalterns
stationed in the barracks which " go with "
Cathedrals. Don Alfonso—well, he is one of
those old bachelors who live also in Georgian

houses outside the Close. I think this matter worth mentioning, not merely out of gratitude for the enjoyment I had of the performance, but because it seems to me to be the right line to take when producing a foreign opera in English. The usual method with us is to imitate the native style of singing and production, to try and make it as like the original as possible. The fact is ignored that Englishmen can never truly enter into the Italian, the French or the German way of looking at things, any more than those others can see things exactly as we do. Our attempts at doing opera in the foreign manner usually result in little more than an exaggeration of the faults of that manner. The spirit is inevitably lost. Something must always go in translations, and it is far better that the letter of the original should be altered to suit the understanding of the singers and their audience, provided the spirit of it is preserved intact. That has been done in Mr Johnstone Douglas's production of *Così fan Tutte*, in the 'Old Vic' performance of Mozart's operas and, with some violations, in Sir Thomas Beecham's edition of *Figaro*. The result has invariably been a popular success, which is, after all, not a bad criterion. Some of these performances have been called hard names, amateurish, squalid, sophisticated; but they give us more of the real Mozart than the unco-ordinated efforts of polyglot singers to follow various traditions, which have grown up during more

than a century, on the vast and unsuitable stage
of Covent Garden, even though the actual quality,
of the singing may there reach a considerably
higher standard.

I have called *Cosi fan Tutte* the most delicious
of Mozart's Italian operas. That does not
imply that it is a greater work than *Don Giovanni*
or *Figaro*. Indeed the assessment of comparative
greatness is best left to those critics who cannot
praise one thing without damning another. In
Così fan Tutte Mozart exhibits none of the moral
indignation which shows through the surface of
heartlessness and libertinage in *Figaro* and *Don
Giovanni*. The later opera is less human than
the other two, since it deals with frankly artificial
characters. It is both less ambitious in what it
sets out to do and more of a unified whole in the
end. *Figaro* is too complicated, even when a deal
of Beaumarchais's original intrigue has been cut
out, and *Don Giovanni* is muddled by the hasty
patching of the second act, apart from the
continual tug-of-war between the comic and the
tragic aspects of the story. But *Così fan Tutte*
is as clear as the sunny sky beneath which its
fête galante is enacted. Nowhere is Mozart's
music more limpid or more witty. Nothing in
Figaro or *Don Giovanni* can surpass the subtle
characterization of the two ladies, one sentimental,
the other more practical in her romanticism.
There are few more amusing jokes in music than
the electric vibrations given out by the wood-

wind during the magnetic cure of the lovers, or the lamentation of Don Alfonso, when he breaks the sad news of the officers' departure to the front. Here Mozart seems almost to mock at his own trick of emphasizing a weak beat in the bar. In sum the music is the most delicate and pointed ever written for the stage. It sounds no depths and its emotional moments, though not insincere, are in proportion to the levity of the subject. Let us therefore make no comparisons, but, like Wagner, set it down to Mozart's credit that he could not write for *Così fan Tutte* the same kind of music which he wrote for *Figaro* or *Don Giovanni*[1] Wagner evidently appreciated *Così fan Tutte* at a time when no one else did, and his tribute is the more forceful in that it comes from the man who laid aside *Siegfried* in order to write *Tristan* and *Die Meistersinger*. These two men—if not alone, at least more than any others—understood that each opera they wrote must have its own characteristic music, that the love of Eva and of Susanna on the one hand and the love of Isolde and of Fiordiligi on the other each required a different idiom for its expression.

Così fan Tutte was produced, without marked success, on January 20, 1790. Mozart's financial gain from it amounted to two hundred ducats,

[1] Wagner's actual words are, " How deeply I love Mozart because he *could* not invent for *Titus* music like that for *Don Giovanni*, or for *Così fan Tutte* music like that for *Figaro!* What a disgrace that would have been to Music ! "—*Opera and Drama*.

which did not even suffice to pay off his debt to
Puchberg. A month later all hope of official
advancement in Vienna disappeared, even though
Mozart may not have been aware of it. For on
February 20, the Emperor Joseph II died and
was succeeded by Leopold II, who displayed his
interest in music, so far as he may be said to have
had any, by frowning on all who had been
patronized by his predecessor. Salieri, whom
Joseph had esteemed above Mozart, resigned his
position and was succeeded by Joseph Weigl.
Da Ponte fell into disfavour and left Vienna.
After a series of adventures, more astonishing
than anything in his opera-books, he arrived in
London, where, like many before and since, he
lost money by producing opera. He turned
bookseller, specializing in Italian books, but again
became bankrupt owing to the treachery of men
he had trusted and befriended. He escaped to
America, where he made a living by teaching
Italian, and wrote his autobiography, the con-
fessions of a penitent sinner—with one eye on the
pupils. He died in his ninetieth year on August
17, 1838, having made his peace with the Church
he had so long flouted both by word and by deed.

The year 1790 was the least productive of
Mozart's musical career. His own catalogue up
to December contains nothing more than the
two last quartets, already mentioned, and the
arrangements of Handel's *Ode for St Cecilia's
Day* and *Alexander's Feast*. The disfavour of

the new Emperor, who refused his petition for the post of second Kapellmeister,[1] added its quota to the discouragement of his own ill-health and poverty, and his anxiety for Constanze, who spent the summer at Baden taking a cure. His correspondence during the year consists of further appeals to Puchberg, who helped him with small sums, and affectionate letters to his wife, full of buoyant hopes, which had in reality nothing on which to float. In May he had two pupils and wrote to Puchberg that he would have liked to increase the number to eight. In order to avoid the expense of two establishments, however humble, he joined Constanze at Baden, pawning his valuables to pay his way.

In the autumn he saw a chance of making money at Frankfurt, where the Emperor was to be crowned on October 9. Mozart was not commanded to attend upon his Imperial master, but he borrowed 800 florins from a moneylender, who was to receive in return 1,000 florins, and set out in company with Hofer, the violinist who had married Josepha Weber. With his usual generosity and improvidence he not only paid for Hofer's expenses, but was apparently prepared to share equally with him the visionary profits of the journey. At Frankfurt he gave a concert

[1] Mozart urges his claim on the grounds that Salieri, "the very able Kapellmeister, has never devoted his attention to the genuine style of Church music, whereas, since my boyhood, I have completely mastered this style." He also asked, with no more success, to be appointed teacher of the pianoforte to the Emperor's children.

of his own works, playing two pianoforte concertos himself. These were probably the two " Coronation " concertos, as they are called after the event which was the occasion of the festivities, in F major (K. 459) and D major (K. 537). It is possible, indeed likely, that the two symphonies performed at this concert were two of those written in 1788.

From Frankfurt Mozart went to Offenbach, where he attempted to interest André, the music publisher, in his works. André, however, would have none of them—until Mozart was dead. Then he purchased all the manuscripts his widow would sell. Next he went to Mannheim, where *Figaro* was being given for the first time. He helped at the final rehearsal, though only after his entrance had been barred by one of the actors, who took him for " a little journeyman tailor." " You'll surely allow Kapellmeister Mozart to listen ! " he said to the embarrassed actor. From Mannheim he paid a sentimental visit to Schwetzingen, where he had heard a great orchestra for the first time twenty-seven years before. Through Heidelberg, Augsburg and Munich he travelled over familiar ground to Vienna, which was reached on November 10. We do not know what Hofer's share of the proceeds was. But we know that Mozart had borrowed in the meantime a further 1,600 florins against a promissory note for 2,000. Actually he received 600 florins, the first 1,000 going to pay off the debt contracted before. He certainly had not gained that freedom from anxiety, for which he expresses a longing in his letters to Constanze, a freedom which would allow him to work in peace.

Yet he did not accept a proposal from Robert May O'Reilly, the Director of the Italian Opera in London, that he should come to England for six months, during which time he was to write two operas. For this he was offered a fee of £300 and would be at liberty to make money by giving concerts, though he must not write for other theatres. His failure to seize this opportunity cannot be explained with certainty. Ill-health, reluctance to leave Constanze again, or possibly her refusal to travel with him in her present condition, may account for it. Perhaps the combination of all three made him too weary to care what happened or whither he went—and it was easiest to stay where he was.

In December Haydn left Vienna to pay his first visit to London at the invitation of Salomon. The two composers, who had acted and re-acted so often upon one another, might have travelled and made history together. But they parted and never met again.

Chapter X

THE LAST YEAR

In December, 1790, Mozart's creative fire was rekindled by a commission for a string quintet from a patron whose identity is unknown. In response to this request he wrote the quintet in D major (K. 593) before the end of the year, and followed it up in April, 1791, with the quintet in E flat (K. 614). The two works were published with a note to the effect that they had been written " at the earnest solicitation of a musical friend."

As in the earlier quintets, two violas are used. The writing is free and elastic, without ever becoming loose ; it combines the most polished grace with great boldness in the clashes of its polyphony, so that the music has both strength and refinement. The first movement of the E flat quintet, the last chamber-work he composed, shows more than any other the direction in which Mozart's ideas of symphonic structure were moving in his last years. The whole movement is built up out of a single concise theme, which blossoms in a thousand unexpected ways, while beneath its cheerful and wayward merriment there is an undertone of calm thoughtfulness which binds the whole together. This principle of developing a movement or even a whole work out of a single germ-theme, of which the most notable example is the C minor Symphony of Beethoven, is quite distinct from the other principle of building a movement out of two different and purposely contrasted themes. The principle was not altogether new, since it was the basis of the fugue, which is the development of a single musical idea to its fullest logical conclusion. But its application to the sonata-form is novel ; and, although the tendency has already appeared before—for example, in the first movement of the " Haffner " Symphony—this last quintet provides the clearest example of it, and is one more proof that in his final year the composer was developing a musical style new both in manner and in structural form.

The flame, once relighted, flickered up intermittently throughout the year, fanned by the most curious breezes. Among the lesser commissions were several for music for clockwork instruments. Musical boxes, consisting of revolving cylinders with pegs which impinged upon resonant prongs and made them sound, were the latest rage in Vienna—the only thing corresponding to our modern mechanical music-makers, the gramophone and the player-pianoforte. For these toys and for a chiming clock Mozart wrote several pieces, of which the F minor Fantasia (K. 608) is the most important and is, indeed, sometimes to be heard at pianoforte recitals. Like these machines themselves, Mozart needed to be wound up, so to speak, by a definite order for music. Then the music poured out with extraordinary facility, and even for the most insignificant occasions, its quality was usually superlative.

In June he composed a setting of " Ave verum corpus " for Stoll, the choirmaster at Baden, where Constanze, who was as usual in poor health, was taking another cure. Stoll had been kind to the Mozarts and showed his admiration of Wolfgang's music by performing some of his early Masses in his church. The " Ave verum corpus " was, no doubt, a token of thanks for these kindnesses, one of such charm and simple piety that it, alone of all the composer's Church music, has survived in general use.

In the meantime an even stranger commission had been received. Emmanuel Schikaneder, who, it will be remembered, had played Gebler's *Thamos, König in Ägypten* with Mozart's incidental music many years before in Salzburg, had come to Vienna in 1789 and taken over the management of the " Theater in Starhembergischen Freihause auf der Wieden." In spite of its imposing name this playhouse was little more than a barn and stood just outside the walls of the city.

Schikaneder was a remarkable man. Born at Regensberg (Ratisbon) in 1751 of the poorest imaginable parents he spent his early years as a vagabond fiddler. He became an actor and was sufficiently successful to achieve the management of a company of his own by the time he was twenty-seven. He had no education whatever, yet he was not devoid of taste, as will be seen from the fact that his repertory included plays by Shakespeare (*Macbeth*, *Hamlet* and *King Lear*), Schiller and Lessing, and Gluck's *Orfeo*. Indeed he contributed a good deal towards the creation of German a national drama in the last years of the century. But his chief activity was the production of popular comic pieces, in which the spectacle played an important part. He was clever enough to see that the general public was tired of the foreign works, which were fashionable in Society and at Court, and that money was to be made out of genuinely national entertainments. His ambitious attempts to draw the public and the variety of the means he employed make one think of him as an eighteenth-century equivalent of Mr C. B. Cochran or Herr Reinhardt. At Regensburg he gave an *al fresco* spectacle in which a camp of a hundred tents with soldiers on horseback was the chief attraction. It was an immense success and attracted three thousand spectators. At Pressburg, with less happy results, he anticipated Rostand's *Chantecler* with a piece in which the heroine was a goose (this is the least original feature), while the remainder of the cast consisted of other members of the poultry-world. When he came to Vienna, he was acute enough to see that comic operas of a popular type with spectacle thrown in would draw the money. In 1790 he produced *Der Stein der Weisen* (*The Philosopher's Stone*), adapted from a tale by Wieland, with music by several hands. In the next year Wranitzky's *Oberon*, based upon the story used later by Weber, was produced.

In May of this year he approached Mozart with a request for a similar " magic " opera. It was an odd task to set the elegant composer of smart Italian operas. For what was wanted was a sort of pantomime with plenty of comic songs for Schikaneder, who took the clown's part in his productions. However, the Court would have none of him now, so Mozart accepted Schikaneder's commission. He was probably influenced in the swallowing of any pride he may have felt about it, by the fact that Josepha Hofer was in the company and her husband in the orchestra, and above all by the fact that Schikaneder was a brother-Mason. Schikaneder was to supply the libretto, which was based on another of Wieland's tales. The plot dealt originally with the simple situation of a fairy queen, who gives to a young prince a portrait of her daughter, who has been abducted by a wicked sorcerer, and a magic flute, by the aid of which he will be able to rescue the captive. The sequel may be imagined. However, when the libretto had reached this stage—and the music was apparently composed piecemeal with it as it progressed—Schikaneder's rival, Marinelli, having perhaps got wind of his purpose, produced a *singspiel* called *Kaspar der Fagottist oder die*

Zauberzither,[1] which was based upon the same story. So Schikaneder scratched his head, called to his assistance Ludwig Giesecke, one of his actors, and, without altering what had already been done, turned the whole plot round and achieved a *peripeteia* that would have astonished the most ingenious of Greek dramatists. The fairy-queen became the villainness of the piece, and the sorcerer, who had not yet appeared on the scene, was turned into the head of a beneficent community of Egyptian priests.

Carl Ludwig Giesecke, who shares with Da Ponte and Schikaneder the claim to be the most remarkable character who came into contact with Mozart, deserves a paragraph to himself. His real name was Metzler, and he was born at Augsburg in 1761, his father being a tailor. After reading law at Göttingen University, he took up the study of botany and mineralogy, and came to Vienna possibly with a view to further study. He had no means, however, and, falling in with Schikaneder, he became a member of his company and played small parts. It may have been on adopting the stage as a temporary profession that he changed his name. There is, however, a less respectable explanation in the story that he had to leave his native town on account of some

---

[1] In this piece the prince is given a magic guitar, while his attendant, Kaspar, who corresponds to Papageno in Mozart's opera, receives the lower-pitched wind-instrument indicated in the title, and with it resorts to fooling of a kind which may best be left to the imagination. The piece met with great success.

unspecified indiscretion. He wrote the libretto of *Oberon*, which has already been mentioned. So he was the person to whom Schikaneder would naturally turn in his difficulty. Yet nothing was heard of Giesecke's share in *Die Zauberflöte (The Magic Flute)*, as the new piece was called, until 1818, when Giesecke returned to Vienna with a collection of geological specimens, which he had gathered together during a residence of seven years in Greenland and which he now deposited in the Imperial Museum. During this visit he mentioned casually to a group of friends in a restaurant that he was the real author of *Die Zauberflöte*, and his statement was published to an astonished world thirty years later by Julius Kornet, a tenor, who was one of the party present when the statement was made. In the meantime Giesecke had been elected to the newly created professorship in Mineralogy in the Royal Dublin Society, despite the fact that he knew almost no English. Having been appointed to the Order of the Dannebrog he was known as Sir Charles Lewis Giesecke, and—as if to put the final touch to the respectability of the one-time actor— Raeburn painted his portrait, which hangs in the gallery of the Society at Dublin. By the time he returned to Vienna he was, therefore, a scientist with an European reputation in his particular line, besides being a charming man who was able to " fall on his feet " wherever he went. Although, therefore, Schikaneder announced *Die Zauberflöte* as the outcome of his unique inspiration, there seems no reason to doubt Giesecke's claim to a share in it, since he could hardly, in his position as a scientist, have taken any great pride in his authorship of that gallimaufry of nonsense, which is the libretto of *Die Zauberflöte*. We may rather suppose that he was glad enough to remain anonymous when he acted as Schikaneder's ghost, and merely mentioned his participation in the affair years afterwards, when the opera had achieved fame, as a matter of interest to his friends.

Schikaneder intended a spectacular pantomime with a good low-comedy part for himself, but, like Mr Dobson's ode which turned to a sonnet, the piece was somehow transformed into a moral drama dealing with the ultimate mysteries of life and death. This astonishing result was due primarily to the change of plan which, as we have seen, occurred early in its composition. The sorcerer turned priest became the head, or whatever may be the correct title, of a Masonic Lodge, thinly disguised as an order of the Egyptian priesthood. Of what comes after the point in the libretto where the change was made, it seems likely that Schikaneder was responsible only for such scenes as immediately concerned his own part of Papageno, while Giesecke wrote the rest. Giesecke was also a Freemason, and, though no claim can be made on the score of literary merit for any of the libretto, it seems more probable

that the young man from Göttingen would have
been possessed of the erudition and wide reading
which is displayed, than the self-educated actor-
manager.   Giesecke resorted for the ritual and
the philosophy of the temple scenes mainly to a
curious novel by the Abbé Terrasson, called
Sethos.[1]   This book was regarded as the chief
authority upon the Egyptian mysteries, from
which Freemasonry borrowed much of its symbolism.

On the face of it the results of Giesecke's and
Schikaneder's collaboration present about as
hopeless a ⁺ask as any operatic composer was ever
set—which is saying a good deal ! There are
almost no dramatic situations, the humour is
mainly of the feeblest kind, the characters are
utterly unreal, and there is no love-scene in the
whole length of it, if we except the comic duet
between Papageno and Papagena, in which they
set up as the ideal of marriage a nestful of simple
bird-like creatures, doubles of themselves. Tamino
and Pamina take love for granted and hardly
speak of it to one another.   Their ideal of
marriage is a finer thing, a true companionship
which will enable them to face all the chances of
life and death with fortitude.   But it is Mozart,
not the librettists, who brings this ideal to our
view, an ideal which Mozart must himself have

---

[1] For a full account of *Sethos* and of Giesecke's probable contribution to
Die Zauberflöte the reader must be referred to E. J. Dent's *Mozart's Operas*,
where the origins of the story are fully investigated.

had before him and which was never realized by Constanze, who was amusing herself at Baden while the composer worked in the little summer-house provided for him by Schikaneder near the theatre.

Mozart had dismissed his single servant, for economy's sake, and accepted the hospitality of Schikaneder, who in turn was glad to have his composer under his eye. He knew Mozart's dilatory ways and was also pleased to be in a position to see that he got for himself the music he wanted. It is safe to say that Mozart never revised any of his compositions so often as he did Papageno's songs, which had to be re-written many times before the impresario was satisfied. It is said that Schikaneder was Mozart's evil genius and led him into bad ways, into drunken-ness and immorality, which further undermined his health. There is no proof of it. The company of the players may have been free and easy, but there is no evidence to support the idea that they were a set of debauchees.[1] It is more than probable that Mozart may have occasionally drunk more than was good for him and may also have forgotten now and then his duty to his dear " Stanzi " in Baden, with whom he corresponded

[1] Maurice Kufferath in his admirable monograph on *The Magic Flute* states definitely that Schikaneder looked after his troupe like a father. " He had elaborated a system of management which has served as a model for the systems still in use at the present day. One may note in it severe and wise regulations regarding the morality of the players, and their loyalty and courtesy in their mutual relations. For the first time in the history of the theatre, we see in his management a system of fines and forfeits inflicted on

in the same vein of childish humour as ever. But it is difficult to believe that *Die Zauberflöte* is the work of a man who was fast sinking into vicious ways. It is said that Mozart had a dual personality, that he was Dr Jekyll in his music and Mr Hyde in his private conduct. Yet, while I do not maintain that he had no weaknesses, there is not a shred of real evidence that he was an immoral man, unless what was the merest peccadillo in his day is to be accounted to him as damnation. I think we may take it that there is no need to resort to the extraordinary theory of dual personality, but accept Mozart as in social matters an ordinary human being—a Tamino, indeed, in his ideals, but one who could not always pass the test of silence when a pretty woman spoke to him. If he was a man of this kind, and no other could have conceived the music of *Die Zauberflöte*, we may be sure that he spent many sorry hours of repentance, not perhaps for his faithlessness to Constanze, but for his failure in loyalty to his ideals.

So it was that, almost as if by accident, Mozart was able to attain to his early ambition of writing a German opera. For *Die Zauberflöte* is the first

the artists to form a fund for the assistance of singers and actors who were in need or out of work."

The rumours against Schikaneder were set in motion mainly by the widowed Constanze, who was furious that he should have reaped the profits of her husband's opera. There is no truth in her accusation that he had robbed Mozart of his share. He made a bargain to pay one hundred ducats for the music and he fulfilled his bargain. It may seem little enough payment for a masterpiece ; but then would a million be too much ?

truly German opera, *Die Entführung* notwithstanding. The earlier work is little more than an
Italian *opera buffa* written in German, the
character of Osmin alone being truly native to
the northern country. In *Die Zauberflöte* the
mating of Mozart's German nationality, the
romantic side of him, with his Italian upbringing,
the classical, has produced, like the wedding of
Faust to Helen, a new and wonderful offspring.
To *Die Zauberflöte* we can trace the sources of the
whole of the nineteenth-century school of German
opera. To put it more exactly, Mozart's last
opera gathered unto itself all the energy of the
many and various spasmodic attempts to create a
national opera in Germany, and out of it created
a style which was the model for future development. *Die Zauberflöte* represents the youth of
this school, Weber's *Der Freischütz* and Beethoven's *Fidelio* in their several ways its manhood,
while its fullest growth, tending already towards
the senile decay of *Parsifal*, is to be seen in the
works of Richard Wagner's maturity. It is to be
noted that this school springs entirely from a
popular and, to use a modern word, low-brow
form of entertainment, just as such national
opera as we may be said to possess, exemplified
by Sullivan's comic operas and Vaughan Williams's
Hugh the Drover, originated from that vulgar
form of entertainment, the ballad-opera, of which
Gay's *Beggar's Opera* is a rather more sophisticated
specimen. There is only one reason why on such

a foundation we have not built our *Zauberflöte*, our *Fidelio*, our *Ring*, and that is the simple one that we have produced no composers capable of doing it.

Die Zauberflöte not only enjoyed an immediate success on its first production, but has been esteemed in Germany ever since above all Mozart's other operas. Beethoven, who disapproved of *Figaro* and *Don Giovanni*, found in the idealism of *Die Zauberflöte* the basis of German music and the highest summit of Mozart's achievement. Wagner set it no less high. Goethe contemplated a sequel to the opera, but realized that, Mozart being dead, a sequel was unthinkable, and wrote the second part of *Faust*. A sequel there was, for the temptation to follow up the success of *Die Zauberflöte* was great, and in 1798 Schikaneder produced *Das Labyrinth, oder der Kampf mit den Elementen*. His choice of a composer fell, oddly enough, upon Mozart's old enemy, Peter von Winter, the pupil of the Abbé Vogler. The success of *Die Zauberflöte* resulted in a spate of magical entertainments, of which a contemporary critic writes : " Words and music are equally contemptible, so that one knows not whether to award the palm of silliness to the poet or the composer." Germany had, indeed, to wait a generation for a composer who was able to follow the lead given by Mozart and Schikaneder, and even *Der Freischütz* falls far below its parent.

The popularity of *Die Zauberflöte* was due,

apart from the topical interest of Freemasonry in Vienna at this time, to its skilful combination of high ideals, which would appeal to the thoughtful, with simple and obvious humour. That the combination was largely fortuitous does no more than account for the very obvious structural faults of the libretto. The sequels and innumerable imitations serve to prove, however, that the successful accident could not be repeated intentionally—at any rate without the assistance of one of the chief elements, namely the composer. It is Mozart's music which raises the symbolism of *Die Zauberflöte* above the plane of the merely childish, enriching it with overtones of thought and of emotion, which were certainly not contemplated by the authors of the book. It carries us into the world of the imagination, where the mysteries of life and death are reviewed in simple terms and in a manner which is beyond the power of words alone. Here is one of the supreme justifications of the operatic form as an independent art, something different from both music and drama. For neither music, even in combination with poetry, nor drama alone could produce the impressive and exalted effect of a work like *Die Zauberflöte*. Its faults are due to the accidents of its creation, not to any inherent flaw in the form of opera as such.

The "interpretations" of the meaning of Mozart's last opera are innumerable, and I do **not** propose to enter into them in detail. Sarastro and the Queen of the Night have been said to symbolize almost everything, according to the interpreter's ideas of good and evil, from the Church of Rome to the Jacobins. The suggestion that the opera represented the successful struggle of German art against Italianism is interesting, for the Italians damned the work outright, calling it " *musica scelerata* without melody." How far our understanding of the work in England has fallen short until recent years is shown by the fact that it was always performed in Italian under the title of *Il Flauto Magico!*

The primary meaning of the work is, of course, Masonic. It symbolizes the struggles and the final victory of the Freemasons over their enemies. Streatfeild summarizes it thus : " Freemasonry in the opera is represented by the mysteries of Isis, over which the high-priest, Sarastro, presides. The Queen of the Night is Maria Theresa, a sworn opponent of Freemasonry, who interdicted its practice in her dominions, and broke up the Lodges with armed force. Tamino may be intended for the Emperor Joseph II, who, though not a Freemason himself as his father was, openly protected the brotherhood ; and we may look upon Pamina as the representative of the Austrian people. The name of Monostatos seems to be connected with monasticism, and may be intended to typify the clerical party, which though outwardly on friendly terms with Freemasonry, seems in reality to have been bent upon its destruction.[1] Papageno and Papagena are excellent representatives of the light-hearted, pleasure-loving population of Vienna."

All this is, no doubt, true, and this interpretation may have been clear enough to the audiences at the first performances of the opera. But this symbolism has long lost its meaning and, if the opera relied on it alone, it would have lost all its attraction. For, in any work of art that is to last, symbols can only be successfully employed when they have also a natural meaning which will be clear to the uninitiated.

Appreciation of *Die Zauberflöte* does not, however, depend upon any initiation into secret mysteries, but merely on the initiation, which all must undergo to a greater or less extent, into experience of life. The hearer of the opera will have no difficulty in perceiving in it a finer allegory, the purification of the soul by self-denial, the achievement of wisdom and happiness in the face of trial and suffering, and the attainment to a perfect union of two persons in a marriage that is more than a physical connection, and in a love that is stronger than death. From the solemn opening chords, to which the trombones lend the peculiar impressiveness that has already been noted, and the magnificent fugue of

---

[1] Streatfeild is unnecessarily diffident in this statement. The Church of Rome was inimical to Freemasonry, as to all secret societies. Incidentally it has always seemed to me that the greatest inconsistency in the libretto is the fact that the supposedly so wise and kind Sarastro should have put such an obvious villain as Monostatos in charge of Pamina !

the overture to the noble chorus of thanksgiving at the end, the music, if we except the comic interludes, moves on a plane of high exaltation, which had never hitherto been reached. The clue to its mood must be sought, as Professor Dent suggests, in that letter to Leopold Mozart, in which Wolfgang reveals his views upon human mortality. The gay and careless Papageno, who is unable to control himself in the face of temptation, danger or disappointment, but is nevertheless admitted, in a lower degree, to the company of the elect, on account of his good humour and true innocence, makes a perfect contrast to the lofty idealism of the main theme. Mozart's character stands here fully revealed, on the one side as earnest, thoughtful and idealistic, on the other as lively, indulgent, though not with conscious selfishness at the expense of others, and even naughty in word and action.

It will be noted that it is not the music alone which makes *Die Zauberflöte* Mozart's masterpiece, great though the music is. The ideas which it embodies contribute to its position in our esteem something which, with the possible exception of certain scenes in *Don Giovanni*, is absent from all his earlier operas. The change signifies not merely that Mozart had become at last a German composer through and through, but that he was also anticipating the development which music was to undergo in the generation after his death. *Così fan Tutte* belongs to the *fin de siècle*, but with

Die Zauberflöte he leapt at a bound into the succeeding century.

Yet it is the music alone which makes *Die Zauberflöte* the masterpiece it is, for, while in the Italian operas the composer had the assistance of clever and well-constructed books, the concoction of Schikaneder and Giesecke would be an inconsequent and tedious piece of nonsense, if Mozart's genius had not given to it a meaning far above the dreams of its authors. The overture, which was written, like the preface to a book, after the main work had been completed, at once informs us by its solemn opening that we are not about to witness a piece of mere pantomimic foolery. Then follows one of the finest and most freely developed fugues ever written, which makes it clear that we are to take life happily, though not thoughtlessly and without care, while the interruption of its cheerful course by the thrice-repeated summons to initiation once more reminds us of the solemnity of our existence.

I have already remarked upon the *rôle* of the trombones in Mozart's other dramatic works. But, whereas in *Idomeneo* and *Don Giovanni*, they are used only occasionally to give a particular colour to certain scenes, in *Die Zauberflöte* they form the background of all the serious parts of the opera. They add grandeur to the opening of the overture and to the three chords ; their soft tones give the right touch of solemnity to the warning of the genii, " Sei standhaft, duldsam und verschwiegen ! " (" Be steadfast, patient, and be silent ! ") and make a wonderful background to their juvenile voices ; it is their terrifying sound that drives away the three ladies, emissaries of the Queen of the Night, who come to tempt Tamino to break his oath, and that confounds the enemies of Truth and Light at the end of the opera ; in the temple scenes they are the basis of the noble music and, as we have noted, emphasize by the association of their use in Church-music the ritual aspect of the initiation. In fact they are the musical counterpart of Sarastro and the Priests of Isis, and they proclaim, as occasion serves, their dignity, which stands aloof from mortal actions, their wisdom, which is full of human sympathy, and their wrath. The most wonderful use is made of them in Sarastro's air, "O Isis und Osiris," and in the scene of the ordeals. In the air they combine with the basset-horns (tenor clarinets) bassoons, violas and lower strings to produce a sombre colouring, which is suddenly lightened in the most remarkable way when the tenors of the chorus respond at an octave higher to the last phrase of Sarastro's invocation, which has sunk down to the very bottom of the bass compass. It may be added here parenthetically that the trombones are not used in Sarastro's second air, " In diesen heil'gen Hallen," where the Priest is represented in a more human and fatherly aspect.

In the scene of the ordeals, when Tamino and

Pamina pass through fire and water, the trombones with the other brass and drums play alone disjointed chords, while Tamino's flute is heard winding above them like the steady voice of a courageous soul in torment. This passage looks very curious on paper, but its stark economy produces in performance an effect of awe, which makes the hearer shudder despite the usual ineffectiveness of the staging of this difficult scene. The passage has resemblances to that in the last movement of the Ninth Symphony, where by a similar use of bare rhythm Beethoven has attempted to evoke the military ideal. But somehow—perhaps merely because he has produced an effect which we have come to associate with a village band, by the use of a thumping drum and cymbals—this must be accounted one of Beethoven's failures. The sublime and the ridiculous are notoriously close neighbours, and Mozart has come down on one side of the fence, while Beethoven has in this instance landed on the other.

Through this solemn world which was intended to be no more than a make-believe fairyland of the most banal kind, but which Mozart transformed into "the unknown region" of man's ideals and aspirations, move Tamino and Pamina, not a mere man and woman, since warm life-blood does not run in their veins as it does in the veins of Don Juan and Elvira, nor yet a fairy-tale prince and princess—but the embodiments of the idealistic side of human nature. Both of them appear, according to ordinary standards and by comparison with the best of Mozart's other dramatic characters, devoid of personality. But this lack of individual interest is inherent in a work which aims at setting forth large ideas allegorically rather than at the delineation of human characters in action. It is a fault, if we must call it such, which appears also in *Fidelio* and even in *The Ring* and *Parsifal*. We must, in fact, look for a literary parallel to *Die Zauberflöte* in works like *The Pilgrim's Progress*, where the characters are symbolic and are defined not in detail but in essentials, rather than in such works as the plays of Shakespeare.

These two figures are guided by the three genii and assisted in time of trouble by resort to the magic flute, the symbol of art. It is useless to attempt to resolve the inconsistency which makes the flute a gift from the wicked Queen of the Night and the attendant genii apparently as much her emissaries as the three coquettish ladies. We must accept the libretto as it stands and make allowance for the results of the change of plan. The music of Tamino himself shows something of the same inconsistency. His first air, which was written before the change had been made, is impulsive and full of passion of the rather conventional kind exhibited by other of Mozart's tenors, Belmonte and Ottavio. The second solo, which occurs in the *finale* of Act I, is very different in spirit. It is grave and thoughtful, and it will be noted at once that the flute solo is very different from the instrumental *obbligati* for wind instruments in other of Mozart's operas.

It has been already pointed out that these airs are in the nature of concertos for voice and orchestra. They occur mainly in the serious operas and the most conspicuous exception, Constanze's great air in *Die Entführung*, goes to prove how "seriously" Mozart regarded the scene in which it occurs, and that he did not think of it as an incident in a conventional *opera buffa*. He might well have treated Tamino's air in the same manner, but fortunately—since such an elaborate and formal affair would have been out of keeping with the general style of *Die Zauber-flöte* (which, of course, Mozart might have seen for himself)—it happened that Schack, the tenor who sang Tamino, could play the flute, and it was decided that he should play it. The result was, of course, that the flute had to stop whenever he sang and any idea of a concerted piece was ruled out. The flute provides a prelude and interludes during the air. I have already noted the remarkable effect produced by this instrument in the ordeal scene. It only remains to be added that this use of the flute as a symbol of art is a curious paradox, since we know that Mozart definitely disliked the instrument. Chance forced him to give it this high place in his masterpiece, but, had he not held this prejudice, the flute might well have played a larger part than it actually does.

Pamina is drawn as a young girl, and at first appears to be on a level with Papageno, into whose naïve ideas she enters with zest in her first scene. But when she is caught in her attempt to escape from Sarastro's castle, the essential nobility of her character comes out and is thrown into relief by the comic and ignoble terror of Papageno, who, in spite of his previous punishment for lying, seeks to invent excuses with which Pamina will have nothing to do. This is almost the only active incident in her part, which is for the rest a passive one. She is not of the heroic build of Beethoven's Leonore, a type we should hardly expect from Mozart. He had, indeed, when Da Ponte gave him the opportunity, created in Donna Anna a heroine who could stimulate others to action and even take action herself, but, even if his librettists had hinted at such a thing, he would hardly have been likely to look so far ahead into the development of human ideas as to make a heroic figure of Pamina. For his ideal woman was evidently to be the helpmeet of man, the sharer of his joys and sorrows, but not a participant, much less the principal agent, in the activities and dangers of life.

Contrasted with Tamino, the figure of the idealistic artist, is Papageno, who stands for the commoner man, the man in the street. Thoughtless, unintellectual, untouched by any desire for the things of the spirit, he is impulsive in his merriment (you cannot call it joy) and in his woe (you cannot call it grief or sorrow). He responds immediately and by instinct to any stimulus he receives, and his mind has no control, as has Tamino's, over his physical reaction to emotions, whether pleasant or the reverse. He is a jolly fellow and likeable, in spite of his partiality for the kind of low and punning wit which disfigures so many of Shakespeare's clowns and, we may add, so many of Mozart's and Beethoven's letters. His relations with Papagena, which are simply physical, though perfectly healthy, and have no ideal higher than the raising up of a large family of beings like themselves, are a presentation of the ideas of marriage held by the ordinary man. It is a marriage subject to fewer difficulties, but also incapable of attaining to so high a degree of happiness as that other. Such, in contradistinction to his ideal embodied in Tamino and Pamina, must have been Mozart's relations with Constanze, merry and playful, but wanting for the husband in those more elevated moments of mutual understanding for which his spirit must have craved.

Papageno has, as a symbol of self-expression, to correspond with Tamino's flute, a set of bells. With this instrument he expresses such ideas as enter his simple mind, ideas typical of the kind of man he is. His art, if we may call it such, is popular and vulgar, as opposed to the high and aristocratic art of Tamino. There may not have been anything actually original in the use of a glockenspiel, but there certainly is great originality in the way Mozart has used it. The elaborate accompaniment which it supplies to Papageno's second song, " Ein mädchen oder weibchen," is wholly delightful, and shows Mozart's ability to make at once the most of any new material that came to his hand. His previous compositions for various clockwork instruments had, perhaps, prepared him for this delightful ebullition of his genius. At one of the performances, as he relates to his wife, he played the glockenspiel himself, while Schikaneder (as Papageno) played a dummy on the stage. He could not resist playing a trick on the singer and added an unexpected *arpeggio* after Schikaneder had stopped his dumb-show. In the next verse the same thing happened again, and Schikaneder refused to go on, so Mozart added another chord, whereupon the actor, who was evidently an adept at " gagging," slapped his dummy instrument and cried out, " stop it ! " —much to the amusement of the audience.

Papagena has nothing to sing except her part in the philoprogenitive duet, and is quite insignificant from the musical point of view. The other comic character—for we can hardly take his villainy seriously—is Monostatos, who is kept well in the background by Schikaneder, lest he should encroach upon Papageno's preserves, and by Mozart, because he is a rather inconvenient person to have in the Temple of Wisdom. However Monostatos has one song, which is quite masterly in its agitated expression of baffled meanness, and the rest of his music is skilful, if only because it keeps him from coming too much to the fore. His place in the general scheme is signified by the remark he makes, when he has been foiled in his attempt on Pamina. "As the daughter won't have me," he says, "I will try my luck with the mother." He is a mere music-hall character of stock type and one of the remains of the original plot which made Sarastro a wicked magician and the Queen of the Night a good fairy.

The Queen is still a good fairy at her first appearance. Her first air is a conventional piece of work, modelled by Mozart, in his inexperience of writing vaudeville, upon the florid air which Mme Hofer sang in Wranitsky's *Oberon*. Josepha Hofer possessed a voice of unusual range and great agility, although, according to a witness quoted by Jahn, she was "a very unpleasing singer." Mozart turned her peculiar ability to good purpose in her second air, where the wide compass and the high florid passages for the voice are used to express the supernatural character and the hellish rage of the Queen. Jahn condemns the *fioriture* as the meretricious adornment of what "might have been a model of pathetic declamation." That was, perhaps, a natural view for a nineteenth-century critic to take at a time when singers were abusing the privileges of the *prima donna* as never before, and when the fine art of *coloratura* had sunk to the level of mountebankery. The brilliant sparkle of this air seems to me fully justified by the hard glittering effect which is obtained by a good singer, just as, in a very different way, the *bravura* airs of the C minor Mass are justified as an expression of praise, the setting-forth to God's honour of the finest achievements of man's art. The repeated high notes, the *staccato* figures and the long *roulade* of triplets in this air give to it a feeling of intense and unearthly passion, which is certainly not to be found in the average piece of *coloratura*, while the declamatory passages certainly have the strongly "pathetic" effect which Jahn admires.

The number of diverse characters and incidents in *Die Zauberflöte* and the general looseness of its construction made it quite impossible for the composer to knit the whole work together in the logical, but complex, manner, in which he had been able to treat Da Ponte's well-constructed books. The *finale* of each act is a string of episodes, involving frequent exits and entrances and even changes of scene, and the music cannot therefore be worked up to a climax in the symphonic manner of the Italian operas, where the characters are gathered together one by one in a single scene and all the threads of the plot are woven into a wonderful pattern that has its counterpart in the music. Something of this kind happens towards the end of the *finale* of the first act, where the successive entries of Pamina with Papageno, Sarastro, Monostatos with Tamino, and the chorus give an effect of increasing dramatic tension. But this method of working up the excitement is wholly absent from the second *finale*, which is a succession of more or less disjointed scenes, which are never really built together in a whole, the opera being rounded off in a very arbitrary way, which is only saved from absurdity by the magnificence of Mozart's invention. This is one of the respects in which *Die Zauberflöte* constitutes a definite break with the existing traditions of opera, and establishes a new tradition of a looser form which was to be followed by later composers in Germany. Like so many other revolutions, it was due in the first instance to fortuitous circumstances, to the chance of Mozart having to make the best of a poor job.

The other important respect in which this opera differs radically from the Italian model is not the casual result of circumstance. For in setting this German text, Mozart deliberately sought the appropriate musical idiom for his native language instead of making use of the Italian idiom. As any who have heard *Figaro* or *Don Giovanni* sung in German will bear witness, German will not go comfortably to *recitativo secco*, which so admirably suits the swift and uncomplicated Italian speech. It may have been realization of this fact that made Mozart, like

many another, accept the compromise, which was
ready to hand, of having those parts of the drama
spoken which are necessary for its explanation,
but which are at the same time quite unsuited for
expression in music. This interruption of the
music by dialogue is always detrimental to opera
as a musical work, since it interrupts the continuous flow of the music and its development
as a highly organized whole. That Mozart did
regard opera as a form having in its own way a
structural unity as real as that of a symphony is
evident from the sequence of keys in his operas.
Tonality is used both to obtain musical unity—
the main movements in an opera being in the same
or in closely related keys—and to emphasize
dramatic contrasts by the juxtaposition of two
unrelated keys. This principle has been adhered
to by other great opera composers, and an
examination of the works of Verdi (especially of
Aïda, *Otello* and *Falstaff*) on the one hand, and
of Wagner on the other, will show that they have
this, at any rate, in common. The ordinary
listener may not be conscious of the fact, but the
unifying or contrasting effect produced by the
skilful use of tonality must, nevertheless, play its
part in arousing the " pleasure " which is peculiar
to opera for all who are not tone-deaf.

This principle is apparent in *Die Zauberflöte*, as
in the Italian operas, and by its use Mozart has
attempted to link up the broken continuity of the
music. But the peculiarly German quality of the

music, to which I wish to call attention, resides not in this technical matter of musical structure, but in the way those parts of the book which are not definitely lyrical have been set to music. For them Mozart created a new style of accompanied recitative, which is as distinctly German as the recitatives of J. S. Bach or the declamation of Wagner's music-dramas. Yet it is also distinctly individual and Mozartian. The most famous passage is the dialogue between Tamino and the Priest before the Temple of Wisdom. This is a perfect example of German declamation, surpassing even that other fine passage in *Don Giovanni*, which has already been discussed, in aptness, if not in dramatic force. We may be said to stand here on the threshold of the German music-drama, which developed precisely along the lines laid down in this scene, where declamation merges naturally into melody. There is no essential difference in style between this passage and, say, the dialogue between Gurnemanz and Parsifal, but only the superficial difference due to the idiosyncrasies of Wagner's personal idiom. What Wagner aid was to develop the style to its logical conclusion, making the music flow more continuously by providing a rich polyphonic accompaniment to support the voices. Already in *Die Zauberflöte* the orchestra has begun to take that important place in the scheme which is one of the chief characteristics of later German opera. We have already noted how Mozart has used different sections of his orchestra to support the different groups of characters—a method which he had already employed, though to a much smaller extent, in *Cosi fan Tutte*, and a method of which the most complete example is to be found in *Lohengrin*, where the violins are definitely associated with the hero and the wood-wind with Elsa. Yet another kind of contrast is obtained from the orchestra in *Die Zauberflöte* ; for it is used freely and independently in the accompaniment of the " human " parts of the opera, while in those which deal with the mystery of things, it moves gravely and in more solid harmony.

It was natural that, in a work intended for a popular audience, Mozart should abandon, to some extent, the elaborate formulas of the Italian air in favour of the more catchy strophic song. Here again he is resorting to a German form, as he had done before in the songs, as opposed to the airs, in *Die Entführung*. German popular melody is just as much the basis of the grave songs of Sarastro as of the comic ditties of Papageno and Osmin, while use has also been made of that other popular element in German music, the chorale.[1]

There remain the choruses, those noble move-ments in which Mozart's religious convictions

[1] Wagner's *Die Meistersinger* is built up out of the same kind of material, strophic songs of a popular type (given, it is true, the characteristic Wag-nerian twist) and Protestant choral music. Mozart had used melodies of a popular character in his instrumental music, notably in the finales of the violin concertos in G major and D major (K. 216 and 218).

at last found the full expression, that was denied them by the conventions of the Church music of his time, though they had appeared less completely in the choruses of *Thamos* and of *Idomeneo*. The choruses are very concise and are not developed into elaborate contrapuntal movements. By this means they produce the very feeling of austere and elevated devotion which is essential to the opera. They owe, no doubt, something to Gluck's example. Indeed, Mozart was accused of having stolen the March of the Priests, which opens the second Act, from *Alceste*, to which he retorted that he could not have done so, since it still stood in Gluck's score. It is certainly true that Gluck had reached a somewhat similar point of view as that which Mozart reveals in *Die Zauberflöte*, and had done his share in laying the foundations of German opera. But whereas Gluck had arrived at this position by taking thought and, one may justly say, through a lack of true musicianship—he had failed as a composer of Italian opera before he evolved the theories which brought him fame—Mozart never appears to have bothered his head with æsthetics, but arrived at his conclusions by the light of his instinct, that is to say along a path which was entirely musical.

Die Zauberflöte was produced on September 30, 1791, but in the meantime its composition had been interrupted by two other important commissions. In July " a stranger, a tall, thin, grave-looking man," says Jahn, " dressed from head to foot in grey, and calculated from his very appearance to make a striking and weird impression, presented Mozart with an anonymous letter begging him, with many flattering allusions to his accomplishments as an artist, to name his price for composing a *Requiem*, and the shortest time in which he could undertake to complete it." Mozart, as we have noted before, was anxious to prove his capacity as a Church-composer to the new Emperor, who had abolished the innovations in Church music instituted by the Emperor Joseph and re-established the orchestras. So he accepted this commission readily, the more so as he was specifically allowed to compose the *Requiem* according to his own ideas and was to be subject to no restrictions, saving that he must not seek to discover the identity of his mysterious patron.

The composition of the *Requiem* had in turn to be postponed owing to a fresh commission, which had to be taken instantly in hand. Leopold II was to be crowned as King of Hungary at Prague on September 6, and about the middle of August Mozart was informed that he had been chosen to supply a festival opera for the occasion. He had, therefore, to complete the work in the space of three weeks. The libretto selected was Metastasio's *La Clemenza di Tito*. The main situation of the plot resembles that of Corneille's *Cinna*, but the treatment of it and the points on which emphasis is laid, are totally different. Vernon Lee writes of it :

> "What interested Metastasio was not what Titus said, but what Sextus felt ; and into Sextus's feelings he dived, bringing them out with wondrous perfection of gradation, from the first terror of finding himself before his betrayed benefactor, . . . through the stages of sickening and dizzy fear, the agonized hesitation, down to that passionate explosion of feeling, that sweet though anguished flood of tears, with which the traitor sinks down overwhelmed by the generosity of the betrayed. . . .
>
> "To conceive an emotional situation, to develop it, gradually yet swiftly, making each step, each movement, even as a musician would develop a theme, this was Metastasio's aim and his glory. To obtain opportunities for such development was his constant thought ; he was for ever seeking for pathetic situations, he loved to crowd them together. The subjects treated by the ancients and by the French did not satisfy him, they were too meagre for him. He would take the main situations from half a dozen plays and poems, and work them into one plot, combining in his *Titus* the *Cinna* of Corneille and the *Andromaque* of Racine ; weaving together Sophocles and La Motte, Ariosto and Racine, Lope and Herodotus, and then, in the prose argument prefixed to his play, referring the reader with grand vagueness to Strabo, Pliny, Sanchoniathon, any one ; as romantic as Shakespeare or Calderon, while thinking he was correct and classic as Maffei."

To those who have not Vernon Lee's ardent

enthusiasm and historic sense, the dramas of Metastasio probably seem stiff and devoid of the very richness which is here attributed to them, his eclecticism overdone, and his passion a trifle ridiculous in its manner of expression. In the present instance Titus's persistent magnanimity appears, to modern notions of drama, senseless and monotonous. Even so soon as 1791, his *Tito* was regarded, to quote Professor Dent, as " a pompous and frigid drama of Roman history such as had been fashionable in Court circles half a century earlier." Metastasio's book was shortened and remodelled by Caterino Mazzola ; and, since this meant a hasty patching and not a fundamental reconstruction of the drama according to later ideas, the last state of it was far worse than the first, which at least had a unity of style. Vernon Lee is quite ruthless about it : " The powerful opening scene between Sextus and Vitellia is fiddle-faddled into a duet ; the rapid scene of the discovered conspiracy is drawn out into a quintet ; the pathetic meeting of Sextus and Titus is fugued and twisted into a trio, and the exquisite outburst of Sextus's remorse is frittered away in a long *rondo*, in which he repeats a dozen times and to all sorts of tunes—' Tanto affanno soffre un core—nè si muore—di dolore.' " That is to say that an attempt was made to put new wine into the old bottle, to treat an opera-book designed for the very different style of Hasse and Jommelli in the new manner, which had been developed with such astonishing rapidity by Mozart. Perhaps nothing shows so plainly the change which he had brought about in operatic style as the disparity between his music and the libretto of this work, and, still more, between the quality as a whole of *Tito*, which has a good libretto of its kind, and of *Die Zauberflöte*, which has a bad libretto of any kind. There is, of course, bound to be a change in operatic conventions in any period of fifty years, but the particular direction of the advance made during the latter half of the eighteenth century and its magnitude are largely due to Mozart. This change was not made with such a flourish and did not arouse such violent passions as that which Wagner made half a century later, but it was hardly less radical and important in its effect on musical history. The very fact that it was accompanied by none of the polemics in which Wagner indulged has resulted in its extent and importance being ignored, the more so as we have no real standard of comparison, since we never see on the stage a single example of the type of opera from which Mozart broke away. But to Mozart's contemporaries the break must have been conspicuous, and its reality may very well account for the comparative ill-success of his operas with the fashionable public, who tend to conservatism and admire that which most resembles what they have admired before. His Italian operas met with favour among the intelligent few, and *Die Zauberflöte* caught the more popular ear in the way that a great work of art every now and then will do, though apparently only through some caprice of fortune.

La Clemenza di Tito failed, as any work produced under such conditions was bound to fail. It was not the kind of opera which suited Mozart's genius; it had to be written in an incredibly short space of time ; and the composer was already exhausted by overwork and by illness, which was due in large part to a constant lack of proper nourishment and the irregular life, in the matter of meals and so on, he had been living in Schikaneder's company. Whether Mozart could have produced a great " serious " opera if he had been given the time and a libretto worked out properly to suit the more modern requirements of his style, is a question which cannot be argued to any satisfying conclusion. He had to work on *Tito* during his journey to Prague with the assistance of his pupil, Süssmayr, who turned out the recitatives according to pattern and probably assisted in the scoring of the music. What we may marvel at is not the failure of the opera, but the fact that it contains music of any lasting merit at all.

The most conspicuous piece in it is the *finale* of the first act, which is sung during the burning of the Capitol. Here, for the first time, Mozart employs his soloists, all six of them, in a concerted movement with the chorus. Professor Dent cites a previous use of soloists and chorus in the *finale* of an opera by Salieri, but says that it is not a success. Mozart's *finale* is entirely successful and provides the first example of the many grand heroic scenes in subsequent Italian operas, where the solo voices vie with the chorus and at the last blend with them to bring down the curtain on a terrific climax of sound. The second act of *Aïda*, and in a rather different way the third act of *Otello* provide familiar instances. Apart from this *finale*, the opera contains two charming little duets, which may be said to owe their popularity to the fact that they are not of the stiff and formal kind which Metastasio's book presupposes in the music, and a fine concert-air—for such it always was and has actually become in practice—for contralto with basset-horn *obbligato*, " Non più di fiori." As in *Die Zauberflöte*, Mozart made use of the basset-horn to give a sombre colouring to some of the music of *La Clemenza di Tito*, though in this instance he was probably as much concerned to give a show piece to Stadler, for whom also he wrote the florid *obbligato* for clarinet in Sextus's air, " Parto, ma tu, ben mio."

Of all the people with whom Mozart came into contact, Anton Stadler seems to have been the meanest and most despicable. He sponged on Mozart consistently, borrowed money from him, whenever he learnt that there was any to be borrowed, and, when there was no money, induced Mozart to pawn his valuables in order to supply him with funds—all this, despite his knowledge of Mozart's own penury, in the name of his brotherhood as a Mason. For Stadler also belonged to the society. Yet every time his deceit and his dishonesty were discovered, Mozart forgave him, as he seems to have forgiven anyone who wronged him, through sheer good nature. For this wretch, whose portrait shows him as an ill-favoured, sneeking type of humanity with shifty eyes full of cunning and a mouth made for lying, Mozart composed, besides the *obbligati* already mentioned, a concerto for clarinet and orchestra (K. 622), which was one of his last works, and the beautiful clarinet quintet (K. 581), which was written in September, 1789.

Whatever may be said about Stadler's character as a man, he was undeniably a fine clarinettist, and if his association with Mozart was disastrous to the composer's pocket, it was of great service to one branch of his art. We have to thank this little rat of a man not only for the quintet and the concerto—just as we owe the clarinet quintet and sonatas of Brahms to his fortunate conjunction with Mühlfeld—but also the development of the clarinet and its big brother, the *corno di bassetto*, as independent voices in Mozart's later works. These instruments play an important part in all the operas after *Cosi fan Tutte*, and the basset-horn gives a peculiar colouring to the music of *Die Zauberflöte*, as we have already noted, and to the *Requiem*. The clarinet was of comparatively recent invention and, apart from the fact that its very novelty offered Mozart one more chance of giving character and originality to his music, its *timbre* was sympathetic to him and provided a high voice in the wood-wind group other than the flute, whose tone poor in overtones aroused aversion in him. He, therefore, welcomed the clarinet, whose wide compass and variety of colour in its different registers was an added advantage, and developed its possibilities to their full extent. There is hardly anything that can be done with the instrument which he did not do, and he was undoubtedly indebted to Stadler's accomplishment as a player for his rapid mastery of its technique.

Mozart left, indeed, little for others to discover about the possibilities of the instrument, and it is noticeable how Brahms follows in his quintet the technical manner of the Stadler quintet, different though the content of the two works is. Mozart's quintet is, compared with his string quintets, light and graceful. Its style is conditioned by the characteristics of the wind instrument. For while it blends admirably with the strings, the clarinet is bound to stand out from them, and has to be used as a contrasting solo voice rather than as one of a group in which each member has equal rights. The wide sweep of the clarinet's compass, its aptitude for elaborate figures and the rhapsodical character which these give to the music, are fully exploited by Mozart. The instrument enters with a sweeping *arpeggio*, which at once asserts its individuality, and throughout the work it treats the material in its own characteristic way, avoiding any slavish imitation of the strings. The result is a work of peculiar charm, developed freely along the lines which best suit the combination of instruments. Indeed, the quintet is one of the best examples of Mozart's euphony, of his unfailing flair for finding the right treatment for any given combination, and his ability to touch lightly upon the deepest chords of emotion.

There is tender sentiment in the first movement, which deepens a little in the slow movement, where the instruments *sing* for our enchantment as they rarely do even in Mozart's music.[1] In the Minuet with its remarkable *Trio* Mozart is once more on the borderline of the *scherzo*, in Beethoven's sense. But it is the final variations which show his genius most clearly. Taking a simple melody of the nursery-rhyme type,[2] he develops from it a movement, in which we catch glimpses of all manner of hidden mysteries and deep meanings. Yet the essentially naïve quality of the material is never lost to sight. Mozart does not twist the theme out of recognition, or develop it in the grand manner until the final

---

[1] The historically minded, who may think this high-falutin,' have their compensation ; for they can hold up this movement, which is in the form of an air, as an excellent example of the influence of Italian vocal music upon the instrumental music of Germany in the eighteenth century.

[2] It resembles somewhat the tune of " Ah, vous dirai-je maman ? " on which he had written a set of pianoforte variations (K. 265) during his visit to Paris in 1778.

transfiguration, like a nobleman descended from lowly ancestors, does not recognize its origin in the humble little theme. Yet he is not content merely to embellish the melody with graceful ornaments, which was all that he did in his youthful variations for pianoforte, but has pressed from it the last drop of significance. All the feeling which this tune evoked in Mozart's soul is here set forth for us, and no better answer could be given to the question, " What do you mean by Mozartian ? " than the performance before the enquirer of these variations from the clarinet quintet.

To turn from this work, so blithe and full of spirit, to the *Requiem* Mass is to face a contrast so painful that I have lingered, a little garrulously perhaps, over the quintet, in order to defer as long as possible the consideration of Mozart's last and strangest work. The mysterious manner in which the *Requiem* was commissioned has already been related. The oddness of it made a deep impression on Mozart's imagination, and when, at the very moment of his departure to Prague for the production of *La Clemenza di Tito*, the stranger reappeared to enquire how the work was progressing, it seemed to Mozart, already overwrought mentally and physically, that here was in very truth a visitant from another world come to summon him away. The idea became an obsession, and he could not banish from his mind the conviction that he was composing the *Requiem* against his own death.

The explanation of the mystery was simple, though strange enough. The messenger was the steward of Count Franz von Walsegg, a minor nobleman who had a small Court at Stuppach. This gentleman had ambitions in the direction of musical composition. But since he had the good sense to realize his own inability to write music, he commissioned others, who had the necessary training, to supply him with compositions, which were well paid for and then passed off on his Court as the products of his own genius. His wife had died recently, and he evidently felt that this was an occasion on which he would be expected to turn out, under the stimulus of his grief, a really first-rate work. So he had the further good sense to apply for a *Requiem* in her honour to one who had the reputation of being a first-rate composer. He seems to have been disappointed at the low price of fifty ducats which Mozart demanded ; for he promised him a further sum on the completion of the work. Perhaps, like many art-patrons, he could not believe that a work was good unless it was also expensive.

In the present instance the deceiver—if we suppose his Court was really taken in by him—was himself deceived. For of the *Requiem*, which was handed to him some time after Mozart's death, a part is not of his composition. Count von Walsegg was, indeed, the victim of a clever forgery. Constanze, left destitute with two children, did not scruple to get the balance of the money promised by delivering to von Walsegg a score completed by Süssmayr in a hand almost indistinguishable from his master's. Then, much to the discomfiture of the amateur, who had the *Requiem* performed as a work of his own composition in December, 1793, she allowed it to be given under her husband's name. When she further arranged for its publication by Messrs Breitkopf and Härtel, the Count, who had at any rate bought and paid for the rights of the work, felt that this was going too far and brought an action against Mozart's widow. However, the action was settled out of court and the Count even allowed his copy to be used for the revision of the proofs.

There is, indeed, no more romantic story in the whole history of music than that connected with the *Requiem* Mass. It has all the materials for imaginative embroidery—a dying composer, a mysterious visitant, an uncompleted work. There is, too, for those who like scandal, the double deception practised by Constanze on the Count and by the Count upon the world—that is to say his own little Court. No wonder that legends grew about the already fantastic facts like barnacles upon a moored hulk! It took an inquest by experts to sift the true from the false, and to find some common measure in the various conflicting statements made by Constanze and by Süssmayr. The experts pronounced for the authenticity of the greater part of the work, wherein they had the support of Beethoven, whose sole comment upon the essay of its chief detractor was to scribble upon it the words : " Oh ! you arch ass ! "

But there are even now some who do not accept this decision. MM. de Wyzewa and de Saint-Foix state categorically and without argument, since the *Requiem* does not come within the scope of the main part of their book, that the *Requiem* and *Kyrie* are the only movements which Mozart certainly completed. " As to the rest of the work," they continue, " everything tends to the belief that Mozart wrote only the *Recordare*, the *Confutatis* and the first notes of the *Lacrimosa*, which themselves must have been revised and scored by his pupil." Similarly Mr William Watson seeks to prove that Mozart's share in the work was negligible, though he admits somewhat inconsistently that Süssmayr was incapable of writing the music, which is consequently attributed to him.[1]

The facts are, briefly, that on his return from Prague in September Mozart completed *Die Zauberflöte* by writing the overture, the march and chorus of the Priests, Papageno's song in Act II and the *finale*, besides orchestrating the whole, and then started work on the *Requiem*. The first two numbers were completed and exist in

[1] See " An Astounding Forgery," by William Watson, in *Music and Letters*, January, 1927.

Mozart's handwriting. There also exist sketches for all but four of the remaining numbers, which consist of the whole of the voice-parts together with the figured bass and sufficient indications of the instrumentation for a capable musician, with whom the composer had discussed his ideas many times over, to complete them in accordance with his intentions. Of the four other numbers, the beginning of one (the *Lacrimosa*) is admittedly by Mozart, while the final section of the work has been set to the music of the *Requiem* and *Kyrie*. This leaves to Süssmayr's credit three whole numbers (*Sanctus, Benedictus,* and *Agnus Dei*) and part of one other (*Lacrimosa*), besides the completion of Mozart's sketches. An examination of the sketches in detail proves that all the things which strike us in a performance of the *Requiem* as being most remarkable, were either fully worked out or at least clearly indicated in Mozart's own hand. For example in the *Confutatis*, the whole of the first violin part of the latter half of the movement (from the words " oro supplex ẹt acclinis,") which is one of the most arresting passages in the whole work, is complete in the sketch, and the entry of the basset-horns and bassoons is cued in. While, therefore, a large part of the actual score is Süssmayr's handiwork, the essential things, those which make it great music, are indisputably Mozart's own.

Of the movements of which no sketches by

Mozart are in existence, the *Sanctus* and *Osanna* may be certainly attributed to Süssmayr. This number is competent and mediocre. If it appeared in a work about which there was no dispute, it might pass for authentic Mozart in an uninspired moment. The same may be said of the *Benedictus*. But here a doubt arises, for the first five notes of its theme appear in the first of the exercises set by Mozart for a niece of the Abbè Stadler in 1784, while there is also a resemblance to it in the fifth of the pianoforte variations (K. 500) written in 1786. Mr Oldman, who has kindly supplied me with this information, adds : " But there is not much in this. The thematic figure itself may well have been a commonplace of the time. Judged as a whole the three pieces of music are as different as they well could be." So I think this resemblance may be set down as fortuitous and the *Benedictus* safely judged to be genuine Süssmayr.

The *Agnus Dei*, alone of the movements which do not appear in Mozart's sketches, reaches the level of the authentic parts of the work, and long before I had examined the evidence in any detail I was convinced by hearing the music that no one but Mozart himself could have written the opening section of the movement. It is not unreasonable to suppose that Süssmayr had before him some sketches which have not survived. At least it is certain that nothing in Süssmayr's acknowledged works warrants the opposite supposition that he was capable of writing the first part of the *Agnus Dei*. Even Gottfried Weber, Beethoven's " arch ass," who first seriously disputed the authenticity of the *Requiem*, confessed that in the parts which are with reason attributed to Süssmayr, " there were flowers which never grew in Süssmayr's garden." Personally I believe —and I have found, since I first expressed this opinion, more support for it from various sources than I expected—that Mozart wrote the first strain of the *Agnus*, even as he wrote the first few bars of the *Lacrimosa.* It is altogether so typically Mozartian in feeling, and the figure of the violin accompaniment is so characteristic and original that it is almost impossible to accept it as a brilliant imitation. Süssmayr may very well, on the other hand, be responsible for the sickly-sweet sentimentality of the second strain (" dona eis requiem.") My conjecture has further support from the way in which the movement proceeds. For the subsequent treatment of the first strain is of the ordinary kind, which might be expected of the pupil, and is devoid of those surprising turns which the master alone could imagine. All this is, of course, mere conjecture and is not susceptible of proof, for Süssmayr may, like many another third-rate composer, have risen for once above his normal level.

Yet even when we deny to Süssmayr the credit for all those things which impress us most deeply in the *Requiem*, we must acknowledge our admiration for the way in which he carried out his task. /No one but a sound musician, who was thoroughly conversant with his master's style and his intentions in the particular work, could have made so good a job of the patching together of the scraps that Mozart left. His ability shows at its best in the finishing of the *Lacrimosa*. But, quite apart from details, he deserves our gratitude for having realized for us as a complete whole the masterpiece, which still existed for the most part only in Mozart's mind when he died. Had Süssmayr not immediately finished the work, while the spell of his master's genius was still strong upon him, we should be the poorer, and the *Requiem* would be a mere mass of fragments impossible to perform. /

Having cut a path, which all may not, perhaps, be ready to follow, through the undergrowth of controversy which surrounds the *Requiem* Mass, we can pass on to the examination of the work itself. With the exception of the *Ave Verum* composed for Stoll at Baden, Mozart had written no Church music since the unfinished Mass in C minor of 1782. It has already been remarked that Mozart regarded the commission for the *Requiem* as an opportunity to prove his capacity in this direction. To this desire on his part may be due his adherence to the conventional style in the opening movements, the *Requiem* and *Kyrie*. Yet although no new ground is broken in these sections. from the very first bars of the instrumental introduction, with its sad burden for the wood-wind accompanied by the heavy tread of staccato chords on strings and organ, we are aware of being in the presence of a deeply felt and personal sorrow. The first mournful petition for eternal rest, against which the strings sob out a broken figure, is followed by a moment of consolation, when after the lovely second subject has been hinted at, a solo soprano intones a quotation from the Psalms ("Te decet hymnus, Deus, in Sion") to an old chorale theme. The entry of the soprano voice at this point is magical in its effect. Mozart had done the same kind of thing before in the C minor Mass, and a comparison of the two movements will exemplify better than anything else the enormous advance in sensitiveness and subtlety of expression which he had made during the nine years that saw the creation of all his most important works. In the *Requiem* there is complete assurance and mastery, the use of the *chorale* itself at this point being in itself a stroke of genius.[1] This new material is then developed by the chorus in a passionate supplication that their prayer may be heard, after which the second subject is displayed in all its beauty. This movement proves, as Jahn says, " the old forms, with their fixed laws and strongly marked features, to have more than a merely abstract or historical value ; it proves them to be in fact, when

[1] Jahn points out that Mozart had made use of this same melody as a *cantus firmus* in the early cantata, *Betulia Liberata*.

artistically conceived and scientifically handled, capable of giving appropriate expression to the deepest emotion in which the human heart finds vent."

The *Kyrie* is an even more remarkable instance of this power of expression within a form circumscribed by strict rules. For it is an elaborate double fugue, the subjects of which have been discovered by the industrious Jahn in an " Hallelujah " chorus in Handel's *Joseph!* Yet, while the debt to Handel is clear at any rate in the general style—if not in the conscious choice of the subjects, which are after all of the ordinary kinds that suggest themselves for fugal treatment— the manner of working out the material is entirely original, and, in this context, the first subject seems to look forward into the next century towards the first movement of Beethoven's last pianoforte sonata. The development of the music leads to a climax of the greatest agitation by way of a series of extraordinary chromatic passages, which Gottfried Weber contemptuously and expressively termed *Gurgeleien*, before sinking to a more resigned and dignified mood at the close.

It is quite possible that in choosing to follow the conventional practice in his treatment of these opening movements, Mozart was influenced as much by artistic motives as by the desire to show his mastery of the old Church style. He may, in fact, have seen that the *Dies Irae*, which follows, required the contrast of a formal introduction in order to set off to the fullest possible extent the more brutish emotions aroused by its verses as compared with those of the Liturgy proper. For this poem, which dates to the middle of the thirteenth century, is an interpolation in the Mass for the Dead. It embodies all those terrible ideas of the pains of Hell and the tortures of the eternally damned contrasted with the hardly won bliss of the righteous, which were so vivid to the mediæval imagination and proved the chief mainstay of the Church's power. The *Dies Irae* is, indeed, the counterpart in words of those strange pictures of the Last Judgment, which still awe the spectator by the crude violence of their horrors, even though he may be amused by the blue and yellow devils pitch-forking emaciated bodies in every contortion of physical anguish into the fiery mouths of enormous dragons. You may still see these scenes enacted in the stained glass windows of many churches, notably at Fairford, whose windows must be among the latest to be installed while the belief in this kind of physical torment after death was still a living reality to all good Christians.

But when this belief had waned, at least among the more thoughtful, it still held its power to stimulate the artist. One cannot believe that Rubens accepted the facts, which he depicted with such magnificent gusto in his " Fall of the Damned," as anything more than the material for a fine decoration. So the *Dies Irae* appeared to

Mozart an opportunity for a splendid and terrible musical design, in which, as in Rubens's picture, the horrible details, relics of a past tradition, would be subordinated to the unity of the whole and would, therefore, sink into insignificance and so lose their brutality. But there entered another factor—the delusions under which Mozart laboured concerning the work on which he was engaged. For once, a note of hysterical passion sounded in his music, ordinarily so disciplined and so detached from any morbid reference to his own personal feelings. It is this note of hysteria which makes the *Requiem* one of the most painful works to contemplate, painful in the way that the cry of an animal caught in a snare or the Pathetic Symphony of Tchaikovsky, who was expert in the expression of self-pity, are painful.

The contrast between the *Requiem* and the serene nobility of *Die Zauberflöte* is as remarkable as their resemblances. Both works treat of the same supreme ordeal which mankind has to face ; the one with the calm and intellectual philosophy of the Mason, the other with the more emotional faith, with its complement of troubling doubts, of the Catholic. Their common factors are in the general style of the music as well as in the predominance in the orchestration of the basset-horn and trombones,[1] although the instrumentation of

[1] It is to be observed that in those movements, for the completion or composition of which Süssmayr is responsible, the use of the trombones becomes more and more conventional and the orchestration generally thicker. In *Die Zauberflöte*, in *Don Giovanni* and in those parts of the *Requiem* which

the opera is far more elaborate than that of the Mass. The *Requiem* shows a falling-off, if not always from the musical standard, at least from the untroubled confidence of *Die Zauberflöte*, which is not unnatural in a man wasted by disease and face to face with the inevitable foe whom in better days he had been able to regard with an unflinching eye.

The words of the *Dies Irae* insist upon the very terrors of death, which that noble profession of faith denies. The sick man fell under their spell and his music became filled with the agony of death as no other work has been, with the possible exception of *The Dream of Gerontius*. Moving and wonderful though the *Requiem* is, and the more moving on account of the circumstances in which it was composed, it is to *Die Zauberflöte* that we should look for the true expression of Mozart's philosophy of life and death.

When Mozart returned to Vienna after the production of *La Clemenza di Tito*, Constanze, who had accompanied him to Prague, retired once more to Baden. On September 30 *Die Zauberflöte* was produced. The fate of the opera hung

---

he finished, including the rather unsuccessful *Tuba mirum*, Mozart employed the trombones with restraint, reserving them for special effects. Süssmayr uses them as a normal part of the orchestra in support of the voices, as Mozart had himself done in his C minor Mass, following the ordinary practice of Church musicians at the time.

in the balance during the first act, as well it might have done, for that first audience must have been very puzzled by it. Mozart, who conducted, was in a state of panic and rushed round to the stage, where Schikaneder tried to comfort him. During the second act, however, the audience took to the work and its success was assured. It grew in popularity at every performance and all Vienna flocked to the small, unfashionable theatre to see the latest thing.

The success came just too late. Mozart set to work with feverish haste upon the *Requiem*. He still wrote cheerfully to Constanze, describing the success of his opera, and found time to take his son, Carl, who was boarded out at Perchtholdsdorf, out for a day's amusement.[1] But gradually the obsession of his morbid fancies grew upon him. Even so early as September (the exact date is not given) he wrote a strange letter in Italian, which seems to be addressed to Da Ponte in response to a suggestion that he should quit Vienna and seek his fortune in England. This letter runs as follows :

" My dear Sir,

I wish I could follow your advice, but how can I do so ? I feel stunned, I reason with difficulty, and cannot get rid of the vision of this unknown man. I

---

[1] He seems to have been as affectionate a father as he was a son and husband, though Carl did not occupy a large place in his thoughts, if we may judge from the letters, wherein he is sent nothing beyond a loving message or the recommendation for a dose of rhubarb.

see him perpetually; he entreats me, presses me, and impatiently demands the work. I go on writing, because composition tires me less than resting. Otherwise I have nothing more to fear. I know from what I suffer that the hour is come; I am at the point of death; I have come to an end before having had the enjoyment of my talent. Life was indeed so beautiful, my career began under such fortunate auspices; but one cannot change one's own destiny. No one can measure his own days, one must resign oneself, it will be as providence wills, and so I finish my death-song; I must not leave it incomplete.

MOZART.[1]

VIENNA,
September, 1791."

These are the expressions of a man on the verge of a nervous breakdown. Since he could take no rest, the inevitable consequences followed. In the middle of October Constanze returned from Baden, alarmed by reports of his condition. She summoned a physician and took away the score of the *Requiem*. By way of a diversion, he composed a Masonic Cantata (K. 623) with words by Schikaneder, which was finished by the middle of November. He managed even to conduct its performance. But the improvement in his health was only momentary. He started work on the *Requiem* once more, spasmodically, turning from one movement to another.

His melancholy returned with redoubled force,

[1] Prof. Dent's translation.

303

and his morbid fancies bred others more monstrous than themselves, so that there is nothing strange, but only something terrible and pitiful, in his delusion that he had been poisoned by his old rival, Salieri, whose genuine delight in *Die Zauberflöte* he had noted with much pleasure a few weeks before. During the last weeks of the month his exhausted brain gradually gave way, until only one function of it, the musical, was working with any efficiency. To the very end he could speak rationally of music ; follow in imagination the performances of *The Magic Flute*, noting by his watch the passage of its scenes ; and add to the *Requiem* a touch here and there until the unfinished *Lacrimosa* became blurred by the tears in his own eyes. Music was his life and was the last faculty left to him in life. Early on the morning of December 5, the fitful gleam was extinguished and with it life passed from his body.

Constanze, who had taken so little care of her husband during his life, being preoccupied with her own illnesses, was prostrated with grief. She retired to her bed after inscribing in an album, which was found on Wolfgang's bed, the record of his death, of their eight years of unbroken bliss, and of her one desire—to join him at once and for ever. She was, no doubt, as sincere as her shallow nature allowed, for she belonged to that class of person whose emotions flare up readily enough, but burn out quickly for lack of solid

material. She probably contributed something
to Mozart's exhaustion ; for everything points to
her being one of those invalids who borrow such
health as they have from others, whose vitality
is thereby sapped. She was not the woman
to give a delicate and sensitive husband the
physical support he needed, any more than she
could enter into true companionship with his
mind.

The widow received many visitors, among them
van Swieten, who advised her not to be extravagant over the funeral. His advice was followed
only too well. It did not occur to Mozart's rich
friend that he might suitably have spent a little
of his wealth upon giving the composer a decent,
not to say a worthy, burial. So on the afternoon
of December 6, a few friends and admirers—van
Swieten, Süssmayr and Salieri among them—
assembled for a service at St. Stephen's Church.
After which, as a severe storm was raging, the
mourners dispersed, leaving the body of Mozart
to be huddled by the sexton into a pauper's grave
in the churchyard of St. Mark's. The grave was
not marked, and, when Constanze was well
enough to visit it, no one could tell her where
her husband lay. Its exact site has never yet been
ascertained with certainty. But, in truth, Mozart
never was in need of the kind of marble monument
which adorns the grave at Salzburg shared by
Constanze and the father-in-law, who detested
her—a singular instance of poetic justice ! For

Mozart had created his own monument—a living and mobile memorial, which has spread world-wide now, and is set up with honour everywhere in the hearts of those who love his music.

CONCLUSION

LIKE the runner who brought the news of Marathon to Athens, Mozart fell exhausted at the moment of triumph. Those who are interested in *post-mortem* details will find support for entering in a certificate of the cause of his death such various diseases as typhus, meningitis, influenza, phthisis and many other items from the medical dictionary. For laymen it will be sufficient to say that Mozart died of continual overwork and only less continual under-nourishment during the twenty-five years since Leopold dragged him round Europe as a show for amateurs of the abnormal. But it matters really very little of what Mozart died. What does matter is when he died—in the thirty-sixth year of his life, in the last decade of the century. Of no man, who has been cut off thus in his prime—not of Schubert or Mendelssohn, of Shelley or Keats, not even of Purcell—can we say with so much assurance that his death deprived us of a new development in art, the nature of which cannot even be imagined. It has been argued that Mozart died, having completed his task, dried up his well of inspiration and worked from his particular vein the last ounce of ore. How far this is from the truth will be perceived by anyone who cares to examine the works of his last year and to compare them with those of even the year or two before. He will be astonished at the new turn which Mozart's genius had taken, and at the recuperative powers of his brain, which could achieve such a development while his physical strength was quickly failing. There is no reason whatever why, if success had come a few months earlier and the composer had been able to take the rest and to obtain the food he required, he should not have lived on to an age nearer to the average span of human life. He suffered, so far as is known, from no organic complaint, only from a delicacy of physique which was unable to endure the exceptional strain put upon it—a strain which made his body receptive to and unable to combat whichever of the malignant diseases it was that actually killed him. Had he not been subjected to that strain, he would have had a reasonable expectancy, as the actuaries say, of at any rate twenty-five more years of life. He would have been only seventy-one, when Beethoven died. Of that age—the age of the Wagner of *Parsifal*—it might have been reasonable to talk of an exhausted mind, a well dried up, a vein worked out—or whatever metaphor happens to fall from the florid pen of the writer. But of thirty-five it is ludicrous.

On the other hand a distinguished critic has suggested that, had Mozart lived on, the face of musical history during the last century would have been fundamentally changed. " He would have done something in opera and symphony," says this authority, "compared with which his own *Zauberflöte* and ' Jupiter ' would have appeared as tentative experiments, and yet something which would have been quite independent of the hectic tone which Beethoven introduced decisively into nineteenth-century music with the ' Eroica.' It is not quite idle to speculate about this, because now, looking back over what has been essentially Beethoven's century of music, it is quite clear that something was lost from music at the beginning of it which may be fairly attributable to Mozart's untimely death. The loss seems to account for some at least of the vague groping of twentieth-century music. One cannot, for example, hear such things as the quartets of Jarnach and Hindemith, or Sibelius's sixth symphony without feeling that the composers are searching in their different ways after types of musical expression which, obliterating that lush emotionalism characteristic of all the great output of the nineteenth century, would recapture something of the pure thinking in sound which makes the *finale* of the ' Jupiter ' one of the mountain peaks of music."

That is one, and a possible, answer to the question, What would Mozart have accomplished if he had lived to the normal span ? But I do not think it is quite the right one. Mozart was moving with the times. It is safe to say that the style of the " Jupiter " Symphony, in so far as it amounts to pure thinking in sound, would not have been adhered to without modification in any symphony Mozart might have composed after 1791. Already in such comparatively insignificant works as the quartet in F major and the E flat quintet the germs of a new style with a distinctly dramatic and hectic tendency are conspicuous, and if the Overture to *Die Zauber-flöte* is an example of pure thinking in sound, does not that description apply also to the even more dramatic C minor symphony of Beethoven? Indeed, the more one examines the last works of Mozart, even if the *Requiem* is left out of account in view of the special circumstances in which it was written—circumstances which tended to make it hectic and even hysterical—the more convinced one becomes that Mozart was rapidly approaching a point of view which would soon have brought him to a position in regard to his art similar to that of Beethoven—or, shall we say? to a definitely nineteenth-century standpoint.

For I do not wish to imply that Mozart would ever have become " another Beethoven," or that, impressionable as he was by outside influences, he would have fallen more deeply under the spell of the rising star than he had under that of Haydn—since each man of genius must always remain essentially himself and inevitably loses his claim to the title of genius when he sinks to the level of belonging to someone's school. But I do suggest that, had he lived, he would have developed his new manner in a way which we cannot indeed imagine, but which would have added to his great works in the branches of symphony, of chamber-music and of opera, others which would have stood level in the same class as the great works of Beethoven, instead of being, as are the works we know, in a class distinct from and therefore not really comparable with the works of the younger man. A Mozart living on into the nineteenth century might have made the transition from the " classical " to the " romantic " less abrupt ; he would hardly have influenced the course of musical history by perpetuating a tradition which was already passing away, even in his own works, when he died.

All this is, of its very nature, mere speculation, inconclusive, and therefore, to the notions of some, senseless. It will be more profitable to examine what the actual quality of Mozart's music is. In the first place there is the charm of his music, almost feminine in its nature, but not effeminate as Chopin's is at times. For the most graceful and elegant movement is always built round the scaffolding of a well-defined form, and, as in good architecture, this form is clearly apparent in the finished work, whatever embellishments may have sprung from his fancy to adorn it. Yet the form is rarely stiff, and in the important works, at any rate, never becomes a mere formula. There are, indeed, certain *clichés*, which occur again and again in the bridging of one theme

to another or in the type of ornamentation—just
as cherubs or bunches of fruit or flowers will
recur on different buildings of the same style—
but these formulas, whether they are really
Mozartian or part of the current coinage of the
eighteenth century, are merely the superficial
characteristics of the idiom of a person or an age.
It is of these formulas that Wagner was thinking,
when he spoke of " the clattering of dishes." Yet
his own music is not less full of similar mannerisms,
which serve to fill up those inevitable gaps
between the moments when he had something
really important and vital to say. Indeed, one
criterion of the greatness of music is the frequency
of these moments and their well-arranged relationship to one another. For a song or a short piece
of instrumental music may be a single and
indivisible flash of inspiration, one of these
" moments " complete in itself and impossible
to subject to any addition or subtraction. But
a long work, such as an opera or a symphony,
must provide breathing-spaces (if only for the
sake of the listener), when the composer falls
back upon the common idiom of his time. We
cannot absorb continuous " originality " by the
hour, and when a composer, as some of the
modern German school attempt to do, presents
us with a sort of meat-extract of his ideas, from
which all charm and adornment and everything
that is not considered by the composer to be
absolutely of the essence of it has been boiled

away, the resulting flavour is unpalatable and uninteresting by reason of the very strength of its concentration.

Mozart is the supreme example of the composer who could work with perfect freedom within the limits of a four-square form. He had learnt discipline in the highest sense, which is that he knew exactly when he might break the rules. He could give free play to his fertile imagination without running the risk of his music losing shape, and on this account he has the advantage of Schubert, who was far more prolific in melodic invention. Indeed, though it is a commonplace to speak of Mozart's " tunefulness," when one comes to examine his music, it is remarkable how little sustained melody there is in it compared with that of Haydn or Schubert, and even of Beethoven or Wagner. I say " even," because the two composers last named are, on the whole, more inclined to build up their music from short themes than from long, flowing melodies. Yet the one could make that noble melody in the ninth symphony—and mar it by his handling of it !—while the other could give us the fervent lyricism of Walther's *Preislied*. There is nothing in Mozart's music comparable with these things. For all its appearance of melodic beauty, it is made of little scraps, often like many of Beethoven's quite insignificant in themselves, which are so joined together in euphony and are made to throw out so many tender shoots or delicate ornaments, that one is astonished on analysing the material to find how little there really is to go upon. Of course, exceptions abound. To take familiar instances, there are the slow movement of the *Kleine Nacht-Musik*, and the flowing and unbroken line of " Deh ! vieni non tardar," which is perhaps the loveliest single thing Mozart ever wrote. But these are exceptions, and they occur more frequently in the operas, that is to say in vocal music, than in the symphonies and quartets.

It is a commonplace of modern criticism to regard Mozart and Wagner as the two poles of music, opposites in every respect. The anti-Wagnerian of to-day, both here and in Germany, fights under the banner of Mozart. But this antithesis between classic purity and turbulent emotionalism is really a false one. It is a survival from the old pretty notion of Mozart as a dear little innocent, in whose mouth butter would not melt. How far from the human reality of the composer this picture is ! So also is the notion that his music is no more than elegant, gay, graceful, and undisturbed by deep-felt passion. His music is intensely emotional, and its moving effect is produced by precisely the same technical means, to which Wagner's music owes most of its lusciousness, that is, by the use of chromaticism within the range of diatonic harmony. To his contemporaries the outstanding quality of Mozart's music was its melancholy ; he was compared with, among painters, Domenichino. It was only less overwhelming than Wagner's was to a later generation by reason of the smaller forces employed. He did not flood his audience with wave upon wave of tremendous sound until their senses were stunned, but his music seemed far more moving than it does to us who have the whole of nineteenth-century music interposed between us and it. Yet, now that that century has passed and we are realizing that its ideas and ideals are not the only ones or even the best to which man can aspire, we have reached a position at which the music of the eighteenth century, above all of Mozart, is infinitely more appealing than it was to the average listener of thirty years ago.

But there are, nevertheless, two fundamental differences that divide Mozart from Wagner, and they are differences rather of temperament than of technique. For Wagner had, no less than Mozart, a wonderful sense of structure, and developed the symphonic form to the utmost limit of freedom without allowing it to become shapeless. The first difference lies, then, in the fact that Mozart's sensuousness is impersonal, whereas that of Wagner is always egotistic and, one might say, self-indulgent. That is the dividing line between the music of the two centuries, of which each of these composers is typical, though Mozart was tending at the end of his life towards the latter attitude of mind. For we can hardly listen to the *Requiem* without feeling something of that same almost physical heart-ache which *Tristan und Isolde* causes in those who are not insensitive or who do not stubbornly refuse to admit to the " weakness " of being moved in that way. The pain is sharpened when we are aware of the circumstances in which the two works were composed ; and, although this knowledge is external to the music and makes it neither better nor worse as music, the very fact that it enlarges our understanding of their meaning proves that they belong to the same category of self-expressionism, whereas *Tristan* and *Figaro* cannot be said to have any such common denominator.

It is true, of course, that everything a composer writes, that is worth writing, comes from the inner experience of his life. *Figaro* is the work of the man who was Wolfgang Mozart and who married Constanze Weber, and of no other, just as *Tristan* is the work of Richard Wagner, who loved, among others, Mathilde Wesendonck. But, while we feel that *Tristan* is a " human document " intended to win us to Wagner's side of the argument, and a justification of his conduct, *Figaro* is devoid of any ulterior motive. It is not that Mozart had no " case " to put ; he had, in his different way, quite as much cause for a grievance against the world as ever Wagner had. But it was not the way of his nature or of his time to use as material for his art personal feelings in what are, after all, small and unimportant matters compared with the eternities.

CONCLUSION

The second respect in which Mozart's music differs fundamentally from that of Wagner is the complete absence from it of any self-consciousness. Wagner composed according to æsthetic theories which he had worked out in his mind and on paper. At least, he thought he did ; for there were times when the pure musician in him overmastered the theorist. Mozart never seems to have bothered his head about theories at any time. He mastered the technique of composition in all its branches, and his inspiration did the rest. He held no views about what an opera or a symphony should be or do. A symphony was for him just a piece of musical thinking to be expressed in the best possible way. That way was the form he had learnt from his elders, but it must yield to the needs of the free expression of his thought. His development of the symphonic form owed nothing to any intellectual ideas on the subject.

In opera his intuitive sense of dramatic effect guided his inspiration no less surely. Although there are passages in his letters, notably in those about *Idomeneo*, which may be quoted in support of theories, those theories are never formulated by him explicitly in words, but existed as part of his common sense somewhere at the back of his consciousness. We cannot but feel the vast difference that this attitude of mind makes, when we hear the music of the two men. When, however, Wagner can forget himself and lose self-consciousness, as he does, to take an example, in the quintet in *Die Meistersinger*, his music suddenly ceases to be " Wagnerian " and becomes just music no different in any respect, save in its idiom, from the music of Mozart.

These two characteristics of Mozart's music—its impersonal quality and the absence from it of any self-consciousness—make it all the more absurd to talk of immorality or its opposite in connection with his art. For, whatever may be said about the place occupied by moral qualities in the art of the nineteenth century, in the case of Mozart's music the question does not arise since these qualities have no place in its composition. On the other hand, it is difficult to believe, as Professor Dent has suggested in *Terpander*, that a work of art, having that lasting value which is one of the necessary qualifications for the title of " great," can be created, as it were in a vacuum, by an intellectual process, without any basis in the emotional experience of the creator. This is to divorce art from morality, sincerity, and indeed from all human feeling with a vengeance ! And it is this divorce, which follows as an excessive reaction upon a century of wedded life between morality and art, that accounts in part for the barrenness of that school of modern music, which is consciously and deliberately based upon this intellectual principle.

There is a middle way between these extremes, which is to admit an indirect connection between the artist's moral character and his creations.

For it is hardly possible that a man whose soul is utterly devoid of nobility can give sincere utterance—and I think sincerity *does* enter into the matter—to noble ideas ; although it does not follow that flaws in the character of the artist— Mozart's " naughtiness ", Beethoven's petty dishonesties, or Wagner's pusillanimity—will inevitably cause corresponding flaws to appear in everything he creates. For it is one of the miracles of artistic creation that, like the refiner's fire, it burns away all that is worthless or irrelevant and leaves the pure gold. But this presupposes the raising of the inspiration to an incandescent heat capable of performing this act of welding and of purification. When incandescence is reached, provided that the artist is master of his material and can subordinate the details to the unity of the whole design, the actual subject-matter loses whatever moral significance it may have and is merged in the artistic significance of the perfect whole, which is one and indivisible. It is true to say that in so far as a work of art strikes one as indecent, it falls short of being truly artistic. In those drawings of the Fall of the Damned, to which reference has already been made, it is possible to find details which would be shocking if they appeared in the work of a lesser artist—as, indeed, are many details in the pictures of Jerome Bosch. But Rubens's power of design and his organization of rhythm is so great that these details no longer stand out or catch the eye, but merely add their quota to the pell-mell horror of the scene depicted. They are, moreover, approached, although with a gusto that rejected nothing in human experience, from an entirely impersonal point of view. Rubens aimed at producing a magnificent design, not at preaching a sermon or pointing a moral.

Although we cannot attribute to him the robust appetite of the Flemish painter, Mozart accepted no less the whole experience of the life of his time and rejected nothing. But such was the heat of his creative inspiration at its highest that he touched nothing which he did not turn to the adornment of his art. No one, unless gifted with a prudish curiosity to seek out impropriety, could find anything to offend him in *Figaro* or *Don Giovanni*. These operas are neither models of good conduct nor the products of a licentious imagination. They are works of art. If we feel, as we can hardly fail to do, that there runs through them an under-current of moral indignation, we may be sure that it flows unconsciously from the background of the composer's mentality, that is from the moral character which lies beyond conscious intellectual processes. The moral indignation is not put there deliberately like the philosophical theories in *The Ring* or the *nobilmente* at the head of a movement by Elgar.

It was, therefore, just of Brahms, more percipient than most of his contemporaries, to speak of Mozart's " purity," by which he meant that he found in Mozart's music a perfect union of form and feeling, from which all dross had been purged away. This perfection was only attained by the strictest intellectual discipline, and at first sight Mozart may seem to provide one more example for those psychological investigators, who maintain that a man and his art go by opposites, that the composer puts into his music those qualities which are absent from his character. Mozart was, indeed, as undisciplined in some respects as either Beethoven or Wagner. May not this very fact prove, however, not that his music is the opposite of his character, but rather that the sense of proportion, which is so evident in his symphonies, also ruled his conduct to the extent of making him regard as of little account the petty affairs which occupy so much time in the life of the average man? He was, moreover, like most significant artists, " of more than ordinary organic sensibility ", to use Wordsworth's phrase, and was no exception in finding that it cost an effort to overcome that shrinking from affairs which is characteristic of the artist—an effort which he did not always bring himself to make. This is always a dangerous plea to enter in favour of the artist, since it has so often been advanced by men who would excuse themselves from the performance of worldly duties on the score of artistic creations which are worthless or even non-existent.

But Mozart never entered that plea for

himself. He was, indeed, unconscious of his " indiscipline ", since he had—and for this, at least, he owed a debt to his father—a complete self-control in all those things which seemed to him to be of importance. Despite the gaiety and elegance, which are perhaps the first qualities to make themselves evident to the hearer of his music, Mozart was intensely serious about everything that really mattered. And music always mattered most. Even as a child he wrote with the utmost gravity about the performances he heard in Italy ; and, when he grew up, religion, in the widest sense, and the broad issues of moral conduct always evoked from him an earnest expression of his convictions, which is at times tinged with youthful priggishness. This fundamental seriousness in his character prevented him from indulging in his music the vulgar fun which sometimes shocks the reader of his letters.

The note of seriousness is sounded, too, in his estimates of his own work. Like all men of great genius, Mozart was sure of his own worth. But his confidence has a serenity which is unique. It is not pitched in the lofty key of Beethoven, nor has it the aggressive quality of Wagner's self-assurance—though he indeed had to surmount more definite and actively hostile obstacles. It is essentially quiet and modest. We feel not only that he knew his worth, but also the exact measure of it, neither more nor less. His attitude in this respect is best exemplified in that phrase in his letter to Da Ponte, which puts into words for once the poignancy that is in his music : " I have come to an end before having had the enjoyment of my talent."

Besides this note of what Warde Fowler calls " manly seriousness ", there are two other main notes in Mozart's music, which the same writer describes thus : " First, a joyousness, a sense of the fragrance of life ; never boisterous, but always buoyant and fresh. Secondly, a certain gentle tenderness, never sentimental, but always natural and inevitable,—a sense of ' the tears that are in things ',—which we may perhaps compare with tenderness of the man who wrote ' sunt lacrimae rerum ', and which has never been realized in music in the same way as by Mozart, except now and again in the songs and slow movements of Brahms."

These notes also find their counterpart in Mozart's character. The tenderness is slightly febrile, the expression of a mind affected by physical delicacy. It is saved from weakness by the earnestness of his purpose, even as that quality holds the note of boisterousness in check. The three characteristics, indeed, inter-act upon one another and, though one of them may for a moment occupy the centre of the stage, the others are close by in the wings ready to enter and take their part. They not only make for the perfection of his music, but also define its limitations. For even in his most serious moments Mozart never rises to that grandeur of tragic feeling which makes most people regard Beethoven's as "greater" music. He might well, at a maturer age, have given deeper and more sustained expression to the tragic feeling, which appears occasionally in the music he left—in one or two scenes of *Don Giovanni* and *Die Zauberflöte* and in the Quintet and Symphony in G minor. But he could not have scaled the heroic heights, which Beethoven reached, without some sacrifice of proportion. Nor was his the mind or physique to do it. The absence of the heroic note from his music must, therefore, be regarded as the defect, or rather the limitation of his qualities.

It is this absolute sense of proportion, this completely disciplined expression of whatever he had to say, whether gay or grave, even more than its lyrical and poetic quality, that has restored Mozart's music to favour at the present day. After a century overshadowed by the mighty figure of Beethoven, it is natural and, indeed, healthy that there should be a reaction against an influence which, besides its merit in widening the scope of music, also had the fault of breaking down the sense of proportion and allowing too conscious a place in art to ethical and other qualities, which should be no more than incidentals. After a century, during which musicians for the most part have accepted one particular approach to their art as the one and only road, it is natural and healthy that composers should be seeking other ways of approach, other standards of measure. The eighteenth century, whether exemplified by the severer art of the big-wigs of its first half or by the riper and in a sense more human developments of the succeeding generation, provides one point of departure for those in search of new paths. The unrest of our time has directed the attention of the serious to an earnest struggle with problems of polyphony, which may have originated in a desire to escape " back to Bach " from the *impasse* of Romanticism and the practical difficulties of existence, but which reminds us rather of an earlier experimental period in the evolution of music, when the Netherlandish composers, under the oppression, equally severe if of a different nature, of hard circumstance, spent their energies in working out all the mathematical possibilities of given musical problems. The less earnest have, on the other hand, directed themselves to a more frivolous kind of experimentation, breaking the rules for the fun of it, like children knocking down the brick palaces they have built, and proving by the results only that it is very easy to turn out music of a sort, if you refuse to be subject to any discipline in your methods.

When, however, tranquillity returns and with it a greater peace of mind, it may very well be that musicians, still mistrusting the grandiose ideals of the nineteenth century, will find in the poetry of Mozart and the prose of Haydn in their balance and freedom, their buoyancy and seriousness, the best models for new forms in which to express new ideas.

GRAFFHAM,
    August 11th, 1926.
NORTH CHAPEL,
    August 11th, 1927.

APPENDIX I

CASANOVA AND "DON GIOVANNI"

A curious piece of evidence bearing upon the much-discussed patching of the second act of *Don Giovanni* has recently been brought to light. Among some papers at Schloss Hirschberg in Czecho-Slovakia have been discovered two sheets of paper containing what are without question extracts from a scene in the opera. They are— also, it seems, without question—in the hand- writing of Casanova and have been corrected in the same hand. Casanova was an intimate friend of Da Ponte—they were birds of a feather—and it is known that at the time of the first production of *Don Giovanni*, Casanova was in Prague arranging for the publication of his novel, *Icosameron*.

The first passage consists of two verses :—

Il solo Don Giovanni
M'astrinse a mascherarmi,
Egli di tanti affanni
E l'unica cagion,
Io merito perdon
Colpevole non son. . . .

Ei prese i panni miei
Per bastonar Masetto,
Con Donna Elvira io fei
Il solo mio dover.
Fu tale il suo voler, etc., to *Lasciatemi scappar*
(fugge).

The second extract, which is on a separate page, runs thus :—

Leporello : Incerto, confuso.
Scoperto, deluso,
Difendermi non so,
Perdon vi chiederò.

Donna Elvira
Don Ottavio } *Perdonarsi non si*
Zerlina *può.*
Masetto

Etc., to *Leporello : Il palpitante cuor (fugge).*

Unfortunately Herr Nettl[1] does not indicate how much is covered by the " etc." in each case. But from the quotations given it is perfectly clear that these verses are variants of the air sung by Leporello immediately after the sextet. They are, moreover, two separate variants of this part of the scene, one treating it as a solo for Leporello, the other as a concerted number for all the characters. Neither version agrees in the smallest

[1] The evidence here given is published in the *Alt-Prager Almanack*, 1927, by Herr Paul Nettl, who, however, draws no conclusions from it. My attention was called to the matter by Mr. C. B. Oldman, who has been kind enough to place the material at my disposal.

degree with the actual words or the poetic form of the air as it stands in the libretto, but they are in the same sense, and the second extract shows that Donna Anna is not on the stage. It will be remembered that she goes off at the end of the sextet in the libretto as we know it.

The only other thing that seems to be certain about these extracts is that they are not merely copies in Casanova's handwriting of a scene from *Don Giovanni*. He would, indeed, hardly have copied them out as pieces of poetry worth recording. Their incompleteness, the fact that they are variants of the same scene, and, above all, the numerous corrections in the same writing prove that they are sketches for a scene in the opera. That they are intended for the *Don Giovanni* which we know as Mozart's, and not for some other libretto, can hardly be doubted, since the sense of the words and the situation coincide so closely with what stands in the actual score.

It is clear, then, that Casanova did some work on this scene, and it is highly improbable that he made the sketches for his own amusement and without any practical purpose. How, then, are we to explain this interesting evidence that so great an authority on the subject of *Don Giovanni* had a hand in it?

In order to answer this question, it is necessary to review the known facts about the composition of the libretto. Da Ponte was extremely busy at the time. He had in hand, besides *Don Giovanni*, a libretto for Salieri and another for Vincente Martino. Martino's opera was produced in Vienna on October 1, 1787, and Da Ponte was in Vienna for the performance. He relates in his autobiography that he then joined Mozart, who had already gone to Prague, to assist at the rehearsals for *Don Giovanni*, which was due for production on October 29. He was, however, able to remain in Prague for a fortnight only, as he had to hurry back to Vienna in order to complete the libretto of *Axur* for Salieri.

Da Ponte's other preoccupations have been held accountable for the undoubted muddle which occurs in the second act of *Don Giovanni*, just after the sextet, that is at the very point where these sketches in Casanova's hand have their place. It has been pointed out by Professor Dent,[1] that in order to shorten the already great length of the opera, Mozart must have decided to run the last of the original three acts of the libretto together.[2] He probably decided on this course after the sextet had been finished, for, as it stands, this movement has all the characteristics of a *finale*, and not those of an *ensemble*. It leads up quite naturally to a fall of the curtain. In order to continue the scene according to the new

---

[1] *Mozart's Operas*, p. 248 ff.
[2] The original playbill of a Viennese performance in June 1788 announces that the opera will begin at 5.30 precisely and will end at 8—rather an optimistic calculation for an opera, which takes, even with cuts, a good three hours to perform.

plan, Leporello's air was added and Ottavio's "Il mio tesoro" was then clumsily tacked on with the thread of an absurd piece of recitative, the whole scene making a double anti-climax to the sextet.

If there is anything at all in the new evidence brought to light by Herr Nettl, it goes to prove that the change was made within three weeks of the date announced for the first performance of the opera. There is nothing unlikely in this, since Mozart habitually left the work of consigning his music to paper till the last possible moment. Indeed, it is confirmed by the stories, exaggerated in legend, of the tardy composition of the overture.

I conjecture, therefore, that what happened was as follows. After his arrival in Prague, Mozart reached the sextet, and decided that the length of the opera must be curtailed. He consulted with Da Ponte, who was much too busy to re-write the opening of the last act and make a respectable join to the sextet. But, whatever suggestions he may have made, the librettist was called back to Vienna and asked his friend, Casanova, to give Mozart any assistance he could in spatch-cocking the two acts. On this assumption Casanova is responsible for the recitative after the sextet, Leporello's air, "Ah, pietà, signori miei!" and the recitative which follows it and introduces Ottavio's air, "Il mio tesoro." It is tantalizing that one link in the chain of evidence is missing, for, unless a further sketch in Casanova's hand which bears a more direct verbal resemblance to Leporello's air, is found, we cannot be sure of our ground. But I can see no other explanation of the existence of the sketches which have been discovered at Schloss Hirschberg. At least, my theory relieves Da Ponte, normally so fine a craftsman, of a part of the responsibility for what is a bad piece of work.

APPENDIX II

CHRONOLOGICAL TABLE OF
MOZART'S LIFE AND WORKS

Year.	Age.	Life.
1756		January 17. M. born at Salzburg.
1757	1	
1758	2	
1759	3	
1760	4	
1761	5	
1762	6	January and February. *First journey*. Munich. September to beginning of next year. *Second journey*. Vienna.
1763	7	June. *Third journey*. Munich, Augsburg, Schwetzingen, Mannheim, Frankfurt, Brussels, Paris.
1764	8	April. Arrival in London. Meets J. C. Bach
1765	9	August. Leaves London for Holland.

II

Compositions.	Contemporary Events.
	Outbreak of Seven Years War. Leopold Mozart's *Complete Violin Method.* Domenico Scarlatti dies. Padre Martini's first volume of *Storia della Musica.*
	Handel dies. Charles III succeeds Philip V of Spain, end of Farinelli's political infiuence. George II dies. Cherubini born. Giesecke born. Joseph Haydn appointed *Kapellmeister* to Prince Esterhazy.
K. 1–6. Five minuets and one allegro for piano.	Gluck's *Orfeo.* Michael Haydn appointed *Kapellmeister* at Salzburg.
K. 8, 9. Andante and Sonata in B flat for piano. K. 7. Sonata in D for piano.	End of Seven Years War. Méhul born.
K. 9–15, 17, 109ᵇ. Sonatas for piano with violin or flute and 'cello accompaniment, etc.	Rameau dies.
K. 16, 19, 22. Symphonies in E flat, D and B flat. K. 21. Air : *Va dal furor.* K. 20. Chorus: *God is our refuge.* Eighteen small pieces for piano.	Joseph II succeeds Francis I of Austria.

335

Year.	Age.	Life.
1766	10	May. Arrival in Paris. July. Returns via Switzerland to Munich. November. Arrival in Salzburg.
1767	11	September. *Fourth journey*. Vienna. M. has smallpox.
1768	12	Still in Vienna and neighbourhood.
1769	13	January. Returns to Salzburg. December. *Fifth journey*. Italy.

336

Compositions.	Contemporary Events.
K. 23. Air : *Conservati fedele.*	
K. 24, 25. Piano variations.	
K. 26–31. Piano sonatas with violin accompaniment.	
K. 32. Galimatias Musicum for piano, strings and wind.	
K. 103. Three Sonatas by J. C. Bach arranged as piano concertos.	
K. 33. Kyrie.	
K. 76, 43. Symphonies in F.	Gluck's *Alceste.*
K. 34. Offertorium.	Rousseau's *Dictionnaire de*
K. 35. Oratorio *Die Schuldigkeit des Ersten Gebotes.*	*Musique.*
K. 42. Cantata *Grabmusik.*	
K. 38. Latin comedy : *Apollo et Hyacinthus.*	
K. 37, 39–41. Adaptations of French sonatas as piano concertos.	
K. 99. Cassation in B flat.	
K. 100. Serenade in D.	
K. 36, K. Anh., 24ᵃ. Airs.	
K. 45, 48. Symphonies in D.	
K. 51. Opera buffa : *La Finta Semplice.*	
K. 50. German operetta : *Bastien und Bastienne.*	
K. 52, 53. Songs.	
K. 47. *Veni sancte spiritus.*	
K. 49. Missa brevis in G.	
K. 64. Minuet.	
K. 65. Missa brevis in D minor.	Gluck's *Paride ed Hellene.*
K. 65ᵃ. Minuets and trios.	Napoleon born.

Year.	Age.	Life.
1770	14	January–March. Milan. March. Bologna. Meets Padre Martini. April. Rome. May. Naples. June. In Rome. Receives Order of Golden Spur. July. Bologna. Starts *Mitridate* and is elected to Philharmonic Society. October. Milan.
1771	15	March. Returns to Salzburg. August. *Sixth journey*. Milan. December. Returns to Salzburg.
1772	16	August. Appointed *Konzertmeister* at Salzburg. October. *Seventh journey*. Milan.

Compositions.	Contemporary Events.
K. 63. Cassation in G.	
K. 70. Recitative and air.	
K. 66. Mass in C.	
K. 141. Te Deum.	
K. 97, 95, 81, 84, K. Anh. 100.	Tartini dies.
Symphonies in D.	Padre Martini's second volume
K. 80. Quartet in G.	of *Storia della Musica.*
K. 87. Opera Seria : *Mitri-*	Beethoven born.
date, Ré di Ponto (Dec. 26).	
K. 143, 117, 89, 85, 115, 44,	
86. Church Music.	
K. 88, 77–79, 82, 83. Vocal	
music.	
K. 122, 123, 94. Miscellaneous	16th Dec.
K. 74, 75, 73, 110, 112, 98,	Archbishop Sigismund of
114, K. Anh. 216. Sym-	Salzburg dies.
phonies.	Grétry's *Zémire et Azor.*
K. 118. Oratorio : *La Betulia*	
Liberata.	
K. 113. Divertissement in E	
flat.	
K. 116, 109, 108, 72, 67–69,	
93, 221, 326. Church Music.	
K. 111. Festa teatrale : *As-*	
canio in Alba (October).	
K. 139. Mass in C minor.	Haydn's Passion, Farewell and
K. 124, 128–130, 132–134.	Funeral Symphonies.
Symphonies (K. 134 in A).	Burney's *Present State of*
K. 136–138, 131. Diverti-	*Music in France and Italy.*
menti.	Hieronymus von Colloredo
K. 126. Azione teatrale : *Il*	appointed Archbishop of
Sogno di Scipione.	Salzburg.
K. 155, 156. Quartets in D	Cimarosa's first opera.
and G.	

Year.	Age.	Life.
1773	17	March. Returns to Salzburg. July. *Eighth journey*. Vienna. October. Returns to Salzburg.
1774	18	December. *Ninth journey*. Munich.

Compositions.	Contemporary Events.
K. 135. Dramma per musica : *Lucio Silla* (December 26).	
K. 144, 145, 125, 127, 197. Church Music.	
K. 149–151. Songs.	
K. 381, 163, 164. Miscellaneous.	
K. 165. Motet : *Exsultate, jubilate.*	Burney's *German Tour.* Lorenzo Da Ponte ordained priest.
K. 190. Concertone in C.	
K. 185, 189. Serenade in D with March.	
K. 168–173. Quartets in F, A, C, E flat, B flat, D minor.	
K. 200. Symphony in C.	
K. 345. Two choruses for *Thamos, König in Ägypten.*	
K. 96, 184, 181, 162, 182, 199. Other symphonies.	
K. 157–160. Other quartets and K. 174 quintet in B flat.	
K. 55, 59, 57, 60, 58, 56. Piano and violin sonatas.	
K. 186, 166, 205, 290. Divertimenti in B flat, E flat, D with March.	
K. 167. Holy Trinity Mass.	
K. 175. Piano Concerto in D.	
K. 180, 176. Miscellaneous.	
K. 183, 201, 202. Symphonies in G minor, A and D.	Jommelli dies. Louis XV dies.
K. 191. Concertone in B flat.	Gluck's *Iphigenia in Aulis.*
K. 358, 279, 179, 280–283, 312. Piano compositions.	Goethe's *Werther.*
K. 192–195. Church Music.	

Year.	Age.	Life.
1775	19	March. Returns to Salzburg.
1776	20	In Salzburg.
1777	21	September. *Tenth journey*. Munich. October. Augsburg (Andreas Stein and Maria Anna Mozart). November. Mannheim.

Compositions.	Contemporary Events.
K. 203, 237. Serenade in D with March.	Sammartini dies.
K. 196. Opera buffa : *La Finta Giardiniera* (January).	
K. 208. Dramma per musica : *Il Re Pastore* (April).	
K. 207, 211, 216, 218, 219. Violin concertos in B flat, D, G, D, A.	
K. 220, 222, 212. Church Music.	
K. 213, 204, 187, 215, 121, 102, 214, 210, 209, 217, 152, 292, 284. Miscellaneous.	
K. 242. Concerto in F for 3 pianos.	Gluck-Piccini controversy in Paris at its height.
K. 250, 249. Serenade in D with March (*Haffner*).	Paisiello's *Il Barbiere di Siviglia*.
K. 257, 259, 258. Masses in C.	
K. 243, 260, 42, 225, 224, 244, 245, 262. Other Church Music.	
K. 239, 240, 247, 248, 252, 251, 253, 254, 101. Serenades and Divertimenti.	
K. 256, 255, 126. Airs.	
K. 238, 246, 261, 269. Miscellaneous.	
K. 272. Scena : *Ah! lo previdi*.	Gluck's *Armida*.
K. 270, 287, 289, 267, 286, 188. Divertimenti, etc.	Holzbauer's *Günther von Schwarzburg* at Mannheim.
K. 274, 278, 273, 287, 275. Church Music.	

Year.	Age:	Life:
1778	22	In Mannheim (in love with Aloysia Weber). March. Paris (Grimm). May. Refuses position of organist at Versailles. July 3. M.'s mother dies. September. Leaves Paris. November. Mannheim. December. Munich. (Breach with Aloysia.)
1779	23	January. Arrives in Salzburg with the *Bäsle*. Appointed organist.

Compositions:	Contemporary Events.
K. 271, 271*, 266, 311, 309, 307. Miscellaneous.	
K. 285. Flute quartet in D.	
N.C. 293. Flute quartet in G.	Gluck's *Iphigenia in Tauris.*
K. 313, 314. Flute concertos in G and D.	Voltaire dies. Arne dies.
K. 301, 303, 305, 302, 296, 304, 306. Violin sonatas.	Karl Theodor becomes Elector of Bavaria and transfers his
K. 299. Concerto in C for flute and harp.	court from Mannheim to Munich.
K. 297. Symphony in D.	
K. Anh. 10. Ballet : *Petits Riens.*	
K. 298. Flute quartet in A.	
K. 315. Andante for flute and orchestra.	
K. 354, 310, 331, 265, 353, 395, 330, 332, 333, 264. Piano compositions.	
K. 294, 295, 486*, 308, 322, K. Anh. 9, 8. Miscellaneous.	
K. 316. Recitative and air : *Popoli di Tessaglia.*	Schikaneder's company in Salzburg.
K. 365. Concerto in E flat for two pianos.	
K. 364. Symphony concertante for violin and viola in E flat.	
K. 345. Two choruses and melodrama for *Thamos, König in Ägypten.*	
K. 344. German opera : *Zaïde* (incomplete).	
K. 318, 319. Symphonies in G and B flat.	

Year.	Age:	Life.
1780	24	At Salzburg. Working on *Idomeneo.* End of year. Goes to Munich to produce *Idomeneo.*
1781	25	March. Returns to Salzburg. Leaves for Vienna to join Archbishop. June. Dismissed from Archbishop's service. December. Signs contract to marry Constanze Weber.
1782	26	At Vienna. August 4. Marries Constanze Weber.

Compositions.	Contemporary Events.
K. 320, 335 and 344, 445. Serenade and Divertimento with Marches.	
K. 329, 317, 328, 321, 343. Church Music.	
K. 378. Violin sonata.	
K. 336, 337, 339, 146, 276. Church Music.	Maria Theresa dies. Ditters von Dittersdorf *floruit.*
K. 338. Symphony in C.	
K. 390–392. Songs.	
K. 366, 367. Opera seria (with ballet) : *Idomeneo* (January 29).	Padre Martini's third volume of *Storia della Musica.*
K. 370. Oboe quartet.	
K. 374. Recitative and air : *A questo seno.*	
K. 361, 375. Serenades for wind in B flat and E flat.	
K. 376, 377, 379, 380, 359, 360. Violin sonatas, etc.	
K. 349, 368, 351, 369, 341, 371, 373, 448. Miscellaneous.	
K. 384. *Die Entführung aus dem Serail* (July 16).	Johann Christian Bach dies. Metastasio dies.
K. 412. Horn concerto in D.	Farinelli dies.
K. 397. Piano fantasia in D minor.	Sarti's *I due litiganti* in Milan.
K. 387. Quartet in G (first of *Haydn* set).	
K. 388 and 385, 408. Serenades (K. 385, *Haffner Symphony*).	
K. 413, 414, 415. Piano concertos in F, A, C.	

Year.	Age.	Life.
1783	27	June. Mozart's son Raimund Leopold born. (died in infancy). August–October. In Salzburg with Constanze. November. In Linz en route for Vienna. (During this year meets Da Ponte in Vienna.)
1784	28	At Vienna. M.'s second son, Karl, born (died 1859). M. initiated into Freemasonry.

Compositions.	Contemporary Events.
K. 394, 398, 352, 399, 401. Piano composition including two preludes and fugues.	
K. 383, 119, 403, 402. Miscellaneous.	
K. 417. Horn concerto in E flat.	Salieri's *Il ricco d'un Giorno.*
K. 427. Grand Mass in C minor (unfinished).	
K. 421. Quartet in D minor (*Haydn*).	
K. 396. Piano fantasia in C minor.	
K. 407. Horn quintet in E flat.	
K. 447. Horn concerto in E flat.	
K. 428. Quartet in E flat (*Haydn*).	
K. 422, 430. Sketches for *l'Oca del Cairo* and *Lo Sposo deluso.*	
K. 425. Symphony in C (*Linz*).	
K. 429. Masonic Cantata: *Dir Seele des Weltalls.*	
K. 416, 418–420, 432, 435, 431. Concert airs.	
K. 405, 441, 423, 424, 426, 444. Miscellaneous.	
K. 449–451, 453, 456, 459. Piano concertos.	Beaumarchais's *Mariage de Figaro* in Paris.
K. 452. Quintet in E flat for piano and wind.	Grétry's *Richard Cœur de Lion.*
K. 458. Quartet in B flat (*Haydn*).	

Year.	Age.	Life.
1785	29	At Vienna. February–April. Leopold stays with M.
1786	30	At Vienna. October. M.'s son, Leopold, born (died in infancy).

Compositions.	Contemporary Events.
K. 454, 460, 455, 457, 461–463. Miscellaneous. K. 464. Quartet in A (*Haydn*). K. 465. Quartet in C (*Haydn*). K. 466, 467, 482. Piano concertos. K. 469. Oratorio : *Davidde penitente*. K. 471. Masonic cantata : *Die Maurerfreude*. K. 472, 473, 474, 476. Songs including *Die Zufriedenheit* and *Das Veilchen*. K. 475. Piano fantasia in C minor. K. 477. Masonic funeral march. K. 478. Piano quartet in G minor. K. 468, 479, 480, 481, 483, 484. Miscellaneous. K. 486. *Der Schauspieldirektor* (Schönbrunn, February 7). K. 488, 491, 503. Piano concertos. K. 492. *Le Nozze di Figaro* (May 1). K. 493. Piano quartet in E flat. K. 495. Horn concerto in E flat. K. 499. Quartet in D. K. 502. Piano trio in B flat. K. 504. Symphony in D (*Prague*).	Frederick William II succeeds Frederick the Great of Prussia. Karl Maria von Weber born. November, Vincente Martin's *Una cosa rara* in Vienna.

Year.	Age.	Life.
1787	31	January. Arrives in Prague with Constanze at invitation of Duschek for performance of *Figaro*. Middle of February. Leaves Prague for Vienna. April. Receives libretto of *Don Giovanni* from Da Ponte. May. Receives visit from Beethoven. May 28. Leopold Mozart dies. September. Leaves again for Prague. Middle of November. Returns to Vienna. December. Appointed chamber-musician and Court-composer in Gluck's place by Joseph II.
1788	32	May 7. First performance of *Don Giovanni* in Vienna.

Compositions.	Contemporary Events.
K. 505. Scena and rondo : *Non temer amato bene.*	
K. 485, 490, 489, 494, 496, 487, 147, 148, 178, 497, 498.	
K. Anh. 136, K. 500, 501, 357, 506. Miscellaneous.	
K. 515. String quintet in C.	
K. 516. String quintet in G minor.	
K. 522. Musical joke for string quartet and two horns.	
K. 523, 524. Songs : *Abendempfindung* and *An Chloë.*	
K. 525. Eine Kleine Nachtmusik.	
K. 527. *Don Giovanni* (29 October in Prague).	
K. 528. Scena and air : *Bella mia fiamma.*	
K. 512, 513, N.C. 496. Other concert airs.	November, Gluck dies.
K. 517–520, 529–531. Other songs.	
K. 509, 511, 521, 526. Miscellaneous.	
K. 537. Piano concerto in D.	C. P. E. Bach dies.
K. 527. Two new airs and duet for *Don Giovanni.*	First collected edition of Goldoni's plays.
K. 542. Piano trio in E.	
K. 543. Symphony in E flat.	
K. 548. Piano trio in C.	
K. 550. Symphony in G minor.	
K. 551. Symphony in C (*Jupiter*).	

2A.

Year.	Age.	Life.
1789	33	April 8. Leaves Vienna for Berlin with Prince Lichnowsky via Prague, Dresden, Leipzig. April. In Potsdam. May. Short stay in Leipsig. May 19. In Berlin at performance of *Die Entführung*. May 28. Leaves Berlin, travelling via Dresden and Prague. June 4. Arrives in Vienna. End of July. Constanze leaves Vienna for Baden. December 31. Private performance at M.'s house of *Così fan tutte*, attended by Haydn.
1790	34	Constanze again in Baden. September 23. Leaves Vienna for Frankfurt for Coronation of Emperor. Middle of October. Leaves Frankfurt, travelling via Mannheim, Augsburg, Munich. November 10. Arrives in Vienna.
1791	35	March. Receives commission from Schikaneder for fairy opera. June. Joins Constanze in Baden.

Compositions.	Contemporary Events.
K. 564. Piano trio in G. K. 566. Reinstrumentation of Handel's *Acis and Galatea*. K. 533, 536, 538–541, 545–547, 549, 552–563, 567, 568. Miscellaneous. K. 572. Reinstrumentation of Handel's *Messiah*. K. 575. Quartet in D. K. 577, 579. Rondo and air for insertion in *Figaro*. K. 581. Clarinet quintet in A. K. 570, 571, 573, 574, 576, 578, 580, 582, 583, 585, 586. Miscellaneous.	Storming of the Bastille.
K. 588. *Così fan tutte* (Vienna, January 26). K. 589. Quartet in B flat. K. 590. Quartet in F. K. 591, 592. Reinstrumentation of Handel's *Alexander's Feast* and *St. Cecilia's Day*. K. 593. Quintet in D. K. 594. Fantasia in F minor for mechanical organ. K. 355, 410, 411, 236, 106. Miscellaneous. K. 595. Piano. concerto in Bb. K. 608. Fantasia in F minor for mechanical organ.	Leopold II succeeds Joseph II. Haydn's visit to England and composition of Salomon symphonies. Meyerbeer born.

Year.	Age.	Life.
		July. M.'s son Wolfgang born (died 1844). July. Receives anonymous commission for requiem. August 18. In Prague for command performance of *La Clemenza di Tito*. September 2. Conducts *Don Giovanni* in Prague. September. Returns to Vienna. October. Constanze again in Baden. November 20. M. ill. End of November. Constanze returns to Vienna. December 5. M. dies.

Compositions.	Contemporary Events.
K. 614. Quintet in E flat. K. 615. Final chorus for Sarti's *Le Gelosie Villane*. K. 618. Motet: *Ave verum corpus*. K. 620. *Die Zauberflöte* (first performance September 30 in Vienna). K. 621. *La Clemenza di Tito* (first performance September 6 in Prague). K. 622. Clarinet concerto in A. K. 623. Masonic cantata. K. 627. Hymn: *Adoramus te*. K. 626. Requiem Mass. K. 591–607, 609–613, 616, 617, 356, 619. Miscellaneous, mostly dance music.	

INDICES

GENERAL INDEX

359

INDEX

INDEX OF COMPOSITIONS

I. VOCAL MUSIC

INDEX

INDEX